George St. Clair

Buried Cities and Bible Countries

George St. Clair

Buried Cities and Bible Countries

ISBN/EAN: 9783337099695

Printed in Europe, USA, Canada, Australia, Japan

Cover: Foto ©ninafisch / pixelio.de

More available books at **www.hansebooks.com**

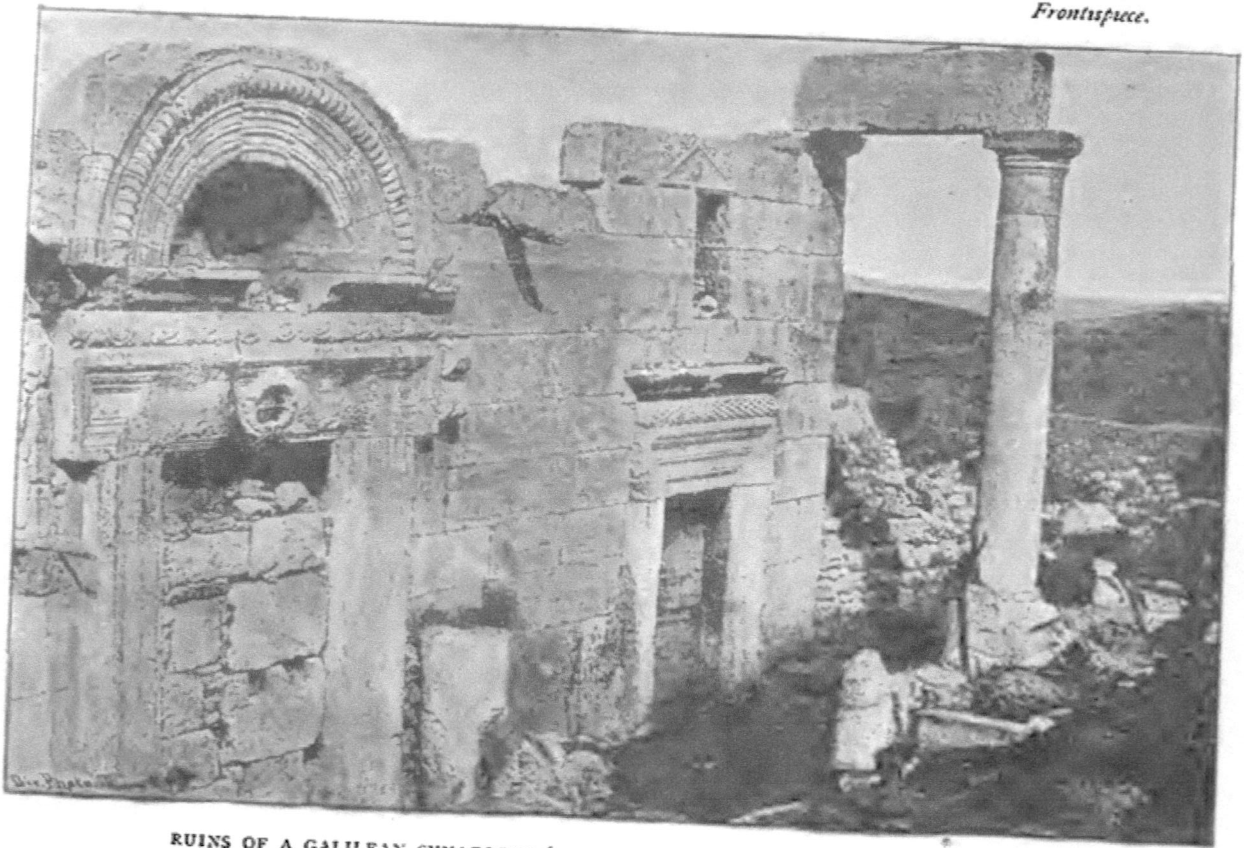

RUINS OF A GALILEAN SYNAGOGUE (KEFR BIRIM).   (*By favour of the Palestine Exploration Fund.*)

BURIED CITIES

AND

BIBLE COUNTRIES

BY

GEORGE ST CLAIR, F.G.S.

MEMBER OF THE SOCIETY OF BIBLICAL ARCHÆOLOGY;
MEMBER OF THE ANTHROPOLOGICAL INSTITUTE, AND TEN YEARS LECTURER
FOR THE PALESTINE EXPLORATION FUND

NEW YORK
THOMAS WHITTAKER
3 AND 4 BIBLE HOUSE
1892

CONTENTS.

LIST OF ILLUSTRATIONS.

PREFACE.

THIS book contains a description of some of the most important modern discoveries bearing upon the Bible, the selection being made to meet the wants of those who have no time to follow the course of exploration, and no taste for technical details. The preparation of such a volume has often been urged upon me by those who have listened to my lectures on Palestine Exploration.

In such a work accuracy is of more value than originality; and therefore I have not hesitated to gather information from the best sources, and to use it freely. The authorities and sources will be found in a list at the end of each chapter; and thus, while due acknowledgment is made, the reader will know where to go to for further information.

In one chapter, indeed—that relating to the topography of Jerusalem in Scripture times—I do venture to state my own views, and give my own map of localities; but it is only because my special study of the subject seems to justify my confidence, and compels me to differ from other writers.

I desire to express my special obligation to the Committee of the Palestine Exploration Fund for allowing the use of their plates for the illustrations of this volume;

to Herr Schick of Jerusalem, for leave to use his plan of
the Second Wall, to Wilfrid H. Hudleston, M.A., F.R.S.,
for the geological sketch-map and section, and to W. Harry
Rylands, F.S.A., Secretary to the Society of Biblical
Archæology, for the special favour of an original drawing
from one of the Hamath stones.

GEORGE ST CLAIR.

BURIED CITIES AND BIBLE COUNTRIES.

CHAPTER I.

EGYPT AND THE BIBLE.

I. *The Rosetta Stone : Decipherment of the Egyptian Hieroglyphs.*

To all who are interested in the ancient history of mankind, the decipherment of the Egyptian hieroglyphs is a fact of the highest importance. As early as the fourth dynasty, and probably as early as the first, the Egyptians possessed the art of writing ; but for thousands of years before the present century the hieroglyphs had become a dead language, which nobody could read. Temples and tombs in the valley of the Nile contained records which might be of surpassing interest ; but the clue to them was lost, and the riddle remained unguessed. At length a discovery was made which began to open the way, and has proved to be one of the most remarkable events in the intellectual history of Europe.

In the year 1799, when Napoleon's army was in Egypt, a French artillery officer, by name Boussard, while engaged in certain works on the redoubt of St Julian, at Rosetta, discovered a large slab of black granite, bearing a triple inscription. The first or upper part was in hieroglyphs, the middle one was in the enchorial or popular character, and the lower one in Greek. The hieroglyphic text was partly broken away and lost, but the other two were nearly complete. The Greek text showed that the monument was designed by the priests of Memphis, in honour of the Pharaohs, and particularly of Ptolemy Epiphanes, who was reigning at the time when the decree was made (198 B.C.). The monument stood originally in the temple of Tum, the god of the setting sun; and there were to be copies of it in other places.

Among other things, the priests say of Ptolemy that "he was pious towards the gods, he ameliorated the life of man, he was full of generous piety, he showed forth with all his might his sentiments of humanity." He lightened taxation, so that the people might have plenty; he released prisoners and the defendants in law suits; he ordered that the revenues of the temples, whether in provisions or money, should remain what they had been. As to the priests, he commanded that they should pay no new promotion fees, that those who had been obliged to make an annual voyage to Alexandria should be free from the obligation; and that what had been neglected in temple services should be re-established. Naturally the priests were grateful, and they ordered this testimonial of recognition to be engraved upon stone, in the sacred characters of Egypt, in the vernacular, and in Greek.

All this was speedily made out from the Greek text, and it was thus clear that the other two forms of the inscription must be of the same purport. Here then at last was a key to the long-lost language of the hieroglyphs. The value of the monument was at once perceived, and after having been copied it was set apart and packed up. The victory of the English at Alexandria, and the surrender of the city in 1801, placed the Rosetta Stone in the hands of Mr. W. R. Hamilton, the British

Commissioner, one of the most distinguished and zealous scholars of the day. The treasure was despatched to England, and has found a fitting resting-place in the British Museum.

This seemingly insignificant stone (says Baron Bunsen) shares, with the great and splendid work, " La Description de l'Egypte," the honour of being the only result of vital importance to universal history, accruing from a vast expedition, a brilliant conquest, and a bloody combat for the possession of Egypt. The men of science and letters who accompanied Napoleon's army in Egypt, employed themselves actively in collecting the precious materials for that great work on the antiquities, the topography, natural history, &c., of that wonderful country. When the work appeared, the monuments that it contained, and the learned commentaries by which they were accompanied, aroused the general attention of the European public to Egyptian research, which had been previously all but abandoned. This collection comprised not only the most important monuments of Egypt, but also the great funereal papyrus, and other Egyptian records of the highest value. But the monuments were mute, the hieroglyphics could not be read, and the riddle of the sphinx still remained unsolved. Attempts had been made, but without much success, and it was the Rosetta Stone which, in reality, unloosed the tongue of both monuments and records, and rendered them accessible to historical investigation. This stone was the mighty agency which, by the light it shed on the mysteries of the Egyptian language and writing, was to enable science to penetrate through the darkness of thousands of years, extend the limits of history, and even open up a possibility of unfolding the primeval secrets of the human race.

As engraved copies of the Rosetta Stone became common in Europe—for which object the English scholars had provided without delay—confidence was entertained that the hieroglyphs would be deciphered.

However (says Mariette), we must not imagine that the deciphering of hieroglyphs by means of the Rosetta Stone was accomplished at the first trial, and without groping in the dark. On the contrary, the savants tried for twenty years without success. At last Champollion appeared. Prior to him people thought each of the letters that compose hieroglyphic writing was a *symbol;* that is, that in every single one of these letters a complete *idea* was expressed. The merit of Champollion consisted in proving that Egyptian writing contains signs which express *sounds ;* in other words, that it is *alphabetic.* He noticed that wherever in the Greek text the proper name *Ptolemy* is met with, there may be found, at a corresponding place of the Egyptian text, a certain number of signs enclosed within an elliptic ring. From this he concluded (1) that the names of kings were indicated, in the hieroglyphic system, in a sort of escutcheon, which he styled a *cartouche ;* (2) that the signs contained in the cartouche must be letter for letter the name of Ptolemy (Ptolemaios).

Even supposing the vowels omitted, Champollion was already in possession of five letters—P.T.L.M.S. Again, Champollion knew, according to a second Greek inscription, engraved on an obelisk of Philae, that on this obelisk a hieroglyphic cartouche is visible which must be that of Cleopatra. If his first reading was correct, the P, the L, and the T of Ptolemy must be found again in the second proper name; while, at the same time, this second proper name would furnish K and R. Although very imperfect as yet, the alphabet thus revealed to Champollion, when applied to other cartouches, put him in possession of nearly all the other consonants.

Thenceforth he had no need to hesitate concerning the *pronunciation* of signs ; for, from the day this proof was furnished, he could certify that he possessed the Egyptian alphabet. But now remained the language; for pronouncing words is nothing, if we know not what they mean. Here Champollion's genius could soar. He perceived that his alphabet, drawn from proper names and applied to words of the language, simply furnished *Coptic.* Now Coptic, in its turn, is a language which, without being so well explored as Greek, had for a long time been not less accessible. (It was a spoken language until the sixteenth century, and three spoken dialects remained, sufficiently resembling the old Egyptian to enable all the grammatical forms and structure to be examined.) Therefore the veil was completely removed. The Egyptian language was only Coptic written in hieroglyphs; or, to speak more correctly, Coptic is only the language of the ancient Pharaohs, written in Greek letters. The rest may be inferred. From sign to sign Champollion really proceeded from the known to the unknown, and soon the illustrious father of Egyptology could lay the foundations of this beautiful science, which has for its object the interpretation of the hieroglyphs.

Further, as remarked by Dr Birch, Egyptologists have patiently traced word after word, through several thousands of texts and inscriptions, until they have found its correct meaning. It was ascertained at length that almost every word consists of two portions—hieroglyphs to represent the sound, followed by hieroglyphs expressing its general or specific meaning. Provided with these materials the enquiry advanced. The result is that we are gradually recovering a knowledge of the history of Egypt and the religion of its people, from a time long anterior to the birth of Moses down to the latest period of the empire. The hieroglyphs reveal a rich literature, including not only the annals of the empire, but books on ethics, romances, works on mathematics, medicine, morals, legal and other reports ; while the great religious work is the Book of the Dead.

[*Authorities and Sources* :—" Egypt's Place in Universal History." By Christian C. J. Bunsen. " The Monuments of Upper Egypt." By Auguste Mariette-Bey. " The Monumental History of Egypt." Rede Lecture. By S. Birch, LL.D.]

2. *Kings and Dynasties of Egypt.*

It will be useful to give here a table of Egyptian Dynasties, so that when we come to speak of Israel in Egypt the reader may have some idea of the long antecedent history of the Empire, and the political circumstances of the time. Unfortunately we must be content at present with approximate dates, for the records of the Egyptians are not dated, and the chronology is but very imperfectly known.

*Table of the Egyptian Dynasties.**

Dynasty.	Capital.	Modern Name.	Approximate Date, according to Mariette.	Approximate Date, according to Wiedemann.
		THE OLD EMPIRE.		
I. Thinite	This	Girgeh	5004	5650
II. Thinite	This	Girgeh	4751	5400
III. Memphite	Memphis	Mitrahenny	4449	5100
IV. Memphite	Memphis	Mitrahenny	4235	4875
V. Memphite	Memphis	Mitrahenny	3951	4600
VI. Elephantine	Elephantinê	Geziret-Assouan	3703	4450
VII. Memphite	Memphis	Mitrahenny	3500	4250
VIII. Memphite	Memphis	Mitrahenny	3500	4250
IX. Heracleopolite	Heracleopolis	Ahnas el-Medineh	3358	4000
X. Heracleopolite	Heracleopolis	Ahnas el-Medineh	3249	3700
XI. Diospolitan	Thebes	Luxor, &c.	3064	3510

* From " Records of the Past." New Series, vol. ii.

Table of the Egyptian Dynasties—continued.

Dynasty.	Capital.	Modern Name.	Approximate Date, according to Mariette.	Approximate Date, according to Wiedemann.
THE MIDDLE EMPIRE.				
XII. Diospolitan	Thebes	Luxor, &c.	2851	3450
XIII. Diospolitan	Thebes	Luxor &c.,	...	3250
XIV. Xoite	Xois	Sakha	2398	2800
THE SHEPHERD KINGS.				
XV. Hyksos	Tanis (Zoan)	San	2214	2325
XVI. Hyksos	Tanis	San	...	2050
Diospolitan	Thebes	Luxor, &c.	...	...
XVII. Hyksos	Tanis	San	...	1800
Diospolitan	Thebes	Luxor, &c.	...	...
THE NEW EMPIRE.				
XVIII. Diospolitan	Thebes	Luxor, &c.	1700	1750
XIX. Diospolitan	Thebes	Luxor, &c.	1400	1490
XX. Diospolitan	Thebes	Luxor, &c.	1200	1280
XXI. Tanite	Tanis	San	1100	1100
XXII. Bubastite	Bubastis	Tel Bast	960	975
XXIII. Tanite	Tanis	San	766	810
XXIV. Saite	Sais	Sa el-Hagar	753	720
XXV. Ethiopian	Napata	Mount Barkal	700	715
XXVI. Saite	Sais	Sa el-Hagar	666	664
XXVII. Persian	Persepolis	...	527	525
XXVIII. Saite	Sais	Sa el-Hagar	...	415
XXIX. Mendesian	Mendes	Eshmun er-Român	399	408
XXX. Sebennyte	Sebennytos	Semenhûd	378	387

In the time of Moses the Egyptian power had already
passed its zenith and begun to decay. There had been
an Old Empire, with the City of *This* for its first capital
and Menes as its first king. Dynasty had succeeded
dynasty, during perhaps two thousand years, and the
capital had been changed several times, when the Middle
Empire came in, and the kings ruled from Thebes and
afterwards from Xois. There had now been fourteen

dynasties altogether; and the power of the kingdom was so far weakened that it was unable to keep out the invader. The Shepherd Kings, coming from Midian, or perhaps from Mesopotamia, established themselves in the Delta, and held possession for several centuries. Their conquest, however, did not extend to Upper Egypt, and so the native dynasties reigned contemporaneously, enthroned at Thebes, while the Hyksos kings were seated at Zoan.

It was probably towards the close of the Hyksos period that Joseph was made governor of Egypt, under the latest of the Shepherd Kings. The seventeenth dynasty saw the last of these foreigners, and after their expulsion the New Empire began, near the end of the eighteenth century before Christ. The eighteenth and nineteenth dynasties included several monarchs of great renown; and as the Israelitish sojourn falls chiefly within this period, it will be useful to give here a chronological list.

Monarchs of the Eighteenth and Nineteenth Dynasties, with approximate dates, according to Brugsch.

Eighteenth Dynasty.	B. C.
Aahmes, Amosis ; its founder	1700
Amenhotep I. (Amenophis)	1666
Thothmes I. (Thotmosis)	1633
Thothmes II. and his sister-wife Hatshepsu . .	1600
Thothmes III.	
Amenhotep II., Son of Thothmes III. . . .	1566
Thothmes IV.	1533
Amenhotep III., Son of Queen Mutemna . .	1500
Amenhotep IV., afterwards called Khuenaten . .	1466

Nineteenth Dynasty.	
Rameses I.	1400
Seti I. (Sethos) Menephtah I.	1366
Rameses II. (Sesostris) Miamun	1333
Menephtah II. (Menepthes)	1300
Seti II. Menephtah III., son of Menephtah II. .	1266
Setnakht-Merer-Miamun II.	1233

Rameses II. was the Pharaoh of the Oppression ; and the Israelites left Egypt in the reign of his successor, Menephtah.

3. *The Finding of the Mummies.*

In 1878 the Khedive Said Pasha authorised Professor Maspero to found a Museum at Boulak (a suburb of Cairo), for the reception of all the antiquities found in the country and calculated to throw light on Egyptian history. Under the successive direction of Professor Maspero and Professor Grébaut the collection has become one of the most valuable and most instructive in the world.

In 1881 the museum was enriched by the most important archæological discovery of modern times. On the 5th of July of that year a cave in the plain of Deir el-Bahari, near Thebes, was explored, and its rich contents were bodily removed to Boulak. They consisted of mummies of kings, queens, and princesses, and other persons of distinction, with numerous articles of clothing, papyri, vases, &c. Hieratic inscriptions on the coffins of several of the kings gave the date of the transfer of the bodies from their original sepulchres in the valley of Bab el Malook, near Luxor, to this pit or tomb, and also of the periodical inspection to which the depôt was subjected. The cave is proved to be the tomb of the Priest-Kings of Amen, the usurpers of the throne of the Ramessides, from Her-Hor to Pinotem III.

The reason for bringing so many kings of different dynasties into this tomb is not accurately known ; but the following circumstances afford ground for reasonable conjecture.

"After Rameses II., the last great warrior of Egypt, had laid aside his javelin and bow, in the fourteenth century before Christ, luxury and indolence were followed by their usual concomitants, poverty and discontent. The artizans and labourers, instead of joining in one common effort to improve the condition of the country, had recourse to violence and robbery. The pillage of the tombs for the sake of their precious contents became a common practice, and in the reign of Rameses IX., of the twentieth dynasty, about the eleventh century before the birth of Christ, an inquiry was instituted to ascertain the extent of the depredations. The robbers were arrested and arraigned, and several of them were condemned to die by their own hands—a common mode of punishment in ancient Egypt. It was discovered likewise that the tombs of the Pharaohs, which had hitherto been respected, were, like the rest, subjected to danger."

The preservers, however, were at work as well as the robbers; the priests of the Egyptian Church appear to have shielded the remains of many of the great kings, by hiding them so effectually that they were never found again until the third quarter of the present century.

"It was an extraordinary discovery, not only for Egyptian archæology, but likewise for Egyptian history, and the fortunate discoverer was Professor Maspero, chief conservator of the Egyptian Museum at Boulak. The discovery came about in the following manner. For some years past, so far back as the time of Mariette, it had been observed that objects of value and interest, tablets, papyri, &c., had found their way into the museums of Europe, and some into private hands. There exists a law in Egypt, that tombs and cemeteries are not to be explored except by direct permission of the Khedive, and all traffic in objects of archaic interest is strictly forbidden. Nevertheless a kind of contraband was in existence, the actual source of which was unknown. Another observation had also been made, namely, that the large majority of the objects were of about the same period, and seemed to have a common origin. When His Royal Highness, the Prince of Wales, was in Egypt, he was presented by a certain Mustapha Aga of Thebes, with a valuable papyrus, which the Prince has very generously deposited in the British

Museum. It was subsequently ascertained that the document in question is only half a papyrus (this curious discovery is due to the acute research of Miss Amelia B. Edwards, one of the Honorary Secretaries of the Egypt Exploration Fund), the other, the hinder half, being in the possession of the Museum of the Louvre at Paris. The Prince of Wales' papyrus was written for a queen, Notem Maut, related to the great priest-king of the twenty-first dynasty, Her-Hor—possibly his wife, but more probably his mother. Another, and a remarkably fine papyrus, was bought by Colonel Campbell in 1876, for the large sum of £400. The latter had evidently been obtained from the mummy of the High Priest Pinotem, descendant of Her-Hor. The coincidence was striking, and led Professor Maspero to the conclusion that a tomb of the priest-kings was in the possession of the Arabs of the district of Thebes, a class of persons who live in the tombs, and gain a living out of the produce of their search. Suspicion quickly pointed to the parties implicated. The chief, Ahmed Ab-der-Rassoul, one of five brothers engaged in the traffic of antikas (antiques), was arrested, and shortly afterwards another of the brothers made a confession and conducted the authorities to the hiding-place in which all these treasures were concealed.

"Near the site of an old temple, known as Deir el-Bahari, at the foot of a rugged mass of precipitous rock, so hidden from view that it might be passed by a hundred times without being seen, was a perpendicular shaft, 35 feet deep, and 6 feet in diameter. At the bottom of the shaft, in its western corner, was an opening a little more than 2 feet high and 5 feet wide, the entrance of a narrow passage tunnelled in the rock. This passage or tunnel led due west for 25 feet, and then turned abruptly to the north for 200 feet, ending in an oblong chamber 260 feet long, the entire length of the tunnel being nearly 500 feet. Throughout the whole of this extensive area the floor was encumbered with coffins and funereal gear, packed together so closely that for some distance it was necessary to crawl upon hands and feet to make any progress. The collection within this strange hiding-place consisted of sarcophagi, coffins, mummies, funereal furniture, and funereal ornaments, the gathered fragments of four or five dynasties, more particularly the seventeenth, eighteenth, nineteenth and twenty-first, comprehending a period of more than five hundred years, and ranging between the eighteenth and twelfth centuries before Christ. . . .

" It was a hot forty-eight hours' work, under the burning sun of Egypt, to bring all those objects to the surface, and a toilsome labour, enlisting the services of three hundred Arabs, to convey them to Luxor, and subsequently to pile them on the deck of the Museum steamer which had journeyed up the river to receive them. The passage down the river partook of the character of a funeral ovation : women with dishevelled hair ran along the banks uttering shrieks and funereal chants, others threw dust upon their heads, men discharged guns, and the funeral of a defunct monarch of to-day could not have excited more apparent emotion."

The coffins and mummies included the following :—

RASKENEN, king of Upper Egypt, a descendant of the old Theban royal race, but at this time tributary to the Hyksos or Shepherd kings. According to the Sallier papyrus in the British Museum, he quarrelled with the Hyksos monarch Apopi, in reference to the cession of an important well. This brought about the overthrow and expulsion of the Hyksos, who had ruled the country for five centuries. According to the same authority, Joseph arrived in Egypt during the reign of the Pharaoh Nub (B.C. 1730), and rose to honour under Apopi.

AAHMES I., founder of the eighteenth dynasty.

AMENHOTEP I. (*Amenophis*), coffin and mummy.

THOTHMES I.—The coffin was occupied by the mummy of a priest-king, Pinotem, of the twenty-first dynasty. The mummy of Thothmes was not found.

The first known representation of a horse occurs on a monument of this reign ; and it is supposed that the horse was introduced into Egypt from Asia about this time.

THOTHMES II.—The coffin and mummy were both found. Thothmes II. reigned but a short time.

THOTHMES III., one of the most famous of Egyptian kings. He continued his predecessors' offensive movements against the Hyksos and their allies, and extended his conquests as far as the Tigris. In his reign Egypt was at the pinnacle of its greatness. The walls of his magnificent temple at Karnak are covered with inscriptions recounting his triumphs, and giving a list of the countries and peoples conquered by him. A stela of black granite found at Karnac, and now in the Egyptian National Museum, contains a poem in celebration of the victories of this king. The coffin and mummy found were broken.

HATSHEPSU, the great woman-king, sister and wife of Thothmes II. Becoming regent for her younger brother, Thothmes III., she assumed a king's dress and masculine style. Neither the coffin nor the mummy were found. But it was the practice of the Egyptians in embalming to take out the intestines and preserve them separately ; and the liver of Hatshepsu was discovered enclosed in a cabinet of wood, inlaid with ivory, which was marked with her name.

RAMESES I., founder of the nineteenth dynasty, was found placed in a coffin of the fashion of the twenty-first dynasty, from which the name of the original owner had been carefully scraped off.

SETI I., his successor (coffin and mummy). The superb alabaster sarcophagus of this monarch was already in the Soane Museum, in Lincoln's Inn Fields. When

Belzoni discovered it in 1817, in the original sepulchre in the valley of the kings at Thebes, he was astonished to find the mummy and coffin gone. When the mummy of this Pharaoh was unrolled it was found that the body was long, fleshless, of a yellow-black colour, and had the arms crossed upon the breast. The head was covered with a mask of fine linen, blackened with bitumen, which it was necessary to remove with scissors. This operation brought to view the most beautiful mummy-head ever seen in the museum. The sculptors of Thebes and Abydos did not flatter this Pharaoh when they gave him that delicate, sweet, smiling profile which is known to travellers. After a lapse of thirty-two centuries the mummy retains the same expression which characterised the features of the living man. Seti I. must have died at an advanced age. The head is shaven, the eyebrows are white, the condition of the body points to more than threescore years of life; thus confirming the opinion of the learned, who have attributed a long reign to this king. Seti I. built the Hall of Columns in the Great Temple of Ammon, at Karnac. There exist numerous remains also at Koorneh, Abydos, and elsewhere, of the extensive and magnificent buildings which he erected with the aid of the conquered Semites, among whom the Israelites must probably be included. During his reign a great canal, the first of its kind, was completed, connecting the Nile with the Red Sea.

RAMESES II., the renowned soldier, son of Seti I., known to the Greeks as Sesostris. The oppression of the Israelites, probably begun by Seti I., was continued under Rameses II. In the sixth year of his reign, however, Moses was born. The mummy of Rameses II. was found deposited in a coffin of the twenty-first dynasty, like that of Rameses I. This gave rise to doubts as to which particular Rameses was enclosed, but on unwrapping the mummy an inscription was found, explaining that the

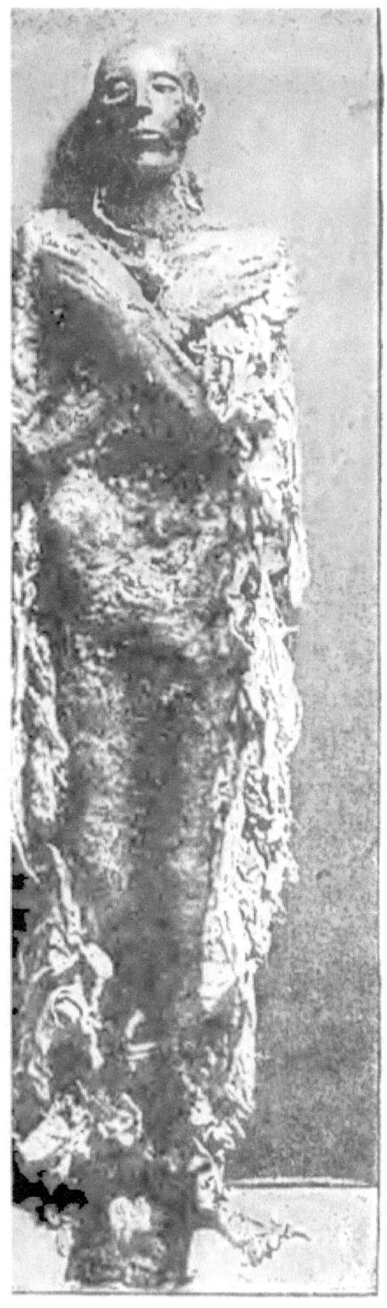

SETI I.

RAMESES II.

original coffin had been accidentally broken, and leaving
no doubt that this was Rameses II. Most striking, when
compared with the mummy of Seti I., is the astonishing
resemblance between father and son. The nose, mouth,
chin, all the features are the same, but in the father they
are more refined than in the son. Rameses II. was over
six feet in height, and we see by the breadth of his chest
and the squareness of his shoulders that he must have been
a man of great bodily strength. Professor Maspero, in his
official report, describes the body as that of a vigorous and
robust old man, with white and well-preserved teeth, white
hair and eyebrows, long and slender hands and feet,
stained with henna, and ears pierced for the reception of
ear-rings. Rameses II. reigned sixty-six years, and was
nearly a hundred years old at the time of his death. He
exhibited great zeal as a builder, and was a patron of
science and art. It was he who built the Ramesseum at
Thebes, and presented it with a library. He also built the
Pylons and Hall of Columns of the Temple of Luxor, and
a score of minor temples in Egypt and Nubia, and made
the marvellous rock-cut temples at Abousimbel.

Rameses II. was succeeded by his thirteenth son,
Meneptah II., who continued the oppression of the
Israelites, and pursued them when they were escaping.

Besides all these monarchs, there were found in the
strange repository at Deir el-Bahari, coffins and mummies
of Rameses III. (of the twentieth dynasty), the last of the
great warrior kings of Egypt, Pinotem I., and Pinotem II.,
priest-kings of the twenty-first dynasty, and several queens,
princes, and notabilities of the same periods. An affecting
story, which brings home to us very vividly the universal
kinship of humanity, is revealed by the contents of the
coffin of Makara, wife of King Pinotem, of the priest-king
dynasty. A little coiled-up bundle lay at the feet of the
Queen, her infant daughter, in giving birth to whom she

gave likewise her life. Thus, and so touchingly, are we led to participate in the affliction of the sick chamber of three thousand years ago. Already had the still-born babe of a queen received a name, Mautemhat, the firstling of the goddess Maut, wife of Amen ; and not a name alone, for she is born to a title strange to our ears, namely, " principal royal spouse."

[*Sources and Authorities :*—The *Times* newspaper, 4th August 1881. The *Times* newspaper, 25th June 1886. " Egyptian Mummies," lecture by Sir Erasmus Wilson ; Kegan Paul, Trench & Co., 1883.]

4. *Egyptians in Palestine before the Exodus.*

When the tribes of Israel were preparing to pass over Jordan, they were told that they were going to possess nations greater and mightier than themselves, a people great and tall, whose cities were fenced up to heaven (Deut. ix. 1 ; i. 28). Of these early inhabitants of Palestine, the spies had reported that Amalek dwelt in the land of the South ; the Hittite, the Jebusite, and the Amorite dwelt in the mountains, and the Canaanite dwelt by the sea and along by the side of Jordan (Num. xiii. 29). We have indeed an enumeration of seven nations dwelling in Palestine at this time, and a testimony to their might :— " The Hittite, the Girgashite, the Amorite, and the Canaanite, the Perizzite, the Hivite, and the Jebusite, seven nations greater and mightier than thou." (Deut. vii. 1). In these passages it is plainly implied that the peoples who occupied Palestine before the Israelitish invasion were in an advanced state of civilisation. Until lately we have known little or nothing about them, beyond the information which these Scripture passages afforded ; but now at last the veil is beginning to lift.

The Hittites.

As there were seven "nations" in Canaan, and the land itself is no larger than Wales, it was long supposed that each of the "nations" was but a small tribe, and was too insignificant to make any figure in history. But we have lately learned that if this was the rule, the Hittites were an exception to it. They were a great people, or perhaps a great confederacy or empire, spread over a vast region in northern Syria and some of the adjacent countries. Their dominion extended more or less over Asia Minor, and the influence of their art and culture reached even into Greece. Their capital was Carchemish, on the Euphrates, the site of which city was discovered a few years ago by Mr Skene, English Consul at Aleppo, and again, two years later, by Mr George Smith, as he was returning from Assyria. The place is now called Jerablus. Another centre of Hittite power was Kadesh, on the Orontes, a city which appears to be referred to in the Bible, for it has been maintained that where Joab and the captains "came to the land of Tahtim-hodshi" (2 Sam. xxiv. 6), it should be rendered "the land of Kadesh of the Hittites," this being the northern border of David's kingdom at that time. The Hittites were thus seated in a region north of Palestine proper; but they appear to have had colonies in the country, and it is these isolated settlements which are classed with the small nations of Canaan by the Bible writer. When Abraham, at Hebron, required a parcel of earth in which to bury his wife Sarah, he bought it of Ephron the Hittite; whence it is clear that there were Hittites owning land in the south. From the mention of Hebron in association with Zoan in Numbers xiii. 22, it is even suspected that the Shepherd Kings who reigned in Zoan were a dynasty of Hittites. At any rate the Hittites were a powerful people, able to hold their own both against the Egyptians and against the Assyrians, and did so in the region of Carchemish for a thousand years.

Thothmes III., "the Egyptian Alexander," who accomplished thirteen campaigns in twenty years, and made Egypt the centre of history, invaded Palestine and gained a victory at Megiddo over the king of Kadesh and his allies. "They fled, head over heels, to Megiddo, with terror in their countenances, and left behind their horses and their gold and silver chariots, and were drawn up, with ropes to their clothes, into this town, since the people had closed the gates of the said town on account of the deeds of the king." "The miserable king of Kadesh" and the miserable king of Megiddo would not have escaped in this way, only that the Egyptian warriors relaxed the pursuit and engaged in plunder. The Pharaoh was beside himself. However, the warriors captured the tent of the miserable king, in which his son was found. Then they raised a shout of joy and gave honour to Amon, the lord of Thebes, who had given to his son Thothmes the victory. After this the neighbouring kings came together to worship before Pharaoh, "and to implore breath for their nostrils." And then came the children of the kings and presented gifts of silver, gold, blue-stone, and green-stone; they brought also wheat, and wine in skins, and fruits for the warriors of the king, since each of the Kitti [Hittites] had taken care to have such provisions for his return home. Then the king pardoned the foreign princes.

A catalogue of the booty includes 3401 living prisoners, 83 hands, 2041 mares, 191 foals, 6 bulls, one chariot, covered with plates of gold, of the king of . . . , 892 chariots of his miserable warriors, one beautiful iron armour of the hostile king, one beautiful iron armour of the king of Megiddo, 200 accoutrements of his miserable warriors, 602 bows, 7 tent-poles covered with plates of gold from the tent of the hostile king. Pharaoh's warriors had also taken as booty . . . bulls, . . . cows, 2000 kids, and 20,500 white goats.

A catalogue is also given of persons and things which Pharaoh afterwards carried off as his property, including 39 noble persons, 87 children of the hostile king and the kings allied with him, 5 marina (lords), 1596 men and maid-servants, 105 persons who gave themselves up because of famine. Besides these prisoners there were taken precious stones, golden dishes, and many utensils of this sort, a large jug with a double handle, 97 swords, 1784 lbs. of gold rings which were found in the hands of the artists, 969 lbs. of silver rings, one statue with head of gold, 6 chairs and footstools of ivory and cedar wood, 6 large tables of cedar wood inlaid with gold and precious stones, one staff of the king worked as a kind of sceptre entirely of gold, one plough inlaid with gold, many garments of the enemy, &c., &c.

These catalogues enable us to form some estimate of the degree of perfection in art and refinement which had been arrived at in Northern Palestine and Syria before the Israelitish invasion. Lists are also given of the towns conquered and the peoples made to submit. Remarking upon these, Brugsch justly says that what gives the highest importance to the catalogue is the undisputed fact that more than three hundred years before the entrance of the Jews into the land of Canaan, a great league of peoples of the same race existed in Palestine under little kings, who dwelt in the same towns and fortresses as we find stated on the monuments, and who for the greater part fell by conquest into the hands of the Jewish immigrants. Among these the King of Kadesh, on the Orontes, in the land of the Amorites—as the inscriptions expressly state—played the first part, since there obeyed him, as their chief leader, all the kings and their peoples from the water of Egypt (which is the same as the Biblical brook which flowed as the boundary of Egypt) to the rivers of Naharain, afterwards called Mesopotamia.

After the death of Thothmes III. the Hittites recovered their independence, and their importance grew from year to year, in such a way that even the Egyptian inscriptions mention the names of their kings in a conspicuous manner, and speak of their gods with reverence. Seti I. came to the throne of Egypt about two centuries after the death of Thothmes, and with him the martial spirit of Egypt revived. Seti drove back the Syrians who had invaded his frontier, and pursued them as far as Phœnicia, where he overthrew with great slaughter "the kings of the land of Phœnicia." He probably suspected the Hittites of abetting his enemies, for, from the overthrow of the Phœnicians, he advanced against Kadesh, professedly as "the avenger of broken treaties." The battle scene is represented on the north side of the great temple of Karnak, where Pharaoh is shown as having thrown to the ground the Hittites, and slain their princes.

Rameses II. was first associated with his father on the throne, and afterwards succeeded him. The great battle of his reign was fought against the Hittites at Kadesh, and was an event of first-class importance. The King of the Hittites had brought together his forces from the remotest parts of his empire, and was aided by allies and satraps from Mesopotamia to Mysia, and from Arvad in the sea. The Egyptian advance followed the coast line, through Joppa, Tyre, Sidon, and Beyrout. On the cliff by the Dog River, Rameses cut his bas-reliefs, and then appears to have advanced up the valley of the Eleutherus. Bringing his army before Kadesh, a great battle was fought, in which the Egyptians claim to be the victors ; but at one point of the struggle the Pharaoh was surrounded and in the greatest danger, and at the close of the fighting a treaty was signed as between equals.

On the great temple at Ibsamboul there is a picture of
the battle of Kadesh, nineteen yards long by more than
eight yards deep.   In this great battle scene there are
eleven hundred figures, and among these there is no
difficulty in recognizing the slim Egyptians and their
Sardonian allies, with horned and crested helmets, and
long swords, shields, and spears.   "The hosts also of the
Hittites and of their allies are represented " (says Brugsch)
" with a lively pictorial expression, for the artist has been

HITTITES (ABOU-SIMBEL).   (*By permission of Messrs, C. Philip & Son.*)

guided by the intention of bringing before the eyes of the
beholder the orderly masses of the Hittite warriors, and
the less regular and warlike troops of the allied peoples,
according to their costume and arms.   The Canaanites are
distinguished in the most striking manner from the allies,
of races unknown to us, who are attired with turban-like
coverings for the head, or with high caps, such as are worn
at the present day by the Persians."   Conder also remarks
that the one race is bearded, the other beardless, and that
this battle picture gives us most lively portraits of the
Hittite warriors in their chariots, and of their walled and
tower-crowned city, with its name written over it, and its
bridges over the Orontes.   The Hittites have long pig-
tails, and their Chinese-like appearance is very remarkable.

Pentaur of Thebes, the poet-laureate of Egypt, had
accompanied Rameses in this expedition, and he celebrated

the achievements of the day in a poem which has come down to us in several editions. It is found on a papyrus roll, and again in conjunction with splendid battle scenes, on the walls of temples at Abydos, Luxor, Karnak, and Ibsamboul.

This prize poem of Pentaur's was written three thousand two hundred years ago, and is the oldest heroic poem in the world. "It may be relied upon," says Dr Wright, "as the earliest specimen of special war correspondence." Besides this narration there is a simple prose account of the same battle, and this is followed by a copy of the treaty of peace which established an offensive and defensive alliance between the empire of the Hittites and Egypt.

I here insert a few incidents from the prize poem of Pentaur, written two years after the battle of Kadesh. Reading between the lines of the boastful hieroglyphs, it is clear that the Hittites must have maintained their ground in the battle, for their king, who, at the beginning of the fight, is "the *vile* king of the Hittites," and "the *miserable* king of the Hittites," towards the close of the battle becomes "the *great* king of the Hittites."

According to Pentaur, the Hittites and their allies covered mountains and valleys like grasshoppers, and no such multitude had ever been seen before. . . . Pharaoh was young and bold, he seized his arms, he armed his people and his chariots, and marched towards the land of the Hittites. . . . Arab spies were caught, who told Pharaoh that the Hittite army was in the neighbourhood of Aleppo ; but "the miserable king of the Hittites" was all the time lying in ambush with his allies north-west of Kadesh. They rose up and surprised the Egyptians. Pharaoh's retreat was cut off. In this crisis he prayed to his god and father, Amon, and was assisted to perform prodigies of valour. He hurled darts with his right hand and fought with his left; the two thousand three hundred horses were dashed to pieces, and the hearts of the Hittites sank within them. The King of the Hittites sent eight of his brother kings with armed chariots against Pharaoh; but six times he charged the unclean wretches, who did not acknowledge his god; he killed them, none escaped. Pharaoh upbraided his worthless warriors, who had left him to fight the battle single-handed, and promised that on his return to Egypt he would see the fodder given to his pair of horses which did not leave him in the lurch.

The battle was renewed the following morning and went sore against the Hittites. Then the hostile king sent a messenger to ask for peace, and to say that the Egyptians and the Hittites ought to be brothers. Pharaoh assembled his warriors to hear the message of "the great king of the Hittites," and by their advice he made peace, and returned to Egypt in serene humour.

On the outer wall of the temple of Karnak we find inscribed the treaty of peace which was made on this or a later occasion, and the terms of the offensive and defensive alliance entered into. It is related that Kheta-sira, King of the Hittites, sent two heralds, bearing a plate of silver, upon which the treaty was engraved. The treaty is between the Grand-Duke of Kheta, Kheta-sira, the puissant, and Rameses, the great ruler of Egypt, the puissant. The arrangement is sanctioned by the Sun and by Sutekh, the chief gods respectively of Egypt and Kheta. There is to be peace and good brotherhood for ever—he shall fraternize with me and I will fraternize with him. The Grand-Duke of Kheta shall not invade the land of Egypt for ever, to carry away anything from it, nor shall Ramessu-Meriamen, the great ruler of Egypt, invade the land of Kheta for ever, to carry away anything from it. If Egypt is invaded by some other enemy, and Pharaoh sends to Kheta for help, the Grand-Duke is to go, or at least to send his infantry and cavalry; and he is, of course, to look for reciprocal aid. If emigrants or fugitives pass from one country to the other they are not to find service and favour, but to be given up ; nevertheless, when taken back, they are not to be punished as criminals. In support of the provisions of the treaty the parties thereunto invoke " the thousand gods of the land of Kheta, in concert with the thousand gods of the land of Egypt." Whosoever shall not observe the provisions of the treaty, the gods shall be against his house and family and servants ; but to whomsoever shall observe them the gods shall give health and life—to his family, himself, and his servants.

" In such a form," says Brugsch, " were peace and friendship made at Ramses, the city in Lower Egypt, between the two most powerful nations of the world at that time —Kheta in the east, and Kemi (Egypt) in the west."

Following upon the conclusion of this treaty we have a happy dynastic alliance. Kheta-sira, the great king of the Hittites, appeared in Egypt in Hittite costume, accompanied by his beautiful daughter, and Pharaoh made this princess his queen. A memorial tablet at Ibsamboul speaks of this as a great, inconceivable wonder—"she herself knew not the impression which her beauty made on thy heart "—and we may fairly infer that her influence contributed to the international friendship which lasted as long as Rameses lived. We do not know the native name of the Hittite princess, but the name given her on her marriage was Ur-Maa-Noferu Ra.

Since it has become evident that the Hittites were a great people, and not a petty local tribe like the Hivites or the Perizzites, scholars have naturally turned again to the Bible references to see what they really imply. On careful examination the Bible passages are seen to be all consistent with the idea that the Hebrew writers were well acquainted with the power and greatness of the

Hittites. Their greatness is nowhere denied ; on the contrary there are some passages which seem plainly to imply it. When Solomon imported horses and chariots from Egypt, he sold them to the kings of Syria and to "all the kings of the Hittites" (2 Chron. i. 16). Again, when Ben-hadad, king of Syria, was besieging Samaria, and the Syrians were smitten with panic, believing that they heard "a noise of chariots, and a noise of horses, even the noise of a great host," what nations did they suppose were alone able to send great hosts into the field with horses and chariots? They said one to another, "Lo, the King of Israel has hired against us the kings of the Hittites and the kings of the Egyptians" (2 Kings vii. 6). Further —to take an instance nearer to the age of Rameses II.—when the future wide inheritance of Israel is promised to Moses and to Joshua, the description runs thus :—"From the wilderness and this Lebanon, even unto the great river, the river Euphrates, all the land of the Hittites, and unto the great sea toward the going down of the sun "—words which had been regarded as a pictorial exaggeration, but which may now be looked upon as literally accurate (Deut. xi. 24 ; Josh. i. 4).

Exploration and research are now making us acquainted with Hittite works of art and with inscriptions in the Hittite character and language ; while, as already stated, we have Egyptian portraits of their soldiers on the Temple wall at Ibsamboul.

Burckhardt the traveller was perhaps the first to discover and describe a Hittite inscription. He gives an account of a stone which he saw in a wall in the city of Hamath, which was covered with hieroglyphs differing from those of Egypt. The discovery was without result at the time ; but when the stone had been seen again, with four others, in 1870, by the American visitor, Mr J. A. Johnson, interest began to be aroused. Similar stones have been

HAMATH INSCRIPTION (HITTITE).

(Specially drawn by W. Har...)

found at Carchemish, at Aleppo, and in various parts of Asia Minor. Some have been removed to the Museum at Constantinople, some are in the British Museum, and some inscriptions remain on rock faces irremovable. A very good collection of illustrative plates will be found appended to Dr Wm. Wright's "Empire of the Hittites." The Hittite hieroglyphs cannot yet be deciphered, although Dr A. H. Sayce and Major Conder may be said to have made a promising beginning. The inquiry has been aided a little by a short inscription in Hittite and Cuneiform characters, engraved on a convex silver plate, which looked like the knob of a staff or dagger, and is known as the boss of Tarkondêmos. We shall probably have to wait for the discovery of some longer bi-lingual inscription before much progress can be made. Meanwhile Major Conder finds much reason to think that the affinities of the Hittites and their language were Mongolian. The inscriptions of course are quite a mystery to the Asiatic folk in whose districts they are found, and they attribute magical virtues to some of them. The particular stone figured above was very efficacious in cases of lumbago: a man had only to lean his back against it and he was effectually cured.

We know something of the religion of the Hittites from their invocation of the gods in their treaty with Rameses II. They adored the sun and moon, the mountains, rivers, clouds, and the sea. But their chief deity was Sutekh, "king of heaven, protector of this treaty," supposed by Brugsch to be a form of Baal, but who is more likely to have been allied to Set or to Dagon. We cannot suppose that their worship was purer than that of the nations round about them ; but it may not have been less pure, nor their life less moral. The appeal to the King of Heaven to protect a treaty is admirable so far as it goes. To what height they could sometimes rise in their conceptions of duty is pleasantly shown if, as seems possible, that beautiful passage in Micah vi. 8 is to be attributed to them—"What doth the Lord require of thee but to do justly, to love mercy, and to walk humbly with thy God." The prophet quotes the sentiment from Balaam, and gives it as Balaam's answer to the question of Balak, king of Moab, who had sent for him to curse Israel. A conversation took place which may be set forth as follows :—

King —Wherewithal shall I come before the Lord, and bow myself before the high God ? Shall I come before him with burnt offerings, with calves of a year old ?

Prophet—Will the Lord be pleased with thousands of rams, or with ten thousands of rivers of oil ?

King—Shall I give my first-born for my transgression, the fruit of my body for the sin of my soul?

Prophet—He hath shewed thee, O man, what is good ; and what doth the Lord require of thee, but to do justly, and to love mercy, and to walk humbly with thy God ? *

In the Book of Numbers we find that Balaam had been sent for from another country, and came from the city of Pethor. Now, in the temple of Karnak, Thothmes III. gives a list of two hundred and eighteen towns in Syria and Aram, which he claims to have conquered, and among them we find Pethor. It was a city on the Upper Euphrates, not far from Carchemish, and so was well within the circle of the Hittite dominion. Balaam, then, may be regarded as a Hittite, or as belonging to the Hittite confederacy,† and since the text quoted shows his idea of the Divine requirements, it indicates the standard of duty which had been arrived at by some among that people.

The rock inscriptions prove that the Hittites possessed a

* See Bishop Butler's "Sermon on the Character of Balaam."

† Rev. H. G. Tomkins argues that he was a Semite, though in close contact with the Hittites.—"Journal of the Anthropological Institute," November 1889.

written language, and this is further shown by their en-graved treaty sent to Rameses II. They appear even to have possessed a literature, for the Egyptian records mention a certain Khilp-sira as a writer of books among the Hittites. One of their cities in the south of Palestine was called Kirjath-Sepher, or Book-Town, so that the place must have been noted for writings of some kind.

The fact that the copy of the treaty sent to Rameses was engraved upon a silver plate, with a figure of the god Sutekh in the middle, shows that the Hittites were an artistic people also. In fact their civilisation was far advanced. " They had walled towns, chased metal work, chariots and horses, skilled artificers. They could carve in stone, and could write in hieroglyphic character. All this wonderful cultivation they possessed while Israel as yet was hardly a nation. Thus the Bible account of the Canaan overrun by Joshua is fully confirmed by monumen-tal evidence." *

[*Authorities and Sources:*—" A History of Egypt under the Pharaohs." By Henry Brugsch-Bey. " The Empire of the Hittites." By William Wright, D.D. " The Hittites : the Story of a forgotten Empire." By A. H. Sayce, LL.D. " Transactions of the Society of Biblical Archæology."]

5. *Semites in Egypt before the Oppression.*

If, as seems probable, the Pharaoh of Joseph was Apepi, the last of the Shepherd Kings, and the Pharaoh of the Oppression was Rameses II., the third king of the nine-teenth dynasty, we have a period of nearly three centuries between Joseph and the " new king who knew not Joseph."

* Major Conder, in the " Journal of the Anthropological Institute," August 1889.

The period appears to be much too long to make the expression "new king" seem natural, while at the same time a shorter period would hardly leave room for the descendants of Jacob to multiply and become a danger to Egypt. This perplexity is removed by the recent discovery of ancient writings under the extensive ruins existing at Tell-el-Amarna in Upper Egypt—a site about midway between Minieh and Siout, and on the eastern bank of the Nile. From these documents it appears that Semites were in great favour with Amenhotep IV. (Amenôphis), the last king of the eighteenth dynasty, whereas the new dynasty that succeeded abominated this foreign influence.

In the latter part of the eighteenth dynasty friendly relations prevailed between Egypt and Mitanni or Nahrina (Aram Naharaim, Judges iii. 8), a Mesopotamian district which lay opposite to the Hittite city of Carchemish. Amenôphis III. married a wife from the royal house of Mitanni; and the offspring of this marriage—Amenôphis IV.—in his turn married Tadukhepa, daughter of Duisratta, the Mitannian king. He was thus doubly drawn to look favourably upon the Mitannian form of faith, which, like that of the Semites, included the adoration of the winged solar disk. Meantime the Egyptian conquest of Palestine, whose petty kings and governors now ruled as satraps for the Egyptian monarch, had paved the way for strangers from Canaan and Syria to rise into favour at Pharaoh's court. Amenôphis IV. surrounded himself with Semitic officers and courtiers, thus offending the nobles of Egypt; and by forsaking the ancient religion of his country, brought about a rupture with the powerful priesthood of Thebes. Forced to go forth, the "heretic king" built a new capital on the edge of the desert to the north. Here he assumed the name of Khu-en-Aten, "the glory of the solar disk," while his architects and sculptors consecrated a new and peculiar style of art to the new religion, and even the potters decorated the vases they modelled with new colours and patterns.

"The archives of the empire were transferred from Thebes to the new residence of the king, and there stored in the royal palace, which stood among its gardens at the northern extremity of the city. But the existence and prosperity of Khu-en-Aten's capital were of short duration. When the king died he left only daughters behind him, whose husbands assumed in succession the royal power. Their reigns lasted but a short time, and it is even possible that more than one of them had to share his power with another prince. At any rate it was not long before rulers and people alike returned to the old paths. The faith which Khu-en-Aten had endeavoured to introduce was left without worshippers, the Asiatic strangers whom he and his father had promoted to high offices of State were driven from power, and the new capital was deserted never to be inhabited again. The great temple of the solar disk fell into decay, like the royal palace, and the archives of Khu-en-Aten were buried under the ruins of the chamber wherein they had been kept."

It is these archives which have now come to light, and which furnish such extraordinary information concerning the state of Egypt and Palestine in the century before the Oppression. In the winter of 1887 the fellahin of Egypt, searching for nitrous earth with which to manure their fields, discovered some three hundred ancient tablets inscribed with Babylonian cuneiform writing. The tablets are copies of letters and despatches from the kings and governors of Babylonia and Assyria, of Syria, Mesopotamia, and Eastern Cappadocia, of Phœnicia and Palestine, exchanging information with the Pharaoh of Egypt, or making reports as to the state of the country they governed. Among the correspondents of the Egyptian sovereigns were Assurynballidh of Assyria and Burnaburyas of Babylonia, which thus fix the date of Khu-en-Aten to about 1430 B.C. This shows incidentally that the Egyptologists have been quite right in not assigning the Exodus to an earlier period than 1320 B.C., that is to say, the reign of Menephtah, the son and successor of Rameses II.

At the date of the despatches Palestine and Phœnicia were garrisoned by Egyptian troops, and their affairs were more or less directed by Egyptian governors. There were as yet no signs of the Israelites coming into the land. But the Canaanite population was already threatened by an enemy from the north. These were the Hittites, to whom references are made in several of the despatches from Syria and Phœnicia. After the weakening of the Egyptian power, in consequence of the religious troubles which followed the death of Khu-en-Aten, the Hittites were enabled to complete their conquests in the south, and to drive a wedge between the Semites of the East and the West. With the revival of the Egyptian empire under the rulers of the nineteenth dynasty the southward course of Hittite conquest was checked ; but the wars of Rameses II. against the Hittites of Kadesh on Orontes desolated and exhausted Canaan and prepared the way for the Israelitish invasion. Phœnicia seems to have been the furthest point to the north to which the direct government of Egypt extended. At any rate the letters which came to the Egyptian monarch from Syria and Mesopotamia were sent to him by princes who called themselves his " brothers," and not by officials who were the " servants " of the king.

It is wonderful to find that in the fifteenth century before our era, active literary intercourse was carried on throughout the civilised world of Western Asia, between Babylonia and Egypt and the smaller states of Palestine, of Syria, of Mesopotamia, and even of Eastern Cappadocia. And this intercourse was carried on by means of the Babylonian language and the complicated Babylonian script. It implies that all over the civilised East there were libraries and

schools, where the Babylonian language and literature were
taught and learned. Babylonian in fact was as much the
language of diplomacy and cultivated society as French has
been in modern times, with the difference that whereas it
does not take long to read French, the cuneiform syllabary
required years of hard labour and attention before it could
be acquired.

One of the facts which result most clearly from a study
of the tablets is that, not only was a Semitic language the
medium of literary intercourse between the Pharaoh of
Egypt and his officers abroad, but that Semites held high
and responsible posts in the Egyptian Court itself. Thus
we find Dudu, or David, addressed by his son as " my lord,"
and ranking apparently next to the monarch; and there are
in the Egyptian National Collection not only letters written
by officials with Egyptian names, like Khapi or Hapi (Apis),
but with such Semitic names as Rib-Addu, Samu-Addu,
Bu-Dadu (the Biblical Bedad) and Milkili (the Biblical
Malchiel). A flood of light is thus poured upon a period
of Egyptian history which is of high interest for the student of the Old Testament. In spite of the reticence of
the Egyptian monuments, we can now see what was the
meaning of the attempt of Amenophis IV. to supersede
the ancestral religion of Egypt. The king was in all
respects an Asiatic. His mother, who seems to have
been a woman of strong character,—able to govern not
only her son, but even her less pliable husband,—came
from the region of the Euphrates, and brought with her
Asiatic followers, Asiatic ideas, and an Asiatic form of
faith. The court became Semitised. The favourites and
officials of the Pharaoh, his officers in the field, his correspondents abroad, bore names which showed them to be of
Canaanite and even of Israelitish origin. If Joseph and
his brethren had found favour among the Hyksos princes
of an earlier day, their descendants were likely to find
equal favour at the court of " the heretic king."

We need not wonder, therefore, if Amenophis IV. found himself compelled to quit Thebes. The old aristocracy might have condoned his religious heresy, but they could not condone his supplanting them with foreign favourites. The rise of the nineteenth dynasty marks the successful reaction of the native Egyptian against the predominance of the Semite in the closing days of the eighteenth dynasty. It was not the founder of the eighteenth dynasty (Aahmes, who drove out the Hyksos) but the founder of the nineteenth dynasty that was "the new king who knew not Joseph." Ever since the progress of Egyptology had made it clear that Rameses II. was the Pharaoh of the Oppression, it was difficult to understand how so long an interval of time as the whole period of the eighteenth dynasty could lie between him and that "new king," whose rise seems to have been followed almost immediately by the servitude and oppression of the Hebrews. If Aahmes began the Oppression, how was it that a whole dynasty passed away before the Israelites cried out? The tablets of Tell-el-Amarna now show that the difficulty does not exist. Up to the death of Khu-en-Aten the Semite had greater influence than the native in the land of Mizraim.

How highly educated this old world was we are but just beginning to learn. But we have already learned enough to discover how important a bearing it has on the criticism of the Old Testament. It has long been tacitly assumed by the critical school that the art of writing was practically unknown in Palestine before the age of David. Little historical credence, it has been urged, can be placed in the earlier records of the Hebrew people, because they could not have been committed to writing until a period when the history of the past had become traditional and mythical. But this assumption can no longer be maintained. Long before the Exodus Canaan had its libraries and its scribes, its schools and literary men. The annals of the country, it is true, were not inscribed in the letters of the Phœnician alphabet on perishable papyrus; the writing material was imperishable clay, the characters were those of the cuneiform syllabary. Though Kirjath-Sepher (*i.e.,* Book-Town) was destroyed by the Israelites, other cities mentioned in the Tell-el-Amarna tablets, like Gaza, or Gath, or Tyre, remained independent, and we cannot imagine that the old traditions of culture and writing were forgotten in any of them. In what is asserted by the critical school to be the oldest relic of Hebrew literature, the Song of Deborah, reference is made to the scribes of Zebulon "that handle the pen of the writer" (Judges v. 14); and we have now no longer any reason to interpret the words in a non-natural sense, and transform the scribe into a military commander (an officer who arranges men in a row instead of arranging letters and words). Only it is probable that the scribes still made use of the cuneiform syllabary, and not yet of the Phœnician alphabet. At all events the Tell-el-Amarna tablets have overthrown the primary foundation on which much of this criticism was built, and have proved that the populations of Palestine, among whom the Israelites settled, and whose culture they inherited, were as literary as the inhabitants of Egypt or Babylonia.

But apart from such side-lights as these upon ancient history, the discovery of the Tell-el-Amarna tablets has a lesson for us of momentous interest. , The collection cannot be the only one of its kind. Elsewhere, in Palestine and Syria as well as in Egypt, similar collections must still be lying under the soil. Burnt clay is not injured by rain and moisture, and even the climate of Palestine will have preserved uninjured its libraries of clay. Such libraries must still be awaiting the spade of the excavator on the sites of places like Gaza, or others whose remains are buried under the lofty mounds of Southern Judea. Kirjath-Sepher must have been the seat of a famous library, consisting mainly, if not altogether, of clay tablets inscribed with cuneiform characters. As the city also bore the name of Debir, or "Sanctuary," we may conclude that the tablets were stored in its chief temple, like the libraries of Assyria and Babylonia. When such relics of the past have been disinterred—as they will be if they are properly searched for—we shall know how the people of Canaan lived in the days of the Patriarchs, and how their Hebrew conquerors established themselves among them in the days when, as yet, there was no king in Israel.

[The information contained in this section is derived almost exclusively from the writings of Dr A. H. Sayce, who has taken a chief part in England in the decipherment of the Tell-el-Amarna inscriptions. See " Proc. Soc. Bib. Arch." "Records of the Past." New Series, vols. ii. and iii. ; "Victoria Institute Annual Address, 1889." See additional facts in the *Contemporary Review*, Dec. 1890, and opinions in Naville's *Bubastis.*

6. *Israel in Egypt.*

We have seen how well the general political circumstances in Egypt and Palestine, in the centuries before the Exodus, supplement the Bible narrative, explaining on the one hand why the Israelites were oppressed, and showing on the other how Canaan was prepared for their easy conquest. But while the fact that Rameses II. was the Pharaoh for whom Israel built " treasure cities " is demonstrated beyond reasonable contradiction, it is remarkable that the inscriptions do not say anything about the Israelites. We must suppose, with Brugsch, that the captives were included in the general name of foreigners, of whom the documents make very frequent mention. It would be satisfactory, no doubt, to find upon some contemporary Egyptian monument, a record of the arrival of Jacob, or the tasks imposed upon the Israelites, or the destruction of Pharaoh's host in the Red Sea. But the Egyptians were not accustomed to record their defeats, and as to the labours imposed upon the Israelites, they were but a matter of course in the case of captives.

But short of direct mention, the Egyptian monuments and records afford ample confirmation to the Biblical account of the Sojourn. The Scripture references to Egyptian manners and customs are, in all respects, accurate ; and this absolute accuracy could only result from actual contact and intimate acquaintance.

The Bible history of Abraham implies that when he visited Egypt, driven thither by famine, that country was already under a settled government, having a king, and princes who acted as the king's subordinates. It requires us to believe that the king was called Pharaoh, or by some name or title which conveyed that sound to Hebrew ears. And further, it assumes that Egypt was so fruitful and so prosperous, as to be a granary for surrounding nations in years of famine. On all these points the Bible is in harmony with what we learn from other sources.

Again, according to Genesis xii. 12, Abram feared for Sarai his wife, lest the Egyptians should take her from him, and should kill him in order to make the proceeding safer. The possibility of such a thing being done by a people so civilised and cultured as the Egyptians has sometimes been doubted : but M. Chabas has called attention to a papyrus which actually states that the wife and children of a foreigner are by right the lawful property of the king. In the "Tale of the Two Brothers" also—an Egyptian romance of the days of Seti II.—we are told that the king of Egypt sent two armies to bring a beautiful woman to him, and to murder her husband.

In this same tale of The Two Brothers the wife of the elder solicits the love of the younger in almost exactly the same way that the wife of Potiphar tempts Joseph. The whole story of Joseph agrees minutely with what we learn of Egypt from her own records. The outward details of life, the officers of the court, the traffic in slaves, the visits for corn, are all pictured on temple walls and stone slabs. No feature in the Bible narrative is out of harmony with what we know of the country from other sources. "Potiphar" appears to be a good Egyptian name, and Egyptologists have pointed out that its probable equivalent in hieroglyphs signifies "Devoted to the Sun-god." Joseph's new name, Zaphnath-paaneah, means "Storehouse of the house of Life," and was given to him when he entered Pharaoh's service, just as a new name was given to the Hittite princess when she became Pharaoh's wife. The king's absolute authority appears abundantly from Herodotus, Diodorus and others. He enacted laws, imposed taxes, administered justice, executed and pardoned offenders at his pleasure. He had a body-guard, which is constantly seen on the sculptures, in close attendance on his person. He was assisted in the management of state affairs by the advice of a council, consisting of the most able and distinguished members of the priestly order. His court was magnificent and comprised various grand functionaries, whose tombs are among the most splendid of the early remains of Egyptian art. When he left his palace for any purpose, he invariably rode in a chariot. His subjects, wherever he appeared, bowed down or prostrated themselves.* The civilisation of the Egyptians, even at a period long before the Israelitish Sojourn, comprised the practice of writing, the distinction into classes or castes, the peculiar dignity of the priests, the practice of embalm-

---

* See the authorities given in "Rawlinson's Historical Illustrations of the Old Testament."

ing and of burying in wooden coffins or mummy cases, the manufacture and use of linen garments, the wearing of gold chains, and almost all the other points which may be noted in the Bible description.

In Genesis xl. 20, Pharaoh held a feast on his birthday, and the chief butler being restored to favour, gave the cup into Pharaoh's hand. We know from the Rosetta Stone that as late as the reign of Ptolemy Epiphanes it was customary to make great rejoicing on the king's birth-day, to consider it holy, and to do no work on it. That it should be a day on which pardons were granted as an act of grace, is more than probable. Cups such as the king would have taken his wine from are portrayed on the monuments ; baskets such as the baker would have carried his bakemeats in are used even unto this day, and may be seen in the British Museum. Before Joseph entered the royal presence he shaved himself and changed his raiment : and here, again, the monuments and profane history offer us illustrations. The Egyptians only allowed their hair to grow during the times of mourning, and to neglect the hair was considered very slovenly and dirty. When a man of low station had to be represented, the artist always drew him with a beard. The British Museum possesses Egyptian razors of various shapes ; and in a tomb at Beni-Hassan the act of shaving is actually represented.

With regard to the seven years of famine, it is true that Egypt was less likely to suffer in this way than the countries round about; yet still, when the inundation of the Nile fell below the average, it was liable to this scourge. History tells of numerous cases in which the inhabitants have suffered terribly from want, and several famines are even mentioned on the monuments. Professor Rawlinson refers us to a case which furnishes a near parallel to the famine of Joseph. In A.D. 1064 a famine began in Egypt which lasted seven years, and was so severe that dogs and cats, and even human flesh, were eaten ; nearly all the horses of the Caliph perished, and his family had to fly into Syria.

When Jacob goes down into Egypt, he is advised to tell Pharaoh that he and his sons are keepers of cattle, so that the land of Goshen may be assigned to them, shepherds being an abomination unto the Egyptians. The Egyptian contempt for herdsmen appears plainly on the monuments, where they are commonly represented as dirty and un-shaven, and are sometimes even caricatured as a deformed and unseemly race. When Jacob dies, his body is embalmed by the physicians, forty days being taken up with the processes, and seventy days being spent in mourn-ing. The methods of embalming are described by Herodotus and Diodorus, and it is stated that in preparing the body according to the first method the operators commenced by extracting the brain and pouring in certain drugs. Then they made an incision in the side of the body with a sharp Ethiopian stone, and drew out the intestines, filling the cavity with powder of pure myrrh, cassia, and other fragrant substances, and sewing up the aperture. This being done, they salted the body, "keeping it in natron during seventy days," after which they washed it and wrapped it up in bands of fine linen smeared on their inner side with gum. Remarking upon the number of days, seventy or seventy-two, mentioned by the two historians, Sir Gardner Wilkinson says there is reason to believe it comprehended the whole period of the mourning, and that the embalming process only occupied a portion of it.

Subsequently to the burial of his father, Joseph himself died, and his body also was embalmed. At some later period there arose a king who knew not Joseph. This monarch is generally supposed to be Rameses II., and if the identification were correct, the indications of his

character afforded by the Book of Exodus agree exactly
with what the monuments reveal concerning that haughty
oppressor; but, as already stated, the reference is probably
to Rameses I.   The slavery of the Israelites was of a kind
to which all hostile or conquered people were reduced by
the Egyptians.   Thothmes III., during his many campaigns, brought to Egypt unnumbered prisoners of every
race, and made them labour like convicts on the public
works, under the superintendence of architects and overseers.   On the walls of a chamber in a tomb at Thebes
there is a very instructive pictorial representation of such
forced labour, and the Asiatic countenances of the workers
strongly resemble those of the Hebrew race.   The date is
too early, and we may suppose them to belong to some
other nation of the Semitic family; but the picture none
the less shows the method of working under taskmasters.
Some carry water in jugs from the tank hard by; others
knead and cut up the loamy earth; others, again, by the
help of a wooden form, make the bricks, or place them
carefully in long rows to dry; while the more intelligent
among them carry out the work of building the walls.
The hieroglyphic explanations inform as that the labourers
are captives whom Thothmes III. has carried away to
build the temple of his father Amon.   They explain that
the baking of the bricks is a work for the new building of
the provision house of the god Amon of Apet (the east
side of Thebes), and they finally declare the strict superintendence of the steward over the foreigners.   The words
are—(Here are seen) the prisoners which have been
carried away as living prisoners in very great numbers;
they work at the building with active fingers; their overseers show themselves in sight, these insist with vehemence,
obeying the orders of the great skilled lord [the head
architect] who prescribes to them the works, and gives
directions to the masters; (they are rewarded), with wine

and all kinds of good dishes; they perform their service with a mind full of love for the king; they build for Thothmes III. a holy of holies for (the gods), may it be rewarded to him through a range of many years.

The overseer speaks thus to the labourers at the building: " The stick is in my hand, be not idle."

Some of the captives thus set to labour by Thothmes belonged to a people called the Aperiu; and in the days of Rameses II. they are mentioned as still in a condition of servitude, quarrying and transporting stone for the great fortress of the city of Paramessu or Tanis.

Diodorus tells us that Rameses II. put up an inscription in each of his buildings, saying that it had been erected by captives, and that not a single native Egyptian was employed on the work. Again, this king manufactured bricks for sale, and, by employing the labour of captives, was enabled to under-sell other makers. The use of crude bricks baked in the sun was universal throughout the country for private and for many public buildings, and the dry climate of Egypt was peculiarly suited to those simple materials. They had the recommendation of cheapness, and those made three thousand years ago, whether with or without straw, are even now as firm and fit for use as when first put up. When made of the Nile mud or alluvial deposit they required straw to prevent their cracking; but those formed of clay taken from the torrent beds on the edge of the desert held together without straw; and crude brick walls frequently had the additional security of a layer of reeds or sticks placed at intervals to act as binders.

[*Authorities and Sources :*—Brugsch's " Egypt under the Pharaohs." Wilkinson's " Ancient Egyptians." Birch's " Egypt " (Series, Ancient History from the Monuments). G. Rawlinson's " Historical Illustrations of the Old Testament." E. A. Wallis Budge, " Dwellers on the Nile." M. E. Harkness, " Egyptian Life and History."]

7. *Buried Cities of the East—Preliminary.*

If the buried cities of the East had been altogether
destroyed and lost, and we possessed only a brief record of
their disappearance, the subject might not possess much
interest for us, and there would be no material for writing
a book. But we are now witnessing a resurrection of some
of them, and are recovering a story of the past, such as revived Egyptian mummies might be able to tell. Nay, not
only Egyptians who walked about—

> " In Thebes's streets three thousand years ago,
>   When the Memnonium was in all its glory,"

but Chaldean shepherds who watched the stars and were
perhaps the first to give names to the signs of the Zodiac.
The ancient relics and records which are now being recovered from Egypt, Palestine, Assyria, and Babylonia,
revive forgotten stories of human struggle, and furnish
material for new chapters in the history of Art, Science,
Laws, and Language, of Mythology, Morals, and Religion.
They also throw frequent side lights upon the Bible narrative, and enable us to compare the Israelites more fairly
with their contemporaries and predecessors.

The catastrophes which led to the partial destruction,
and the eventual burial of the cities of the East must have
seemed nothing less than pure calamities at the time ; but
one of the results has been the providential preservation of
the remains for the enlightenment of the present genera-
tion. When a buried city is unearthed, it serves to confute
the scepticism which had been growing up, and to rectify the
errors which had found their place in books of history.
We are familiar with the fact that the cities of Herculaneum
and Pompeii were overwhelmed—the former by streams of
lava, the latter by showers of ashes, pumice, and stones,
from the crater of Vesuvius, in A.D. 79. The existence of

those cities had come to be doubted, and for ages they
were spoken of as "the fabulous cities;" nevertheless, after
sixteen centuries, they were brought to light, and they
present us with a picture of Roman life, such as history by
itself could never have supplied.   The site of Pompeii had
always borne the name of *Civita*, or the city; and in 1748,
a Spanish colonel of engineers, having heard that the
remains of a house had been discovered, with ancient
statues and other objects, obtained leave to excavate.   In
a few days his labours met with encouraging reward, and
eventually about one third of the ancient city was uncovered.   We may now walk about in Pompeii, observing
how its houses were built, and how its streets were paved.
We see the ruts worn by the wheels of chariots, we note
the public fountains, the temples, the theatre, which would
seat 10,000 people.   We notice the corn-mills in the
bakers' shops, the vats in the dyers' shops, and in private
houses we observe with interest the many articles of
domestic use.   Excepting that the upper stories of the
houses have been destroyed—either burnt by the red-hot
stones, or broken down by the weight of matter which fell
upon them—"we see a flourishing city in the very state in
which it existed nearly eighteen centuries ago—the buildings as they were originally designed, not altered and
patched to meet the exigencies of newer fashions; the
paintings undimmed by the leaden touch of time; household furniture left in the confusion of use; articles, even
of intrinsic value, abandoned in the hurry of escape, yet
safe from the robber, or scattered about as they fell from
the trembling hand, which could not pause or stoop for its
most valuable possessions: and in some instances, the
bones of the inhabitants, bearing sad testimony to the
suddenness and completeness of the calamity which overwhelmed them." *

Remains of Roman London are found 16 or 17 feet

* Dyer's " Pompeii."

underground, in the neighbourhood of the Bank of England and the Mansion House, although London has not been buried in volcanic ashes. Rome itself is a buried city, for the capital of modern Italy stands upon the ruins of the city of the Cæsars. In Eastern countries the site of an ancient city is sometimes occupied by a squalid village, which is its degenerate successor; in other instances the site is quite deserted, and only a *tell* or mound remains to call attention to it. Ancient sites have also occasionally become submerged beneath the waters of seas or lakes. Thus the Lake of Aboukir in Egypt was drained lately, in order to reclaim the area for cultivation, and when the floor was laid bare from the water, there appeared everywhere traces of streets, of stone-covered ways, and of fields for tillage marked out by lines of shells.

Professor Maspero describes the process by which Egyptian temples become buried. "Just as in Europe during the Middle Ages the population crowded most densely round about the churches and abbeys, so in Egypt they swarmed around the temples, profiting by that security which the terror of his name and the solidity of his ramparts ensured to the local deity. A clear space was at first reserved round the pylons and the walls; but in course of time the houses encroached upon this ground, and were even built up against the boundary wall. Destroyed and rebuilt, century after century, upon the self-same spot, the *débris* of these surrrounding dwellings so raised the level of the soil that the temples ended for the most part by being gradually buried in a hollow, formed by the artificial elevation of the surrounding city. Herodotus mentions this of Bubastis, and on examination it is seen to have been the same in many other localities. At last, when the temple had been thrown down and was forsaken, the rubbish covered it up, and so the ruins have been preserved, to reward the modern explorer."

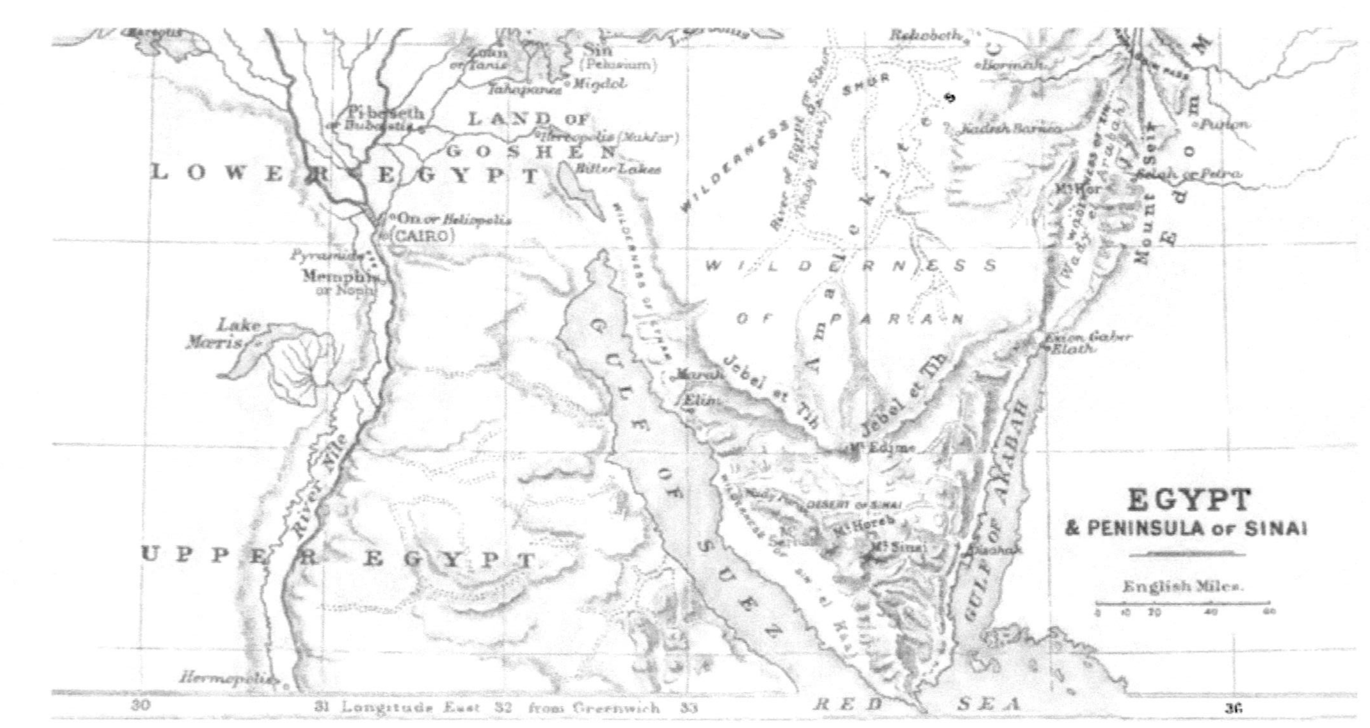

EGYPT
& PENINSULA of SINAI
English Miles.
0 10 20 40 60
LOWER EGYPT
UPPER EGYPT
LAND OF GOSHEN
Zoan or Tanis
Sin (Pelusium)
Tahapanes
Migdol
Pithom or Bubastis
Pi-beseth or Bubastis
Heroopolis (Muktar)
Bitter Lakes
On or Heliopolis
(CAIRO)
Pyramids
Memphis or Noph
Lake Mœris
River Nile
Naucratis
Hermopolis
Rehoboth
Beersheba
Kadesh Barnea
Mount Hor
M.t Hor
Selah or Petra
Punon
WILDERNESS OF SHUR
WILDERNESS OF ETHAM
River of Egypt (Wady el Arish)
WILDERNESS OF PARAN
GULF OF SUEZ
GULF OF AKABAH
Jebel et Tih
Jebel et Tih
M.t Edjme
Marah
Elim
DESERT OF SINAI
M.t Horeb
M.t Sinai
RED SEA
Hermopolis
Ezion Gaber Elath
30 31 Longitude East 32 from Greenwich 33 36

8. *Biblical Sites in Egypt.*

It is justly remarked by Rev. Greville J. Chester that there is scarcely a better or more striking commentary upon the prophets of Israel than the present condition of the ancient Biblical cities of Lower Egypt. For information regarding these cities—or what remains of them, buried in the soil—we are largely indebted to the Egypt Exploration Fund, which was founded in 1883, for the purpose of promoting historical investigation in Egypt, by means of systematically conducted explorations. Particular attention is given to sites which may be expected to throw light upon obscure questions of history and topography, such as those connected with the mysterious Hyksos period (the period of the Shepherd Kings), the district of the Hebrew Sojourn, the route of the Exodus, and the early sources of Greek art. Explorers have been sent out every season, and each year has been fruitful in discoveries. The objects of antiquity discovered are first submitted to the Director and Conservators of the National Egyptian Museum ; and those which can be spared are divided between the British Museum and the Museum of Fine Arts, Boston, U.S.A.

Excavations at San.—San, in the north-eastern part of the Delta, is the Tanis of the Septuagint and the Greek historians, and the Zoan of the Bible. At the time of the Exodus Zoan was the capital of Egypt, and the Pharaoh resided there. The wonders wrought by Moses and Aaron are referred to by the Psalmist as having been manifested in the field of Zoan (Psalm lxxviii. 43). We are told that Hebron was built only seven years before Zoan (Num. xiii. 22), and therefore, since Hebron was flourishing in Abraham's time, Zoan also must have been a very ancient city.

The modern village of San is a small collection of mud hovels, situated on the banks of a canal, which was once the Tanitic branch of the Nile. Near the village there are huge mounds which contain a ruined temple and other ancient remains. The place has been to a large extent explored by Mr W. M. Flinders Petrie, and the Memoir containing his interesting results is published by the Egypt Exploration Fund.

Rameses II., the Pharaoh of the Oppression, seems to have fixed upon Zoan and made it a new capital, because by its position it commanded the northern route to Syria and placed the king, after the conquest of that country, in easy communication with all his dominions. It was also close to the very centre of the Hyksos rule, which was only lately ended.

The Hyksos were the so-called Shepherd Kings, who appear to have come from the Arabian desert, or perhaps beyond, and established themselves in Lower Egypt at a period when native rule was weak. "The monuments of the Hyksos are among the most curious in Egypt; and it is to San that we owe the greater number of those brought to light. They are all distinguished by an entirely different type of face from any that can be found on other Egyptian monuments, a type which cannot be attributed to any other known period; and it is therefore all the more certain that they belong to the foreign race. Another peculiarity is that they are without exception executed in black or grey granite. The Hyksos only held the Delta, and occasionally more or less of Middle Egypt, and so they had no command of the red granite quarries of Assouan, which remained in the power of the native rulers. Whether the black granite came from Sinai or from the Hammamat district is not certain." Mr F. Ll. Griffith, the coadjutor of Mr Flinders Petrie, mentions several interesting monuments of a kind peculiar to this people. One is a group of two men, with bushy plaited hair and long beards: they stand with a tray of offerings in front of them, on which lie fishes, with papyrus plants hanging round. The details are beautifully worked, the flowers and buds being most delicately wrought. The black granite sphinxes made by the Hyksos have been often described. They have the flat, massive, muscular, lowering face, with short whiskers and beard around it, the lips being shaven; and the hair is in a mat of thick, short locks descending over the whole chest, a style copied from the great sphinxes of the twelfth dynasty. It is a curious fact that the inscriptions on Hyksos sphinxes, &c., are always in a line down the right shoulder, never on the left. Mr Petrie suggests that this honouring of the right shoulder by this Semitic people is analogous to the particular offering of the right shoulder continually enjoined in the Jewish law.* The Egyptians missed this idea, and inscribed either side indifferently, showing no preference for the left, although that was their side of honour.

Here at San, or Tanis, was discovered the famous Stone of San or Decree of Canopus, which is now preserved in the National Museum of Egypt. It bears the text of a decree made by the priests of Egypt, assembled at Canopus (which was at that time the religious capital of the country) in the ninth year of Ptolemy Euergetes (B.C. 254). It ordains the deification of Berenice, a daughter of Ptolemy's just dead, and creates a fifth order of priests, to be called Euergetæ, for the better paying of divine honours to the king and queen. The chief value of the monument consists in the circumstance that the inscription is tri-lingual, the characters being hieroglyphic (sacred), demotic (those of everyday business), and Greek (the chief language of foreigners in Egypt); so that, like the Rosetta Stone, it is of great use in helping scholars to decipher the Egyptian

* Exod. xxix. 22 ; Levit. vii. 32, viii. 25, ix. 21 ; Num. xviii. 18.

monuments. There is a plaster cast of this stone in the British Museum.

Mr Griffith finds that the early monuments of Tanis are suggestive of having been brought by Rameses II. to adorn his new capital. The truth about the age of Tanis can only be ascertained when deep excavations are made in the mound itself, or a sufficient examination of the extensive cemeteries has been carried out. But while the explorer is waiting, the cemeteries are in danger of being worked out by the Arabs, and the tombs are being destroyed for the sake of amulets to sell to dealers and travellers.

Tell Nebesheh—About eight miles S.E. of Tanis (modern San) is the low mound of Tell Nebesheh, originally known as Tell Farun—*i.e.*, the mound of Pharaoh, because of the great monolith shrine called Ras Farun, or Pharaoh's Head. Here Mr Petrie found, among other things, the remains of a temple, the altar of which contained important inscriptions. They were engraved by a certain "chief of the chancellors and royal seal bearer," whose name and further titles are effaced. This person was one of a series of officials whose titles were singularly parallel to the English Lord High Chancellor and Lord Privy Seal. The altar appears to belong to the Hyksos period, and it is suggested by Mr Petrie that these officials—who were so powerful that one of them actually appropriated for his inscriptions the royal monuments in a public temple—were native Egyptians, the Hyksos conquerors being only a military horde, without much civil organization, or organizing capacity, and taking over as they found it the native bureaucracy, who managed all the details of the needful administration of the country. So there appears to have been a series of viziers, men who acted for the king over the treasury and taxes, and over the royal decrees and public documents, bearing the king's seal.

After some further discussion of the position and importance of these viziers, Mr Petrie says that yet one further document may be quoted as giving and receiving light on this question : the account of Joseph in the Book of Genesis undoubtedly refers to the Hyksos period, and there we read, " Let Pharaoh look out a man discreet and wise, and set him over the land of Egypt "—not, let Pharaoh give orders to his own officers. " And Pharaoh said unto Joseph . . . . . Thou shalt be over my house, and according unto thy word shall all my people be ruled : only in the throne will I be greater than thou. And Pharaoh said unto Joseph, See, I have set thee over all the land of Egypt. And Pharaoh took off his signet-ring from his hand, and put it upon Joseph's hand, and arrayed him in vestures of fine linen, and put a gold chain about his neck; and he made him to ride in the second chariot which he had ; and they cried before him, ' Abrech ;' and he set him over all the land of Egypt." Here we read of the investiture of a vizier under the Hyksos, creating him royal seal-bearer, and giving him the honour of the second chariot. This we now see was not an extraordinary act of an autocrat, but the filling up of a regular office of the head of the native administration.

Excavations at Tell Basta, the ancient Bubastis. A little to the south of Zagazig, Mr Naville and Mr Griffith have made important discoveries. Bubastis was the seat of the worship of Bast or Pasht, the cat-headed goddess, whose temple is described by Herodotus as the most beautiful in Egypt. It was surrounded, he tells us, by a low wall, having figures engraved upon it. Here, accordingly, in April 1887, our explorers began their work, in the rectangular depression surrounded on all sides by the mounds of houses, which must have been higher than the temple. In a short time they disclosed the site of a grand hypostyle hall, strewn with fallen monolithic columns of twelfth dynasty workmanship, and a hall without columns, but lined, as it

should seem, with elaborate bas-relief sculptures representing a great religious ceremony, and containing tens of thousands of minutely-executed hieroglyphic inscriptions.   The
columns and the architraves of the hypostyle hall, though
of an earlier period, are emblazoned with the ovals of
Rameses II. (nineteenth dynasty).   The inscriptions of the
festival hall commemorate Osorkon II., of the twenty-
second dynasty, 'and his Queen Karoama.   Besides the
two historical landmarks thus determined, various blocks
bearing the names of Usertesen III. and Pepi Merira
testified to the existence of the edifice not only in the days
of the first great Theban Empire, but in the very remote
age of the Pyramid kings of the sixth dynasty.   At the
same time a small tentative excavation at the western
extremity of the site yielded the name and titles of
Nectanebo I., of the thirtieth and last native dynasty.
Such being the outcome of but four weeks' labour at the
close of the season, it seemed reasonable to hope for
important results when the excavations should be resumed.
This hope was more than fulfilled in 1888.   As the work
in this instance was not carried on in the desert, but quite
near to a busy railway station, many travellers visited the
place.   The scene was curiously picturesque.   " Here,
grouped together on the verge of the great cemetery of
Sacred Cats, are the tents of the officers of the Fund ;
yonder, swarming like bees at the bottom of the huge
crater-like depression which marks the area of the temple,
are seen some three to four hundred labourers—diggers in
the trenches and pits, basket-carriers clearing away the
soil as it is thrown out, overseers to keep the diggers at
work, ' pathway-men ' to keep the paths open and the
carriers moving, gangs of brawny ' Shayalin,' or [native
porters, harnessed together by stout ropes, and hauling or
turning sculptured blocks which have not seen the light for
many centuries ; girls with bowls of water and sponges,

to wash down the carved surfaces preparatory to the process of taking paper 'squeezes;' and small boys to run errands, help with the measuring tapes, and keep guard over the tents and baggage. With so many hands at work and so many overseers to keep them going, it is not wonderful that the excavations make rapid progress. The two large pits which were opened last season are now thrown into one, and are being enlarged from east to west, following the axis of the structure. The sides are also being cleared, and before another month shall have expired the whole temple—of which, apparently, not one stone remains upon another—will be visible from end to end. Its entire length is probably about 700 or 800 feet; but measurements, of course, are as yet purely conjectural."

Among the discoveries at this second exploration was a third hall, dating from the reign of Osorkon I., the walls of which were sculptured with bas-reliefs on a large scale, representing the king in the act of worshipping Bast and the other deities of the city. It appears that one great divinity honoured here was Amon; and another was the god Set.

It had not been suspected that Bubastis was the site of an important Hyksos settlement; but from the type of the statues and other things which have been found, that turns out to have been the case.

The chronographers have preserved the names of several of the Hyksos kings, recording them as follows:—Silites (or Salatis), Beon, Apachnas, Tannas (or Tanras), Asseth, and Apophis (in Egyptian, Apepi). Mariette, in his very successful excavations at Tanis, found the name of Apepi written on the arm of a statue, although the statue was of older date. Mr Naville has found, at Tell Basta, a colossal statue which he takes to be the statue of Apepi. It is now in the British Museum. This is particularly interesting, because Syncellus relates that Apepi was the king in whose reign Joseph rose to the high position described in Genesis. One remarkable object found at Tell Basta is part of a seated statue, upon which the royal name reads " Ian-Ra," or " Ra-Ian."   The name is new to us, but when Mr Naville went over to Boulak, where the Museum of Antiquities then was, and showed a copy to Ahmed Kemal-ed-Deen Effendi, the learned Mohammedan official, he exclaimed at once— " You have found the Pharaoh of Joseph. All our Arab books call him Reiyan, the son of El Welid." European scholars do not place absolute reliance on Arab chronicles, which are often fanciful ; yet it is remarkable that the statue of Ian-Ra, Joseph's king, according to the Arabs, should be found at Tell Basta, in close proximity to the statue of Apepi, Joseph's king, according to Syncellus. Mr Naville distinguishes Ian-Ra from Apepi, and thinks he is the same as Ianias or Annas, mentioned by Josephus as the fifth king out of six. Mr Naville has also found at Tell Basta the names of twenty-five Pharaohs who were known already, including Cheops and Chephren, the builders of the pyramids, about 3700 B.C.

That Joseph served a Hyksos king has long been accepted by the majority of Egyptologists as a very probable hypothesis, both chronologically and from the internal evidence of the Biblical narrative. The Arab writers represent the Hyksos as Amalekites of Midian. Mr Naville agrees with those who think they came from Mesopotamia, and already possessed a high degree of civilisation and culture.

Bubastis seems to have been a favourite place of residence with the Shepherd Kings ; and thus Joseph would be but a short distance from his brethren in the land of Goshen, where they looked after the king's herds of cattle.

Saft-el-Henneh or Goshen.—In more than one season Mr Naville carried on operations to discover the locality of Goshen, which had always been matter of conjecture and controversy. He has come to the conclusion that Goshen was a city a little to the east of the modern Zagazig, and situated in a district of the same name. The land of Goshen may be described as a district roughly triangular in shape, with its apex to the south; having Zagazig at its north-west angle, Tel-el-Kebir north-east, and Belbeis at the lower extremity. The town of Goshen appears to have been at Saft-el-Henneh, nearly halfway between the eastern and western points of the triangle. Here we find the name Tel Fakûs, the Phakusa of the Greeks, and apparently the same as Kesem, Gesem, or Goshen. Saft-el-Henneh itself is a large village, standing in the midst of a country peculiarly fruitful, corresponding thus to "the best of the land," which was given to the Israelites.

"At the first glance," says Mr Naville, "one sees that Saft-el-Henneh stands on the site of an ancient city of considerable extent. The whole village is constructed on the ruins of old houses, many of which are still to be seen on the south side."

The monuments discovered at Saft include a colossal statue, in black granite, of Rameses II., which, probably, belonged to a temple of some importance; and a shrine of Nectanebo II., with a dedicatory hymn, and the information that the place where the shrine was erected was called Kes.

The Book of Genesis tells us that Goshen was a pasture land. We may thence infer that it was not thickly inhabited, and not yet organized into a province with its capital, its temples, its priests, and its governor. Since then the name is absent from the earliest Egyptian lists of provinces—namely, those of Seti I. and Rameses II. (the Pharaoh that oppressed Israel)—Mr Naville maintains that the hieroglyphic records which simply omit the name, and the Bible narrative which incidentally shows us the reason why, are remarkably in accord.

Heliopolis.—No excavations have yet been undertaken at Heliopolis, the City of the Sun, which is situated some nine miles from Cairo in a north-easterly direction. It was a very ancient city, of great celebrity as a seat of the worship of the sun god *Ra*, whose symbol in the form of the living bull Mnevis, was there kept and cared for and reverenced. In the Bible the city is called On or Beth Shemesh. Joseph probably served Potiphar in this city; and Pharaoh afterwards gave him to wife Asenath, daughter of Potiphera, a priest of On. There can be little doubt, either, that Moses, who was learned in all the wisdom of the Egyptians, was educated at this seat of learning. We must believe, therefore, that he often looked upon the six obelisks which stood in front of the temple of Ra—one of which remains to this day—for they had been erected centuries before his birth. Four of them were set up by Thothmes III. and his family, about 1600 years before the Christian era, and the other two by Usertesen I. upwards of 3000 years B.C. Two of the Thothmes obelisks were at a later period transferred to Alexandria, to adorn the approach of a magnificent temple erected in honour of the Cæsars; and it is one of these two which has become known as Cleopatra's Needle and now stands on the Thames Embankment. The one obelisk which remains at Heliopolis is the oldest object of the kind in the world.

Scarcely anything is now to be seen of the city itself. It no doubt served as a handy quarry to the builders of Cairo; but since the surviving obelisk is buried 3 or 4 feet in Nile mud, it is not improbable that many small objects of antiquarian interest are buried also. Moreover, the sides of the vast enclosure in which the temple was situated are still marked by mounds or walls of crude brick, and these, on the north side, have their continuation in the ruins of the ancient town. Here are frequently found scarabæi or images of the sacred beetle, with other sacred images, emblems in porcelain, and other antiquities, so that apparently the place would repay a systematic search.

Tell Defenneh, the Biblical Tahpanhes.—In June 1886 Mr Flinders Petrie had the felicity to discover "Pharaoh's House," to which Jeremiah was brought, after the calamities in Judea, and where he hid the great stones, as a symbolical act, in the mortar of the brickwork. It lies in the sandy desert bordering on Lake Menzaleh, about two days' journey from San, some hours distant on the one hand from the cultivated Delta, and on the other hand from the Suez Canal. Here in the midst of the plain are the brick ruins of a large building; and on the first evening of his arrival in the district Mr Petrie heard to his surprise that the building was known as the *Kasr el Bint el Yehudi*, or the Palace of the Jew's daughter. Obviously this might refer to the daughter of King Zedekiah who accompanied Jeremiah in his exile ; and there could now be no doubt that Defenneh represented the ancient Daphnai and Tahpanhes. It was a frontier fortress or advanced post, to guard the great highway into Syria.

By the associations of Tahpanhes we are at once carried to Scripture. " The children of Noph and Tahpanhes have broken the crown of thy head " (Jer. ii. 16). This was after the slaying of Josiah, the deposition of Jehoahaz, the setting up of the tributary Jehoiakim, and the removal of Jehoahaz into Egypt—events which marked the first period of intercourse between Jews and Greeks. " This intercourse, however, was soon to be increased ; three years later, Nebuchadnezzar invaded Judea, and all who fled from the war would arrive at Tahpanhes in their flight into Egypt, and most likely stop there. In short, during all the troubles and continual invasions and sieges of Jerusalem, in B.C. 607, B.C. 603, and B.C. 599 (in which a wholesale deportation of the people took place), and, above all, in the final long siege and destruction of 590-588 B.C., when "the city was broken up," and all the men of war fled, every one who sought to avoid the miseries of war, or who was politically obnoxious, would naturally flee down into Egypt. Such refugees would necessarily reach the frontier fort on the caravan road, and would there find a mixed and mainly foreign population, Greek, Phœnician, and Egyptian, among whom their presence would not be resented, as it would be by the still strictly protectionist Egyptians further in the country. That they should largely, or perhaps mainly settle there would be the most natural course ; they would be tolerated, they would find a constant communication with their own countrymen, and they would be as near to Judea as they could in safety remain, while they awaited a chance of returning.

" The last and greatest migration to Tahpanhes is that fully recorded by Jeremiah, which gives us the pattern of what doubtless had been going on long before. After Nebuchadnezzar had retired with his spoils, Gedaliah, the governor whom he set up, was quickly slain, the country fell into anarchy, and all the responsible inhabitants who were left fled into Egypt to avoid the vengeance of Nebuchadnezzar. 'Johanan the son of Kareah, and all the captains of the forces, took all the remnant of Judah, that were returned (from all nations, whither they had been driven), to sojourn in the land of Judah; the men, and the women, and the children, and the king's daughters [Zedekiah's], and every person that Nebuzaradan, the captain of the guard, had left with Gedaliah the son of Ahikam the son of Shaphan, and Jeremiah the prophet, and Baruch the son of Neriah ; and they came into the land of Egypt ; for they obeyed not the voice of the Lord : and they came even to Tahpanhes' (Jer. xliii. 5-7)." This migration was undertaken in spite of the warnings of Jeremiah.

Pharaoh Hophra, the reigning monarch in Egypt, had been an ally of King Zedekiah's, and so he placed at the disposal of his friend's daughter the palace in this frontier fortress of Tahpanhes, which had been a royal residence sometimes. Here we may suppose the fugitives would have been comparatively contented, and thought themselves safe, only that Jeremiah vehemently prophesied that Nebuchadnezzar would come and destroy the place. This, according to Josephus, he did—" He fell upon Egypt, . . . and took those Jews that were there captives, and led them away to Babylon ; and such was the end of the nation of the Hebrews " (Ant. ix. 7). Josephus is not always believed, and it has even been denied in recent years that Nebuchadnezzar was ever in Egypt at all. But a recently discovered inscription tells us that he was in the country, and penetrated as far south as Assouan ;* and now at last Mr Petrie discovers the palace to have been plundered, dismantled, and burnt, apparently in fulfilment of Jeremiah's prediction.

The existing remains of Tahpanhes are extensive, and show that the ancient city was a large one. Under the corners of the chief buildings were found *plaques* of metal and of stone, engraved with the cartouche of Psammetichus I.; and under the south-east corner the teeth and bones of an ox, sacrificed at the ceremony when the building was founded. Among the antiquities found are beautiful painted Greek vases, plaques, &c., of gold, silver, lead, and copper, articles of carnelian, jaspar, and lapis lazuli.

A most interesting thing is the finding of the brickwork or pavement spoken of in Jeremiah xliii. 8. " Then came the word of the Lord unto Jeremiah in Tahpanhes, saying, Take great stones in thine hand, and hide them in mortar in the brickwork which is at the entry of Pharaoh's house in Tahpanhes, in the sight of the men of Judah ; and say

* See Sayce's " Fresh Light from the Monuments," p. 139.

unto them, Thus saith the Lord of Hosts, the God of Israel : Behold I will send and take Nebuchadnezzar the King of Babylon, my servant, and will set his throne upon these stones that I have hid ; and he shall spread his royal pavilion over them, &c." This brickwork or pavement at the entry of Pharaoh's house has always been misunderstood, and served as a puzzle to translators. "But" (says Mr Petrie) "as soon as the plan of the palace began to be recovered, the exactness of the description was manifest. On the north-west of the fort was a great open air platform of brickwork, such as is now seen outside all great houses, and most small ones, in Egypt. A space is reserved outside the door, generally along the side of the house, covered with hard beaten mud, edged with a ridge of bricks if not much raised from the ground, and kept swept clean. On this platform the inhabitants sit when they wish to converse with their neighbours or the passers-by. A great man will settle himself to receive his friends and drink coffee, and public business is generally transacted there. Such seems to have been the object of this large platform—a place to meet persons who would not be admitted to the palace or fort, to assemble guards, to hold large *levées*, to receive tribute and stores, to unlade goods, and to transact the multifarious business which in such a climate is best done in the open air. At the same time the actual way into the palace was along a raised causeway which rose at the back of this platform.

"This platform" (continues Mr Petrie) "is therefore unmistakably 'the brickwork or pavement which is at the entry of Pharaoh's house in Tahpanhes.' Here the ceremony described by Jeremiah took place before the chiefs of the fugitives assembled on the platform, and here Nebuchadnezzar 'spread his royal pavilion.' The very nature of the site is precisely applicable to all the events. Unhappily, the great denudation which has gone on has

swept away most of this platform, and we could not expect
to find the stones whose hiding is described by Jeremiah."

Another discovery, made some years ago, looks like
evidence that Nebuchadnezzar actually came to Tahpanhes.
A native sold to the Boulak Museum three cylinders of
terra cotta, such as would be used for foundation memorials,
the text on them being an inscription of Nebuchadnezzar's
referring to his constructions in Babylon. These cylinders
were said to come from the Isthmus of Suez, but it is
strongly suspected that they were found at Defenneh, after
the platform had become denuded.

Tell-el-Yahoudeh, the Mound of the Jew.—This place
should be interesting to us, if only from the fact that a
temple was built here, which some have fancied would be
the counterpart of the Temple at Jerusalem. If any considerable remains of the temple can be found, they may
assist materially the right understanding of the descriptions
which have come down to us of the more important structure on Mount Moriah.

Tell-el-Yahoudeh is about twenty miles from Cairo, on
the way to Ismailia, near the Moslem village of Shibeen-el-
Kanater, and is supposed to be the city of Onias.
Josephus tells us that at the time of the conquest of Judea
by Antiochus Epiphanes, Onias, son of the high priest, fled
from the persecution, and took refuge in Egypt (B. C. 182).
Onias, feeling encouraged by a prophecy of Isaiah's that a
time should come when there would be "an altar to the
Lord in the midst of the land of Egypt" (Isaiah xix. 19),
begged the Egyptian king, Ptolemy Philometor, to grant
him permission to build a temple, on the site of a deserted
shrine or fortress. The request was granted, and Onias
built a small city, after the model of Jerusalem, and a
temple, after the pattern of the temple of Solomon.

The mound now existing measures about half a mile
from east to west, and a quarter of a mile from north to

south, and has the appearance of a fortress. It has been more or less ransacked at various times; but would probably still repay a thorough exploration. In the absence of a full investigation there remains a little doubt about the genuineness of the site; but Professor Sayce, on one occasion, found here a fragment of stone, bearing two ancient Hebrew letters; and the decisive proof that it was a Jewish settlement has been furnished by the discovery of a Jewish cemetery, about one mile further east in the desert. The ground there, for the length of more than half a mile, is quite honey-combed with tombs. Here and there a body was found *in situ*, and there were no traces of enbalming, nor any ornament of any kind, but invariably a brick under the head, which was a distinctive mark of Jewish burials. A few tablets had escaped the general destruction, and the names which they contained fully confirmed the conclusion suggested by the mode of burial: " Eleazar " was one name and is purely Jewish: some others were Jewish with a Greek ending, as Salamis, Nethaneus, Barchias; and others still were Greek names of frequent use among the Jews, as Aristobulos, Onesimas, Tryphania.

Tell-el-Maskhuta or Pithom-Succoth.—The Pharaoh who enslaved the Israelites appears to have been Rameses II., son of Seti I., of the nineteenth dynasty. This dynasty only began with Rameses I., the grandfather of Rameses II. The store cities built by the Israelites were called Raamses and Pithom; and when the Exodus took place the starting point was Rameses and the first resting-place Succoth (Ex. i. 11; xii. 37). None of these places were known, and it had hardly been suspected that Pithom and Succoth were so closely associated as they are now found to be. But the site of Pithom has lately been discovered. We all remember Kassassin, where Sir Garnet Wolseley halted the British troops, in the campaign of 1882, just before that silent midnight march to storm Arabi's entrenchments. It is twelve miles west of Ismailia on the Suez Canal. Close by Kassassin is a low mound called *Tell-el-Maskhuta*, the Mound of the Statue. Here, at the end of the last century, was found a red granite monolith, representing Rameses II. sitting between the two solar gods Ra and Tum. In 1860 M. Paponot's men came across another monolith, and it is probable that the pair stood symmetrically at the entrance of some edifice. Further excavation brought to light two sphinxes in black granite, placed also on each side of the avenue ; and then, farther on, a shrine or *naos* in red sandstone, and a large *stele* in red granite, lying flat. All these monuments had been dedicated to the god Tum.

The excavations recently made by M. Edouard Naville, of Geneva, are described in his Memoir written for the Egypt Exploration Fund, from which Memoir we glean the following interesting information. The city was called Pi Tum, which means the house or abode of Tum (the god of the setting sun), and the surrounding district was called Thuku or Thukut, which is equivalent to Succoth. It is a mere philological accident that the Hebrew language has a word succoth, signifying *tents*. The inscriptions appear to show that it was Rameses II. who caused the city to be built; and in this they do but confirm the view previously entertained by Egyptologists. Pithom was both a store city and a fortress, and so was surrounded by very thick walls, part of which are yet preserved. The civil city of Thuku extended all round the sacred buildings of Pithom. We have first of all a square area enclosed by enormous brick walls, the space within being equal to 55,000 square yards. In the south-west angle is a small temple. The wall enclosure is honeycombed with rectangular chambers, well built, the bricks being of Nile mud, and united by mortar. It is a curious fact that some of the bricks contain straw, while others are

without.   These chambers M. Naville believes to be the
granaries into which Pharaoh gathered the provisions
necessary for armies about to cross the desert, and perhaps
for caravans and travellers, who were on the road to Syria.

Pithom, according to the Coptic version of the Scriptures, was the place where Joseph went up to meet Jacob
—"near Pithom, the city in the land of Rameses" (Gen.
xlvi. 28).   It is true that the LXX., supported by Josephus,
make Heroopolis to be the meeting-place; but it is not
unlikely that Heroopolis was a later name for Pithom
itself.   The Greeks were succeeded by the Romans, traces
of whose habitations are to be seen on all sides.

When the Romans levelled the ground for their camp,
they destroyed without mercy an immense number of
inscriptions, which would have been most precious to us
now.   Of those which remain, by far the most important
is the great tablet of Philadelphus, measuring 4 feet 3
inches, by 3 feet 2 inches, which was found near the *naos*.
It is stated in the inscription that the king ordered it to be
erected *before* **his father** *Tum,* **the great god of Succoth.**   It
records what was done for Pithom by the king, and his
queen and sister Arsinoe.   We learn from it that Pithom
and the neighbouring city of Arsinoe, which the king
founded in honour of his sister, were the starting points of
commercial expeditions to the Red Sea; and that from
thence one of Ptolemy's generals went to the land of the
Troglodytes, and founded the city of Ptolemais Θηριῶν, for
the special purpose of facilitating the chase of elephants.
And it was to Heroopolis that the ships brought the
animals (so that if Heroopolis was Pithom, and Pithom
was Maskhuta, the navigable water must have extended
farther northward than it does at present).   We learn also
that close to Pithom there was a city called Pikerehat, or
Pikeheret, apparently the Pi-ha-hiroth mentioned in the
narrative of the Exodus.

It was suggested by the late Dr Birch that the Israelites, besides building store cities, were compelled, like convicts or captives of war, to labour on the forts of Tanis, and on the line of the great wall which protected Egypt on the north-east. This long wall extended from Pelusium southwards, and had been built to keep out the tribes of the desert and other invaders from the Asiatic side. From the "Adventures of Sinuhit," a narrative dating from the twelfth dynasty, it appears to have been of very early construction; for the fugitive there says, "I reached the walls of the prince, which he has constructed to repel the Sittiu and to destroy the Nomiu-Shaiu; I remained in a crouching posture among the bushes, for fear of being seen by the guard, relieved each day, which keeps watch from the summit of the fortress: I proceeded on my way at nightfall." * The wall appears to have been renovated by Seti I. and Rameses II., and strengthened by forts, built after the Canaanite models which the Pharaohs had seen in the course of their campaigns. The Egyptians, not content with appropriating the thing, appropriated also the name, and called these frontier towers by the Semitic name of *Magdilu* or Migdols. In a later reign, an officer who had been sent to recapture two runaway slaves, reports that he did not overtake them until he had got beyond the region of the wall, to the north of the Migdol of King Seti Menephtah.†

[*Authorities and Sources :*—" Biblical Sites in Lower Egypt." By Greville J. Chester, B.A., in the Survey Memoirs, P. E. Fund. "Tel-el-Yahoudeh." By Prof. T. Hayter Lewis, F.S.A., in Trans. Soc. Bib. Archæol., vol. vii. "The Store-City of Pithom." By M. Naville, Egypt Exploration Fund. "Goshen." By M. Naville,

---

* " Records of the Past," New Series, vol. ii.
† Brugsch, " History of Egypt," vol. ii.

E. E. Fund. "Daphnae." By W. M. Flinders Petrie,
E. E. Fund. "Tanis." By W. M. Flinders Petrie,
E. E. Fund. Murray's Handbook, "Egypt."]

9. *The Route of the Exodus.*

As Succoth was the first station of the Israelites in
leaving Egypt, and we now know the locality, we begin to
be able to trace their route. Starting from Rameses—a
city not yet identified, but perhaps near the present
Zagazig*—two courses were open to them. They might
go northward, past the city of Zoan, and then skirt the
coast of Philistia—the route generally taken by the great
conquerors, and by much the nearer way. But there were
objections against taking it, for "it came to pass in the
course of those many days that the king of Egypt died"
(Exod. ii. 23), and the new Pharaoh, Menephtah, son and
successor of Rameses II., was holding his Court at Zoan at
this time,† and had his chariots and his horsemen about
him. Nor must we forget the great wall and its fortresses,
which in that direction would bar the way. "It was a
wall," says Mr Poole, "carefully constructed, with scarp and
counter-scarp, ditch and glacis, well manned by the best
troops, the sentinel on the ramparts day and night."
Prudence would seem to say that this route should not be
attempted. The course actually taken appears to have
been from Rameses eastward, along the valley Tumilat
and the line of the canal which had been made by Seti I.
They then encamped at Succoth, probably for the same
reason that the British encamped there in 1882, namely,

* May it not perhaps have been a new name given to Bubastis, after rebuilding?

† M. Naville, whose excavations at Tell Basta have shown that Bubastis
was a very large city, and a favourite resort of the king and his family, thinks
it quite possible that, at the time we are speaking of, the king was at Bubastis
and not at Zoan.

that there was abundance of forage and water, and a defensible position. The next station was " Etham, in the edge of the wilderness," northward from Pithom-Succoth, we may suppose, for they seem to have been marching (perhaps for a feint) as though they would take the short route through the Philistine country. But then they received the command to "turn back and encamp before Pi-ha-hiroth, between the Migdol and the sea, before Baal-Zephon, over against it by the sea." They obeyed, and to understand the course they actually pursued, we must take into account some recent geological discoveries. It is not the aim of the present writer to put forth original views of his own, but rather to explain the conclusions arrived at by the ablest investigators. In accordance with this design, it will be desirable here to introduce a paragraph from Major Henry Spence Palmer, who shared with Colonel Sir Charles Wilson the command of the Sinai Survey Expedition.

"The character and scene of the Red Sea passage—the greatest event which ancient history records—have in all ages been the subject of controversy, according to the variously proposed systems of topography, and the extent to which men have admitted or denied the operation of miraculous agency. Some, holding to the strict interpretation of such passages as, ' The waters were a wall unto them on their right hand and their left ' (Exod. xiv. 20), ' The floods stood upright as an heap ' (Ps. xv. 8), ' He made the waters to stand as an heap ' (Ps. lxxvii. 15), have inferred that the deep sea must have been literally parted asunder, and that through the chasm thus formed the Israelites passed, with a sheer wall of water on either side of them. By such, the scene of the passage has been fixed at six, ten, fifty, and even sixty miles below Suez, and the position of the city of Rameses has been varied to meet the several theories as to the crossing place. The advocates of these views, apparently anxious to aggrandise the miracle to the utmost, and discarding from fair consideration the physical agency which Scripture expressly mentions as the direct means by which the passage was made practicable, have, however, overlooked or evaded the difficulty of explaining how the fugitives, with their flocks and herds, could have travelled over the sharp coral rocks, and vast quantities of sea-weed which cover the sea-bottom at these points. The obvious difficulty also, that a short way below Suez, the breadth of the sea becomes too great for the passage to have been effected within the limits of time given in the narrative, without some preternatural acceleration of speed, of which Scripture gives no hint or mention, has never been met satisfactorily. There is the yet greater difficulty that a wind strong enough to have produced upon deep water the extraordinary effect which is supposed, would have been much too violent for any man or body of men to have stood up against it. Lastly, there is the impossible supposition that Pharaoh and his host would have been mad enough to rush to their doom in this fearful chasm."

Of late years, however, the theory of a deep-water passage has been practically abandoned. Modern critics prefer an intelligent interpretation, according to known natural laws, of the words of Exodus xiv. 21, 22, which lay stress upon the *east wind* as the direct natural agent by which the sea bottom was for the time made dry land.

Major Palmer mentions the presence of marine shells in the Bitter Lake as showing that it was formerly filled with salt water from the Gulf of Suez. He says further :—" This communication subsequently became broken by the gradual elevation of the neck of land eleven miles long which now separates the lakes from the head of the gulf— an interesting fulfilment of the prophecy in Isaiah xi. 15— "and the Lord shall utterly destroy the tongue of the

Egyptian sea.' Darius, about B.C. 500, restored the connection by cutting a canal through the isthmus, which after
a period of disuse was reopened by Ptolemy Philadelphus,
about B.C. 250. Traces of Darius's canal are still seen, in
a very perfect state, though its bed has since risen above
the level of high water in the gulf. If, as can hardly be
doubted, there was a connection, at least tidal, between the
lakes and the gulf at the time of the Exodus, the only
course eastward from Egypt which would have been
ordinarily practicable for the march of hosts, must have
passed to the north of the Great Bitter Lake, crossing the
belt of dry ground which, interrupted only by the Timsah
and Ballah Lakes, extends between it and the Menzaleh
Lake, and the Children of Israel must have been following
one such route when, at Etham, they were directed to turn
and encamp before Pi-ha-horoth."

These views of Major Palmer's are shared by M. Naville,
by Sir Wm. Dawson, and others, and have been decisively
confirmed by the geological survey of the region. In 1883
the Committee of the Palestine Exploration Fund sent out
Professor Hull, the eminent geologist, accompanied by
Major Kitchener, R.E., and other competent men, and this
party investigated the geology of Lower Egypt, of the Desert
of Sinai, the Valley of the Arabah, and the southern portion
of Palestine. The results were very remarkable. It appears, for instance, that at a distant period of the past
the waters of the seas, lakes, and gulfs of all this region
stood some two hundred feet higher than they do now—
the proof being found in the fact that at the height of two
hundred feet the limestone rocks have been bored into by
the well-known " shell-fish," the pholas, while the sands and
gravels at that height contain shells and corals and
crinoids, of the same species as those which still inhabit
the waters of the Gulf of Suez. With the waters at that
height the whole of Lower Egypt would be submerged,

together with extensive tracts on either side of the Gulf
of Suez. But this occurred in the distant past, probably
many ages before mankind dwelt in these regions at all.
There was, however, a more recent period, as the land
slowly rose out of the waters—and Professor Hull thinks it
may have coincided with the time of the Exodus—when
the waters were just 26 feet higher than they are at
present, and then, although Lower Egypt would not be
submerged, the Gulf of Suez must have extended northward as far as the Bitter Lakes, making an arm of the sea
about a mile wide and 20 or 30 feet deep.

It is suggested by M. Naville that the Israelites, when
they turned back from Etham, came down on the western
side of this arm of the sea, and got into a defile, so that
they appeared to be caught in a trap. Pharaoh thought so,
and said, " They are entangled in the land, the wilderness
hath shut them in ; " and so he pursued them, and thought
to obtain an easy victory.   But Moses had clear knowledge
of what he was to do. Although the waters of the gulf
were for the most part 20 or 30 feet deep, and
quite impassable, there was one place (near the present
Châluf) where they were quite shallow, where the land
now is 26 feet higher than the waters, and where, at that
time, reeds were growing. This part of the gulf was a
shallow sea of reeds : and what the Hebrew Bible really
says is that the Israelites crossed the sea of reeds—*yam
Souph* *—which was the former extension of the Red Sea
northwards. This place was so shallow that when the
north-east wind blew, co-operating with a retreating tide,
it was liable to be rendered dry ; and because the tribes of
the Desert used then to rush in, through this temporary
gateway, and carry off the cattle, and plunder the fertile
district around Pithom, the Pharaohs had established a

* Gesenius gives the meaning, " rush, reed, seaweed ; " and in Exod. ii. 3,
Moses is said to have been laid in an ark of *souph* or reeds.

watch-tower here—one of their Migdols. The Israelites "encamped between the Migdol and the sea:" then the north-east wind arose and made the passage dry, so that they were able to pass over. Their God had made a way for them. If this explanation, which is now very generally received, should be finally established, it must for ever silence all objections as to the credibility of this part of the Scripture narrative.

[*Authorities and Sources:*—"The Store-City of Pithom." By M. Naville, Egypt Exploration Fund. "Sinai." By Major H. Spencer Palmer, R.E. "The Desert of the Exodus." By Prof. E. H. Palmer. "Sinai and Palestine." By Dean Stanley. "Egypt and Sinai." By Sir J. Wm. Dawson.]

10. *The Wilderness Wanderings.*

All questions regarding the actual route of the Israelites and the true Mount Sinai were carefully studied during the Ordnance Survey of the Sinai Desert in 1868-9. The expedition was conducted by Major Henry Spencer Palmer, R.E., and Colonel Sir Charles Wilson, R.E., and the results were published in 1872, by authority of the Treasury, in five massive folio volumes. It may be fairly said that this expedition vindicated the accuracy of the Bible narrative; for the late Prof. E. H. Palmer, who was one of the party, and kept his own daily journal as they went along, assures us that the Bible narrative reads exactly like a daily journal kept by a member of a travelling party. A traveller begins by setting down his first impressions, which are often corrected in his later notes as the result of further experience; and Palmer pointed to such evidences of authenticity in the Bible story.

The results of the Survey of Sinai only concern us here

so far as they relate to discoveries of ruins and relics of the past.

The mining district of the peninsula of Sinai became subject to Egyptian rule at a very early time—probably some 3200 years before the Christian era—and the sculptured records of their occupation spread over a period of some 2000 years. On tablets at the mouth of one of the caves at Magháralh, King Senefru and his successor Cheops (who built the Great Pyramid) are represented, the one conquering a shepherd of the East, the other striking to the earth an Asiatic foe. "On the opposite cliffs" (says Major Palmer) "are the remains of the ancient settlement, comprising the dwellings of the miners, who probably were prisoners of war, and the barracks of their military guards. Flint and stone implements, such as arrow-heads and spear-heads, flint chisels and knives, and rude hammer-heads of greenstone, are found amongst these ruins."

At Sarábit el Khádim, ten or twelve miles further inland, where a new field of mining was discovered about the time that Magháralh began to show signs of exhaustion, there are ruins of two temples, built of well-cut stone, without mortar, the walls and vestibule being covered with Egyptian scenes.

But we are chiefly concerned to know whether any traces remain of the Israelitish Sojourn, and especially any of a character to throw additional light on Scripture. Of course a wandering people, dwelling in tents, would not leave evidence of their passage in buried cities; and what we have rather to look for is deserted camps. One such camp at least is reasonably identified now as Kibroth Hattaavah, where the people were fed with quails (Num. xi. 33). The Scripture narrative says that they journeyed thence to Hazeroth, and abode there. About thirty miles north-east of Jebel Musa, at a spot called *Erweis el Ebeirig,* are some old stone remains to which a legend attaches which very strikingly recalls the Scripture statement, and may very possibly contain some grain of truth. "These ruins" (say the Arabs) "are the remains of a large pilgrim or Hajj caravan, which in remote ages stopped here on the way to Hazeroth, and was afterwards lost in the Tih, and never again heard of." Hazeroth, the name of which still survives in 'Ain Hudherah, is fifteen miles further on towards 'Akabah. The Bádiet et Tih is by interpretation the wilderness of the wanderings, and is a sort of peninsula of higher ground which projects down into the Sinai desert from the north. Major Palmer tells us that the ruins at Erweis el Ebeirig form a class by themselves, differing from all other ancient remains hitherto found in the peninsula. Though there are a few stone houses, the remains consist chiefly of a great number of small enclosures of stone, mostly circular, and extending over several square miles of country. The stones are not set on end; their arrangement is not unlike that which may be seen on spots where an Arab encampment has been, though they certainly cannot be taken for Arab remains. The large enclosures intended for important personages, and the hearths or fire-places, can still be distinctly traced, showing conclusively that it is a large deserted camp. In the neighbourhood, but beyond the camp area, are a number of stone heaps, which, from their shape and position, are probably burial places without the camp, though none have yet been examined.

Between the Tih wilderness and Judea, is the Negeb or "South Country" of Scripture, now a deserted and barren wilderness, but shown by Professor E. H. Palmer to be full of the most interesting traces of former inhabitants and cultivation. In the Scripture narrative of the wanderings we read about Kadesh Barnea, where Miriam died, and whence the spies went up to Eshkol and obtained the grapes. The identification of Kadesh Barnea had long been difficult and disputed, until it was discovered, in the year 1840, by Dr Rowlands to be *'Ain Gadis* (or *Qades*) in Jebel Magráh, on the south-west frontier of the Negeb. The name *Gadis* is identical in meaning and etymology with the Kadesh of the Bible, while the word *'Ain* means a fountain; so that Kadesh Barnea can scarcely be said to have changed its name. The place is a picturesque oasis, and from under a ragged spur of solid rock, regarded by Rowlands as "the cliff" smitten by Moses, there issues an abundant stream. Professor Palmer, visiting the district some thirty years after, failed to find this great spring, but it was discovered again by Rev. F. W. Holland in 1878, and by Dr Clay Trumbull of America in 1881; and Dr Trumbull's book on Kadesh Barnea is now the fullest source of information.

Mr Holland's record of the Sinai Survey Expedition is printed at the end of the volume on the "Recovery of Jerusalem," published by the Palestine Exploration Fund. Mr Holland endeavours to trace the route of the Israelites, to fix the stations, to identify the spot where the battle of Rephidim was fought, and to make more intelligible the entire story. Traditions of the passage of the children of Israel through the country are common enough, he says. The physical conditions of the country are such as to render it quite possible that the events recorded in the Book of Exodus occurred there. The route of the Israelites has not indeed been laid down with absolute certainty, but much light has undoubtedly been thrown upon it by the explorations that have been made. Mr Holland concludes by declaring that "not a single member of the expedition returned home without feeling more firmly convinced than ever of the truth of that sacred history which he found illustrated and confirmed by the natural features of the desert. The mountains and valleys, the very rocks, barren and sun-scorched as they now are, seem to furnish evidences, which none who behold them can gainsay, that this was that 'great and terrible wilderness' through which Moses, under God's direction, led His people."

[*Authorities and Sources* :—" Explorations in the Peninsula of Sinai." By Rev. F. W. Holland (in volume on the "Recovery of Jerusalem"). "Sinai." By Major H. S. Palmer. "The Desert of the Exodus." By Professor E. H. Palmer. "The Desert of the Tih." By Prof. E. H. Palmer (in the volume of Special Papers, P. E. Fund.)]

CHAPTER II.

PALESTINE.

1. Palestine generally.

IT will be a useful preliminary to our study of Palestine if we give here a short list of the expeditions sent out by the Committee of the Palestine Exploration Fund.

We were already greatly indebted to many explorers—Dr Robinson, Burckhardt, Van de Velde, &c., for the geography, and M. Lartet for the geology, but there had never been any organised party in Palestine, properly equipped for a scientific survey. In 1864 Jerusalem was properly surveyed by Captain Wilson, R.E., at the expense of Lady Burdett Coutts, and an excellent map of the city was published. Then the happy idea occurred to Mr George Grove, at that time Secretary of the Crystal Palace Company, but also known for his topographical articles in Dr Smith's "Dictionary of the Bible," that the time was ripe for a systematic survey of the entire country. His energy brought together an influential company at a public meeting in Willis's Rooms, on the 22nd June 1865, the Archbishop of York being in the chair, and a Society was at once formed. The Archbishop of York was elected President, Mr George Grove, Hon. Secretary, and the first Committee included the names of the Duke of Argyll, the Earl of Shaftesbury, A. H. Layard, M.P., Walter Morrison, M.P., Dean Stanley, Sir Henry Rawlinson, Rev. H. B. Tristram, F.R.S., and others equally distinguished. The Archbishop, in his opening address, laid down the principles on which the work of the Society should be based—namely, that it should be a scientific society, carrying out its work in a scientific way, and should abstain from controversy. To these principles the Society has steadily adhered, and it has been (as it has called itself) "A Society for the accurate and systematic investigation of the archæology, topography, geology, and physical geography, natural history, manners, and customs of the Holy Land, for Biblical illustration."

The first expedition was sent out in 1866, under Captain Wilson, R.E., and Lieutenant Anderson, R.E., and landed at Beyrout. During six months this party carefully probed the country from Damascus to Hebron, and finally made its report in favour of commencing excavations at Jerusalem.

In 1867 Lieutenant Warren, R.E., was despatched to Jerusalem, with a party of non-commissioned officers, to commence the excavations. This work was continued until 1870. In 1868 the Moabite Stone was discovered by Rev. F. Klein, and in 1870 M. Clermont Ganneau, an archæologist employed by the Society, found an inscribed stone belonging to Herod's temple.

To the same year 1870 belongs the Survey of Sinai, conducted by Major H. S. Palmer and Captain Wilson, and to 1871 Professor E. H. Palmer's journey through the Desert of the Tih (or Wilderness of the Wanderings).

The Survey of Western Palestine was begun in 1872 ; and when, in a short time, Captain Stewart came home invalided, his place was taken by Lieutenant Conder, who continued the work during a series of years. Meantime, in 1874, M. Clermont Ganneau went out on another archæological mission.

In 1877 the Survey, which had been interrupted by an attack on the party, at Safed, was resumed by Lieutenant

Kitchener, who had been Conder's chief helper, and was completed satisfactorily.

In 1880 the great map of Western Palestine was published ; and in 1881 Conder commenced the Survey of Eastern Palestine, which, however, the Turks did not allow to be completed.

A geological expedition left England in October 1883, under Professor Edward Hull, F.R.S., Director of the Geological Survey of Ireland. Lieutenant-Colonel Kitchener, who accompanied him, surveyed the Wady Arabah.

In 1885 and later years, extensive tracts of country have been surveyed by Herr Schumacher, especially in the Jaulan.

Following upon these various explorations, the Society has poured out an incessant stream of publications, maps, and photographs, and its officers have published important books on their own account.

2. *Physical Features of Palestine.*

" The main object of the Survey of Palestine may be said to have been to collect materials in illustration of the Bible. Few stronger confirmations of the historic and authentic character of the sacred volume can be imagined than that furnished by a comparison of the ' Land and the Book,' which shows clearly that they tally in every respect. Mistaken ideas and preconceived notions may be corrected ; but the truth of the Bible is certainly established on a firm basis, by the criticisms of those who, familiar with the people and the country, are able to read it, not as a dead record of a former world or of an extinct race, but as a living picture of manners and of a land which can still be studied by any who will devote themselves to the task."—*Major Conder.*

Let us begin our present study of the Holy Land by

fixing in our minds a clear notion of its general physiography. Two ranges of hills, running from north to south, one on either side of the river Jordan, stand out as a principal feature of the country. The western range is between 2000 and 3000 feet high, and the eastern range about 1000 feet higher. The Jordan, gathering its waters from three sources, but chiefly from a spring issuing from a cave at Banias, at the base of the Anti-Lebanon, about 1000 feet above the ocean level, descends rapidly, and at a distance of 12 miles passes through the marshy swamp called Lake Huleh, generally identified with the Scriptural Waters of Merom. "Lake Huleh" is 4 miles long, and is very nearly at the same level with the Mediterranean. The Jordan was not known to pass through this swamp as an actual stream until Mr J. Macgregor, in his *Rob Roy* canoe, navigated his way through the reeds. Descending with the stream ("Jordan" means *the Descender*), we come, at a further distance of 10½ miles, to the Lake of Galilee, and here we are 682 feet below the Mediterranean. The lake is 12½ miles long, and nearly 8 miles wide at its broadest part. Between the Lake of Galilee and the Dead Sea the distance, as the crow flies, is 65 miles; but the stream is so tortuous that Lieutenant Lynch found it, in navigation, to be 200 miles. In the course of this distance Lynch passed down twenty-seven rapids which he considered "threatening," besides a great many more of lesser magnitude. The Dead Sea itself is 1292 feet below the Mediterranean, though the level varies by a few feet according as Jordan overflows or runs low. Its length is 47 miles and its breadth about 10 miles. It has no outlet to the south, but gets rid, by evaporation from the surface, of all the water poured into it. Thus the Jordan occupies a gorge which is deep as well as wide, and is, together with its lake basins, the most remarkable depression of the kind on the face of the earth. As

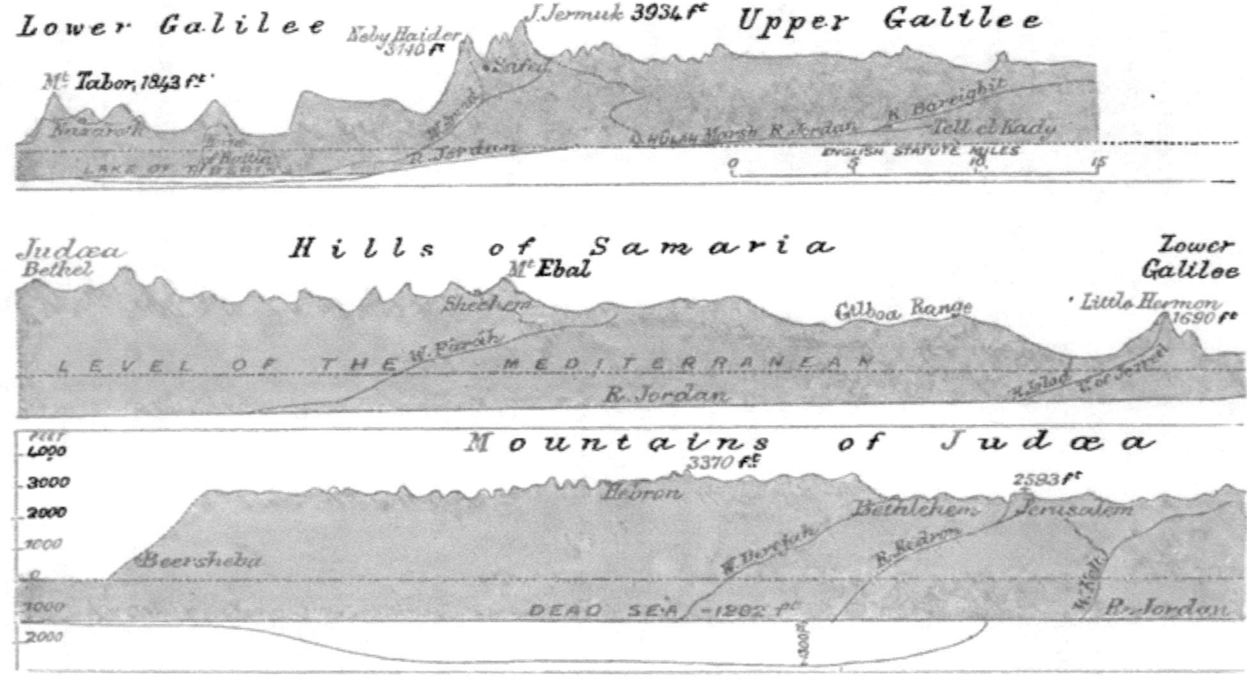

MERIDIONAL SECTION, WESTERN PALESTINE.

(Reduced from Mr Trelawney Saunders' Section by W. H. Hudleston.)

remarked by Mr Ffoulkes, it is a river that has never been navigable, flowing into a sea that has never known a port—has never been a highway to more hospitable coasts—has never possessed a fishery—a river that has never boasted of a single town of eminence upon its banks.

North of the Dead Sea the Valley of the Jordan widens out into an extensive flat called the Kikkar or the Round, the Plain of the Jordan. Northwards of this again, the low ground of the Jordan Valley extends for several miles on either side of the stream, the hills now drawing closer, now opening wider. Following the low ground north-ward, we by-and-bye find an opening to the left, the western range of hills being broken in two by the Valley of Jezreel and the Great Plain of Esdraelon. We may continue our journey westward, and round the promontory of Mount Carmel, where the road is close to the sea, and then southward through the Plain of Sharon into the Plain of Philistia, and onward to the desert of Sinai. Thus it is possible to travel all round without once climb-ing the hills: so that this central region is like an island, with plains around it instead of the ocean. It was, in fact, still more isolated, by having a second separating ring around the first; for on the west was the Mediterranean Sea, navigated by the Phœnicians, who were peaceably disposed; on the south and east were extensive deserts, and on the north were the mountains of Lebanon, sending down their roots to the sea-coast. There was, however, a way through Canaan, from Egypt to Mesopotamia, by the coast route and through the passes of the Lebanon.

The hills of Western Palestine do not afford much level table-land, for the torrents running off on either side, into the sea westward and into the river eastward, cut the ground into deep gorges; these, over-lapping at their sources, leave a central wavy ridge, and if we travel from

north to south anywhere but along this ridge we may
have to cross torrent-beds 1000 feet deep. The eastern
range is cut by gorges even more formidable, of which
the principal are the Arnon, the Jabbok, and the Hiero-
max.

The hills of Western Palestine consisted of grey rock,
and were comparatively bare and infertile; the plains were
gorgeous with flowers, and rich with corn-fields. Beyond
the plain of Esdraelon was wild scenery of mountain and
forest. The eastern hills were green with forest and
pasture; in the central region were the forests of Gilead;
north of Gilead was rich pasturage for wild herds of cattle
—the "bulls of Bashan;" in the south was rich pasturage
too, and the king of Moab at one time was a sheep-master,
paying as tribute the wool of 100,000 lambs and 100,000
rams (2 Kings iii. 4).

From Dan in the north to Beersheba in the south, the
country measured only 140 miles, and from the Jordan
to the sea only some forty or fifty: a small country, even
when we include the eastern hills, yet sufficient for the
tribes of Israel at that time; and in parts extremely
fruitful, a land of milk and honey.

Dan was a natural point for a northern limit, since there
the ascent of Mount Hermon begins, and there we have
one of the sources of the Jordan. The city was situated
on an isolated cone, and the modern name of it is Banias.
On the north side of it there rises a cliff 100 feet in
height, and at the foot of this is a cave, which was a
sanctuary of the god Pan. Two niches in the cliff side
contain inscriptions in honour of Pan. From the worship
of this deity the city was called Panias or Panium. Its
Biblical name was probably Baal Gad. In the time of
Josephus the waters of the Jordan burst forth from the
cave itself, but now they issue at the foot of a heap of
rubbish in front of the cavern, in numerous tiny rills, which

soon unite and form a river. The Castle of Banias is one of the most splendid ruins in Syria. It was surveyed and planned by Colonel Kitchener in 1877. Remains of columns occur in the village of Banias, and Major Conder suspects that the Crusaders who fortified the place may very probably have destroyed the heathen temple and used the pillars in their masonry.

About an hour's distance south of Banias is a mound called *Tell el Kady* (the heap of Dan), and here we have another source of the Jordan. Tell el Kady is one of the most romantic and picturesque spots in the country, abundantly watered, and overlooking the broad valley of the Upper Jordan, with mountain peaks and ridges to north, east, and west. A group of dolmens recently discovered at this spot may be thought to have some connection with the ancient worship.

Beersheba (the *well of swearing*, or the *well of the seven*) was one of the oldest places in Palestine, and is about as far south as a place can be without actually being in the desert. There are at present on the spot two principal wells and five smaller ones, and they are among the first objects encountered on entering Palestine from the south. Conder found the principal well to be 12 feet 3 inches in diameter, and over 45 feet deep, lined with a ring of masonry to a depth of 28 feet. The sides of all the wells are furrowed by the ropes of the water-drawers ; but one discovery was made which was rather disappointing, namely, that the masonry is not very ancient. Fifteen courses down, on the south side of the large well, there is a stone with an inscription in Arabic, on a tablet dated, as well as could be made out, 505 A.H., that is 1117 A.D. The wells have no parapets, and a traveller might easily walk into them unaware. Round the two which contain water there are some rude stone water troughs, which may be of any age.

These being the limits of the country, let us return again to a consideration of its physical aspects.

The physical features of the country naturally depend upon its geological formation. The ranges of hills, east and west of Jordan, are formed almost entirely of beds of cretaceous limestone, which were once continuous. The Jordan Valley coincides with a line of fault ; that is to say, the rocky strata cracked in an irregular line from north to south, and the country west of this fault sank down bodily, so that the higher strata of rocks on that side abut now against the lower strata on the eastern side. With this depression to begin with, the rains and torrents have gradually sculptured the valley into its present form.

The maritime district of Palestine, stretching from the base of Carmel southwards by Joppa and Gaza to the Desert of Beersheba, consists of a series of low hills from 300 feet to 400 feet high, separated by valleys and alluvial plains extending inland to a varying distance. The coast line is bordered by a line of sand-hills, which, when unrestrained by some physical barrier, are ever moving inland with disastrous effect. The district is largely composed of beds of sand and gravel, which have once been the bed of the outer sea ; while along the line of many of the rivers and streams a deposit of rich loam of a deep brown colour covers considerable areas, and yields abundant crops of wheat and maize to the cultivators.

Professor Edward Hull, the eminent geologist, who was commissioned by the Palestine Exploration Society to investigate the geology of the Desert and the Holy Land, reported the results to the Committee, in an elaborate Memoir, in which he treats of the maritime district, the table-land of Western Palestine and the Tih Desert, the depression of the Jordan Valley and its continuation southward to the Gulf of Akabah, the elevated plateau east of Jordan, and the mountainous tract of the peninsula of Sinai. Utilising the labours of his predecessors, Russeger,

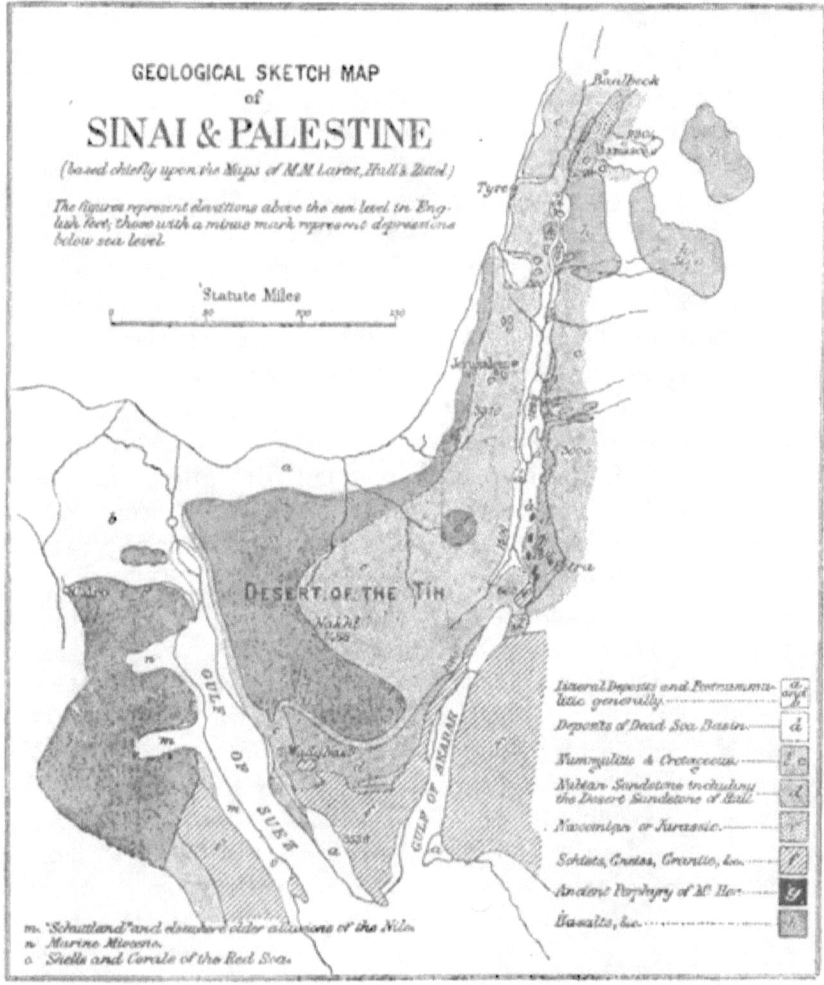

Fraas, Lartet, Vignes, &c., he sometimes confirms their results, and sometimes adds to our knowledge.

By the kindness of Mr W. H. Hudleston, F.R.S., and

Secretary of the Geological Society, I am able to illustrate this chapter with a geological map based chiefly on the maps of Lartet, Hull, and Zittel. To a great extent it tells its own story regarding the features of the country, and the rocks and formations of which the region is constructed. The oldest rocks occupy the greater portion of the Sinaitic peninsula, as well as the mountains bordering the Gulf of Akabah, and extending northward along the eastern side of the Wady el Arabah. They consist of granitic, gneissose and schistose rocks, amongst which have been intruded great masses of red porphyry, dark greenstone, and other igneous rocks in the form of dykes, veins, and bosses. These rocks are probably among the oldest in the world. After these ancient rocks had been consolidated they were subjected to a vast amount of erosion, and were worn into very uneven surfaces, over which the more recent formations were spread ; first filling up the hollows with the lower strata, and ultimately covering even the higher elevations as the process of deposition of strata went on. The oldest of these formations is the Red Sandstone and Conglomerate, which Professor Edward Hull calls the " Desert Sandstone " formation. It forms a narrow strip along the margin of the old crystalline rocks. It is capped with the fossiliferous limestone of the Wady Nash, which shows it to belong to the Carboniferous period—in fact to be the representative of the Carboniferous Limestone of Europe and the British Isles. It is also found east of the Arabah Valley and amongst the mountains of Moab east of the Ghor. This is succeeded by another Sandstone formation, more extensively distributed than the former. It belongs to a much more recent geological period, namely, the Cretaceous ; and is the representative of the " Nubian Sandstone " of Roziere, so largely developed in Africa, especially in Nubia and Upper Egypt This is succeeded by the Cretaceous and Nummulitic

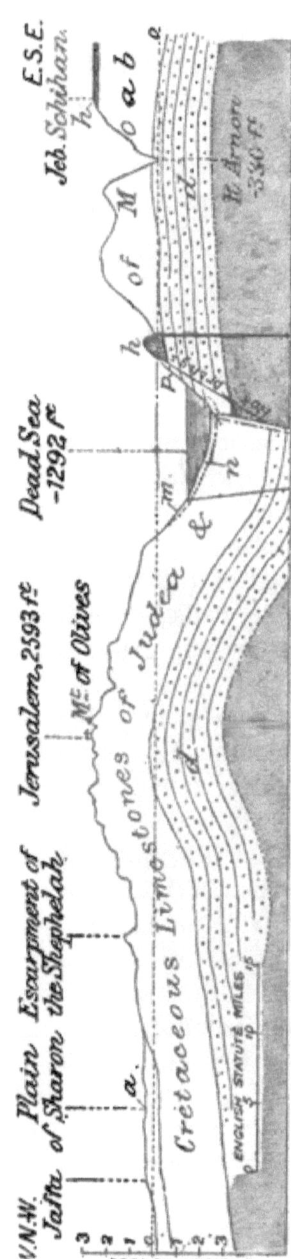

GENERALISED GEOLOGICAL SECTION ACROSS PALESTINE.

o, Level of the Mediterranean : *a*, bed of the maritime plains ; *m*, old lacustrine deposits of the Dead Sea basin ; *n*, deposits now forming beneath the Dead Sea ; *p*, tufaceous deposits of hot springs ; *h*, basalt.

Limestone formations, which occupy the greater part of the map, forming the great table-land of the Tih, from its western escarpment to the borders of the Arabah Valley, and stretching northward throughout the hill country of Judea and Samaria into Syria and the Lebanon.

On the east of the Jordan Valley the Cretaceous Limestone forms the tablelands of Edom and Moab : as far north as the Hauran and Jaulan, where the limestone passes below great sheets of basaltic lava. The Cretaceous Limestone represents the Chalk formation of Europe and the British Isles.

Although the Cretaceous Limestone belongs to the Secondary period, and the Nummulitic Limestone to the Tertiary, they are very closely connected in Palestine, as far as their mineral characters are concerned ; and they both contain beds or bands of flint and chert.

The Cretaceous Limestone underlies nearly the whole of the Jordan and Arabah Valleys, although concealed by more recent deposits, and is broken off along the line of the great Jordan Valley fault against older formations. In other words, on the west we have strata of the age of the English chalk, which dip down very suddenly towards the centre of the valley. On the east we have the Nubian Sandstone, with hard limestone above it geologically coeval with our greensand. It is entirely owing to the presence of this leading line of fracture and displacement, and the subsequent denudation of strata, that this great valley exists, and that the eastern side is so mountainous and characterised by such grand features of hill and dale.

These limestones pass under a newer formation of Calcareous Sandstone in the direction of the Mediterranean, a formation probably of Upper Eocene age, and called by Hull the " Calcareous Sandstone of Philistia."

The formations next in order consist of raised beaches and sea-beds along the coast, and of lake-beds in the Ghor and Jordan Valley ; and these bring us, geologically, much nearer to our own time.

Not only do the physical features of a country depend upon its geological formation, but it cannot be questioned that the character and mode of life of the inhabitants are moulded or modified by the physical features. It is remarked by Professor Edward Hull that the mild patient character of the Egyptian cultivator befits the nature of that wide alluvial tract of fertile land which is watered by the Nile. The mountainous tracts of the Sinaitic peninsula, formed of the oldest crystalline rocks of that part of the world, have become the abode of the Bedouin Arab, the hardy child of nature, who has adapted himself to a life in keeping with his wild surroundings. The great table-land of the Tih, less rugged and inhospitable than the mountainous parts of Sinai and Serbal, supports roving tribes, partly pastoral, and gradually assimilating their habits to the Fellahin of Philistia and of Palestine, who cultivate the ground and rear large flocks and herds.

[*Authorities and Sources :*—Smith's "Dictionary of the Bible." Survey of Western Palestine, Memoir on the Geology. Dr Edward Hull. "The Geology of Palestine." Wilfred H. Hudleston, F.R.S. "*Rob-Roy* on the Jordan." John Macgregor.]

3. *The Dead Sea, Salt Sea, or Sea of Lot.*

It is pointed out by Sir George Grove that the name "Dead Sea" never occurs in the Bible, and appears not to have existed until the second century after Christ. It originated in an erroneous opinion, and there can be little doubt that to the name is due in a great measure the mistakes and misrepresentations which were for so long prevalent regarding this lake, and which have not indeed yet wholly ceased to exist. In the Old Testament it is called the Salt Sea, and the Sea of the Plain (Arabah). By the Arabs it is called El Bahr Lut (the Sea of Lot).

The Salt Sea lies in the deepest part of the great Jordan-Arabah depression, and the ground rises to the south of it, as well as in all other directions. It was shown, in fact, by Colonel Kitchener's survey of the Arabah that the bed of the valley, for the most part, is raised above the level of the Gulf of Akabah. From the border of the Dead Sea southward the ground rises but little for 10 miles, but then begins to rise rapidly, so that at a distance of about 40 miles it is as high as the sea level at Akabah; and 29 miles further south it is 660 feet above that level.

The Jordan Valley, as already stated, coincides with a great fault in the strata. This had been recognised by Lartet, Tristram, Wilson, and others; and Professor Hull has traced the continuation of this fracture, at the base of the Edomite mountains along the Arabah Valley. He agrees with Lartet in thinking that the waters of the Jordan Valley have not flowed down into the Gulf of Akabah since the land emerged from the ocean. The disconnection of the inner waters from the outer is a very ancient event, dating back to Miocene times.

The River Jordan, throughout its course, from the Sea of Tiberias to the Salt Sea, cuts its channel through alluvial terraces, consisting of sand, gravel, and calcareous marl, which sometimes contain shells, semi-fossilised, but of species still living in the lakes of Tiberias and Huleh. These terraces are continuous round the shores of the Salt Sea, and between the base of the cliffs of Jebel Karantul, near Jericho, and the fords of the Jordan, three of them may be observed,

the first being at a level of 650 to 600 feet,
the second   ,,   ,,   520 to 250 ,,
the third   ,,   ,,   200 to 130 ,,

and below the last named is the alluvial flat, liable to be flooded on the rise of the waters. The upper surfaces and outer margins of these terraces indicate successive stages, at which the waters have rested in sinking down to their present level. Originally they reached a level somewhat over that of the Mediterranean, and at that time a great inland lake extended from Lake Huleh southwards into the Arabah Valley, its length being about 200 miles.

In the Jordan Valley, the upper terrace, at the foot of the hills, is called the Ghor, and it is to be distinguished from the Zor, or bottom of the valley, in which the channel of the river, cut still deeper, meanders.

The Salt Sea itself is enclosed on all sides by terraced hills, except towards the north, where it receives the waters of the Jordan. In rising gradually out of the ocean, the region appears to have rested several times at successive levels, and the sea left its mark in deposits of marl, gravel, and silt.

Beyond the southern end of the Salt Sea the banks of the Ghor rise in the form of a great white sloping wall, to a height of about 600 feet above the plain, and are formed of horizontal courses of sand and gravel, resting on white marl and loam. This mural wall sweeps round in a semi-circular form from side to side of the Ghor. The upper surface is nearly level (except where broken into by river channels), and from its base stretches a plain covered partly, over the western side, by a forest of small trees and shrubs, and partly by vegetation affording pasturage to the numerous flocks of the Arabs, who settle down here during the cooler months of the year. It is impossible to doubt that at no remote period the waters of the Salt Sea, though now distant some 10 miles, washed the base of these cliffs, and a rise of a few feet would submerge this verdant plain, and bring back the sea to its former more extended limits.

From this position also, the white terrace of Jebel Usdum—" the salt mountain ", where the Crusaders wrongly placed Sodom—is seen projecting from the sides of the loftier limestone terraces of the Judæan hills. Towards the east, similar terraces of whitish alluvial deposits are seen clinging to the sides of the Moabite hills, or running far up the deep glens which penetrate the sides of the great table-land. In these terraces, the upper surfaces of which reach a level of about 600 feet above the waters of the Salt Sea, we behold but the remnants of an ancient sea-bed, which must originally have stretched from side to side.

Eight hundred feet higher than these terraces there are others composed of marl, gravel, and silt, through which the ravines of existing streams have been cut ; and this indicates that the level of the Salt Sea stood at one time 100 feet higher than the waters of the Mediterranean stand now.

Origin of the saltness of the Dead Sea.—It has been

generally recognised that the waters of lakes which have no outlet ultimately become more or less saline. Of these the most important in the old world are the Caspian, the Sea of Aral, Lakes Balkash, Van, Urumiah, and, lastly, the Dead Sea, or as it was originally called, "the Salt Sea." "The Caspian," says Professor Hull, "owing to its great extent and other causes, is but slightly saline ; but that with which we have here to deal is the most saline of all. It is probable that the water of the ocean itself has become salt owing to the same cause which has produced saltness in the inland lakes, as it may be regarded as a mass of water without an outlet. The cause of the saltness in such lakes I now proceed to explain.

"It has been found that the waters of rivers contain, besides matter which is in a state of mechanical suspension, carbonates of lime and magnesia, and saline ingredients in a state of solution ; and as those lakes which have an outlet, such as the Sea of Galilee, part with their waters and saline ingredients as fast as they receive them, the waters of such lakes remain fresh. It is otherwise, however, with regard to lakes which have no outlet. In such cases the water is evaporated as fast as it is received ; and as the vapour is in a condition of purity, the saline ingredients remain behind. Thus the waters of such a lake tend constantly to increase in saltness, until a state of saturation is attained, when the excess of salt is precipitated, and forms beds at the bottom of the lake. The contrast presented by the waters of the Sea of Galilee on the one hand, and those of the Dead Sea on the other, though both are fed by the same river, is a striking illustration of the effects resulting from opposite physical conditions. In the former case, the waters are fresh, and abound in fishes and molluscs ; in the latter, they are so intensely salt that all animal life is absent.

"The increase of saltness in the waters of the Dead Sea

has probably been very slow, and dates back from its earliest condition, when its waters stretched for a distance of about 200 miles from north to south. . . .

" The excessive salinity of the waters of the Dead Sea will be recognised from a comparison with those of the Atlantic Ocean. Thus, while the waters of the ocean give six pounds of salt, &c., in a hundred pounds of water, those of the Dead Sea give 24·57. pounds in the same quantity; but in both cases the degree of salinity varies with the depth, the waters at the surface being less saline than those near the bottom. . . .

"*As to the depth of the waters*:—The floor of the Dead Sea has been sounded on two occasions : first, by the Expedition under Lieutenant Lynch in 1848, and secondly, by that under the Duc de Luynes. In the former case the maximum depth was found to be 1278 feet ; in the latter 1217 feet, being close approximations to each other. We may therefore affirm that the floor of the lake descends to nearly as great a depth below its surface as the surface itself below the level of the Mediteranean Sea.

" The section given by Lynch indicates that the place of greatest depth lies much nearer the Moabite than the Judæan shore, and the descent from the base of the Moabite escarpment below Jebel Attarus and between the outlets of the Wâdies Mojeb and Zerka Maïn, is very steep indeed. The deepest part of the trough seems to lie in a direction running north and south, at a distance of about 2 miles from the eastern bank ; and while the ascent towards this bank is rapid, that towards the Judæan shore on the west is comparatively gentle. The line of this deep trough seems exactly to coincide with that of the great Jordan Valley fault. From the bottom of the deeper part, the sounding line brought up specimens of crystals of salt (sodium-chloride), and it can scarcely be doubted that a bed of this mineral, together with gypsum, is in course of formation over the central portions of the Dead Sea."

[*Authorities and Sources* :—" Memoirs of the Survey : Geology " Dr E. Hull. Smith's " Dict. of Bible." " Tent-Work in Palestine." By Major Conder, R.E.]

4. *The Cities of the Plain.*

There is now a general consent that Sodom and Gomorrah, Admah and Zeboim were situated north of the Dead Sea, in the Kikkar or Plain of the Jordan. There are old maps which represent these cities as situated at the bottom of the Dead Sea waters, and yet enveloped in flames! Popular ignorance imagines that the bitumen which rises to the surface of the waters is a relic of the agency which effected the destruction. And until recently even the best scholars supposed the cities to lie beneath the shallow part of the sea, south of the Lisan peninsula. All such theories are disproved by the geological investigation, which shows that the Dead Sea is much older than any date which can be assigned to the destruction of the cities, and that the surface of the water has been constantly diminishing in area and sinking to lower levels.

There is nothing in the Bible which should lead us to look for the cities south of the Dead Sea, where the Crusaders placed them, or east of it, or anywhere but north and in the Kikkar. When Abraham and Lot talked together concerning the disputes between their herdsmen, and decided to go different ways with their flocks, " Lot lifted up his eyes and beheld all the Plain of the Jordan, that it was well watered . . . until thou comest unto Zoar." It was clearly shown by Sir George Grove, in Smith's " Dictionary of the Bible," that the Plain of the Jordan here spoken of is not the Arabah, in which the Dead Sea reposes, but the Kikkar or " Round " of country north of it. The position of Abraham and Lot at the time was on a mount east of Bethel; and as the site of Bethel is known, it was not difficult to find the mount east of it. It was reasonably identified by Rev. Canon Williams, and his conclusions were confirmed in 1865 by Colonel Sir C. Wilson. It has been shown that if the cities had been south of the Dead Sea, human vision could not possibly have extended so far, to distinguish anything. But north of the sea, in the Round or Plain, Lot would be able to perceive them. Accordingly, when the friendly conference ended, he journeyed eastward from the mount near Bethel, in order to reach his new home in Sodom.

The vision of Lot had extended across the plain, to Zoar and no farther, because the plain was bounded by the high mountains of Moab. Dr Tristram believes that he has identified Zoar, the fifth city of the Plain, the "little city" to which Lot fled after the convulsion. Standing on Mount Nebo, he detected the ruins a little in front of him, almost in a line with Jericho. The ruins were on a low brow of ground, and thus correspond to the description that Lot rested in this city on his way to the mountains, and afterwards went up into the mountain and dwelt in a cave. The ruins are still called Ziara, which does not differ much from the Greek spelling Ζωαρα, nor very widely from the Hebrew.

Is it possible to discover any relics of the four larger cities? Although destroyed by fire, they may not have been utterly annihilated, any more than Pompeii; but if their remains are hiding beneath the dust, the dust keeps its secret well. Major Conder rode day by day over almost every acre of ground between Jericho and the Dead Sea, and could not detect any mound or sign of a buried city. The whole was a white desert, except near the hills, where rich herbage grows after the rains. The time of year was most favourable for such exploration, because no long grass existed to hide any ruins. But in all that plain he found no ruin, except the old monastery of St John and a little hermit's cave.

This description leaves out of account a remarkable group of *tells,* or mounds of earth and rubbish, strewn over with ruins, existing in the neighbourhood of Jericho. They are seven in number, and one of them is not far from Elisha's Fountain, now called *Ain es Sultan.* One would imagine that the exploration of these mounds might yield valuable results; but nobody undertakes the work. It is true that some excavations made by Sir Charles Warren only proved the existence of sun-dried bricks; and because the mounds occur generally where the soil is alluvial, Conder regards them as piles of refuse bricks, and nothing more; but Sir J. W. Dawson, on visiting the place, noticed numerous flint chips in the mound, and Sir C. Warren, when presiding at my Guildford lecture, publicly expressed the opinion that many small objects of great interest would probably be found if the stuff were sifted.

But if the ruins of the Cities of the Plain are not discoverable, their names appear to linger in the district, slightly disguised as Arabic words, and applying to portions of the ground.

Conder justly remarks that the cities would probably be situated near fresh-water springs, and the great spring of 'Ain Feshkhah, on the north-west of the Dead Sea, is a probable site for one of them. The great bluff not far south of the spring is called Tubk 'Amriyeh by the Bedawin, and the neighbouring valley Wady 'Amriyeh. This word is radically identical with the Hebrew Gomorrah, or Amorah as it is spelt in one passage (Gen. x. 19), meaning, according to some authorities, "depression," according to others, "cultivation."

Admah means "red earth," a description which would hardly apply to the ground near the Dead Sea. But there

is no reason why all the four cities should be close to the
Dead Sea. A convulsion overthrowing cities near the
Sea would probably be felt a long way up the Jordan
Valley, owing to the line of fault. Conder has pointed
out, too, that the term Kikkar is applied in the Bible to
the Jordan Valley as far north as Succoth. A "city
Adam" is noticed in the Book of Joshua as being beside
Zaretan ; the name Ed Damieh applies to the neighbourhood of the Jordan ford east of Kurn Surtabeh, about
23 miles up the valley ; and it has always seemed
possible to Conder that Adam and Admah were one
and the same. I would add a suggestion of my own
in support of the view that Admah was some distance up
the Jordan Valley. The passage Gen. x. 19 describes the
boundary of Canaan, beginning at Sidon, following the
coast line to Gaza, striking thence eastward to the Plain of
the Jordan, and then proceeding up the Jordan Valley to
Dan or Lasha—and the passage may be freely rendered
thus,—" And the border of the Canaanite was from Sidon ;
thence you go towards Gerar, as far as Gaza ; thence you
go toward Sodom ; then by Gomorrah and Admah and
Zeboim, unto Dan."* As Gerar was beyond Gaza southward, the boundary only went toward it ; and as Sodom
was beyond Jordan eastward, the boundary only went
toward Sodom ; there was no need to say it stopped at the
river, for that was obvious. It then follows the course of
the river from the Dead Sea to the source of the stream.

* In this paraphrase I render one of the *vavs* by "then" instead of "and."
This will be allowed me. What will be objected to is the assumption that
Lasha is Laish, especially as Lasha contains a different radical, the *ayin*
(לָשַׁע). But the passage in Genesis may give an archaic spelling ; and as
Lasha signifies "the breaking through of waters," it is eminently descriptive
of the source of the Jordan at Dan. To place Lasha in the south-east of
Palestine, as is done in Smith's "Dictionary of the Bible," is to charge the
description in Genesis with being defective, for how are the limits of a people
defined by tracing two sides of an irregular quadrangle ?

And then the northern boundary is known without description. If this rendering holds good, then Gomorrah was north-west of the Dead Sea, on a line joining Gaza with Sodom ; and the boundary of the Canaanites, after reaching Gomorrah, touched Admah and Zeboim, and continued northward to the grotto at Banias.

Zeboim means "hyenas," and is identical with the Arabic Dub'a. For this reason Conder asks whether it may not have been situated at the cliff just above the plain, near the site of Roman Jericho, for that is now called Shakh ed Dub'a, "lair of the Hyena." If I am right in my reading of Gen. x. 19, Zeboim should be northward of Admah —unless two names so often coupled together may have their order transposed. Grove reminds us that the Valley of Zeboim (the name spelt a little differently) was a ravine or gorge apparently east of Michmas, described in 1 Sam. xiii. 18. It appears to be overlooked in the discussion that Zeboim is mentioned in Nehemiah xi. 34, in the same group with Hadid, Lod, and Ono, among the places occupied by the children of Benjamin, while in Neh. vii. 37, these three places are named between Jericho and Senaah. But if the Lod in this passage is to be regarded as Lydda in the Plain of Sharon, the grouping of the places affords us no guidance.

Sodom alone, as Conder goes on to say, remains without a suggestion, and he finds no trace of it west of the Jordan. He notes, however, that the word Siddim is apparently the same with the Arabic *Sidd*, which is used in a peculiar sense by the Arabs of the Jordan Valley as meaning "cliffs" or banks of marl, such as exist along the southern edge of the plains of Jericho, the ordinary meaning being "dam" or obstruction. Thus the Vale of Siddim might well, so far as its name is concerned, have been situated in the vicinity of the northern shores of the Dead Sea.

Dr Selah Merrill, in his " East of the Jordan," also discusses

the site of the Cities of the Plain. He says :—" Since Zoar
was one of them, a hint as to their situation may be derived
from Gen. xiii. 10, where Lot and Abraham are represented
as standing on a hill near Bethel, and looking down the
Jordan Valley towards the Dead Sea. As this verse is
rendered in our English Bible, the meaning is not clear ;
but it will become so when all the middle portion of the
verse is read as a parenthesis, as follows : 'And Lot lifted
up his eyes and beheld all the Plain of Jordan (that it was
well watered everywhere, before the Lord destroyed Sodom
and Gomorrah, even as the garden of the Lord, like the
land of Egypt), until thou comest to Zoar.' The last
clause qualifies the first. Lot saw all the Plain of Jordan
as far as Zoar, or 'until you come to Zoar.' Zoar was
both the limit of the plain and the limit of vision in that
direction, so far as the land was concerned."

Dr Merrill then shows that nothing could have been
distinguished at the southern end of the Dead Sea ; and
quotes early writers to show that Zoar existed near the
northern end.

Regarding the destruction of Sodom and Gomorrah, it
is not sufficient to say briefly that it was a miracle, and
assume that no further explanation can be given. A rain
of brimstone and fire is spoken of, and it is legitimate to
look for the source of it. With the instance of Pompeii
in our minds it is natural to suggest volcanic agency,
especially as the region north-east of the Dead Sea affords
evidence of volcanic action. But Sir J. W. Dawson (a
well-known American geologist), in his volume on " Egypt
and Syria," ingeniously argues for a petroleum explosion.
The "slime pits" spoken of as abounding in the Vale of
Siddim (Gen. xiv. 10), he regards as petroleum wells, and
then traces a parallel as follows :—" Regions of bitumen,
like that of the Dead Sea, are liable to eruptions of a most
destructive character. Of these we have had examples

in the oil regions of America. In a narrative of one of
these now before me, and which occurred a few years ago,
in the oil district of Petrolia, in Canada, I read that a
borehole struck a reservoir of gas, which rushed upward
with explosive force, carrying before it a large quantity
of petroleum. The gas almost immediately took fire, and
formed a tall column of flame, while the burning petroleum
spread over the ground and ignited tanks of the substance
in the vicinity. In this way a space of about fifteen acres
was enveloped in fire, a village was burned, and several
persons lost their lives. The air flowing toward the
eruption caused a whirlwind, which carried the dense
smoke high into the air, and threw down burning bitumen
all round.

"Now, if we suppose that at the time referred to, accumu-
lations of inflammable gas and petroleum existed below
the Plain of Siddim, the escape of these through the
opening of a fissure along the old line of fault might
produce the effects described—namely, a pillar of smoke
rising up to heaven, burning bitumen and sulphur raining
on the doomed cities, and fire spreading over the ground.
The attendant phenomenon of the evolution of saline
waters, implied in the destruction of Lot's wife, would be
a natural accompaniment, as water is always discharged
in such eruptions; and in this case it would be a brine
thick with mud, and fitted to encrust and cover any object
reached by it."

An important note, with reference to the destruction of
the Cities of the Plain, appears in the statement in Gen. xiv.,
that the Vale of Siddim had bitumen pits or wells, and that
these were so abundant or important as to furnish a place of
retreat to, or to impede the flight of, the defeated kings of
Sodom and Gomorrah. These bitumen pits have disappeared, unless their remains are represented by the singular
pits described by Dr Merrill as occurring near Wady Nimrim.

Their existence in the times of Abraham would bespeak a much greater abundance of bituminous matter than that now remaining ; and it is possible that the eruption which destroyed the Cities of the Plain may have, to a great extent, exhausted the supply of petroleum.

" There is no reason to think " (adds Dr Dawson) "that the destruction of Sodom and Gomorrah was connected with any important change in the limits of the Dead Sea, though it is highly probable that some subsidence of the valley took place, and may have slightly affected its levels relatively to the Jordan and the sea ; but it would appear from Deut. xxix. 23, that the eruption was followed by a permanent deterioration of the district by the saline mud with which it was covered."

In the *Theological Monthly* for May 1890, Rev. James Neil declares that no bitumen pits are to be found anywhere in the neighbourhood of the Jordan. The pits spoken of by Dr Selah Merrill were connected with aqueducts, and used for purposes of irrigation. But the asphalt thrown up from the bottom of the Dead Sea may have been employed to render such pits watertight, and to that extent they would be slime pits. He shows that such pits do exist in the Jordan Valley, extending across it in long lines just north of the supposed site of some of the Cities of the Plain ; and it is a very curious fact that the Bedawin, who are unacquainted with their nature and purpose, have a legend connecting them with a great battle.

[*Authorities and Sources :*—Smith's " Dict. of the Bible." " Tent-work in Palestine." Major Conder, R.E. " The Land of Moab." Rev. Canon Tristram, F.R.S. " East of Jordan." Dr Selah Merrill. " Egypt and Syria." Sir J. W. Dawson.]

5. *"Lot's Wife."*

In connection with the destruction of Sodom, the Bible mentions the fate which overtook Lot's wife, who "became a pillar of salt." The Arabs have legends on the subject; and travellers now and again describe the pillars of salt which have been pointed out to them, and to which the legends attach. The stories are by no means modern. Major Conder, in his "Syrian Stone Lore," brings into brief compass the notions of the Fathers of the Church on the subject. From an early period "Lot's wife" is mentioned as standing by the western shores of the Dead Sea, and Antoninus Martyr is careful to combat the idea that the pillar of salt was destroyed through its being constantly licked by animals. Irenæus also (IV. xxxi. 3) mentions "Lot's wife" as a pillar still standing. Tertullian and Cyprian preserve a very curious Latin hymn on the subject (*cf.* Anton. Martyr, xv.). It seems possibly to be the natural pinnacle, now called Karnet Sahsul Hameid, to which these writers refer. The feminine nature of this statue was supposed to be still perceptible, in spite of petrification.

Perhaps the best account of "Lot's wife" is to be found in E. H. Palmer's "Desert of the Exodus," where a coloured plate helps the realisation.

"While with the Ghawárineh" (says Palmer) "we had heard strange rumours that 'a statue' called 'Lot's wife' existed on the eastern shore of the Dead Sea, but none of them had ever seen it, or could give us a satisfactory description of it. Making cautious inquiries amongst the Beni Hamideh, we found that the statement was correct, and after some little trouble, guides were procured who offered to conduct us to the spot. . . . Our path led us to another plateau, about 1000 feet above the Dead Sea, and on the extreme edge of this was the object of which we were in search—Bint Sheikh Lot, or 'Lot's wife.' It is a tall isolated needle of rock, which does really bear a curious resemblance to an Arab woman with a child upon her shoulder. The Arab legend of Lot's wife differs from the Bible account only in the addition of a few frivolous details. They say that there were seven Cities of the Plain, and that they were all miraculously overwhelmed by the Dead Sea as a punishment for their crimes. The prophet Lot and his family alone escaped the general destruction; he was divinely warned to take all that he had and flee eastward, a strict injunction being given that they should not look behind them. Lot's wife, who had on previous occasions ridiculed her husband's prophetic office, disobeyed the command, and, turning to gaze upon the scene of the disaster, was changed into this pillar of rock.

"Travellers in all ages have discovered 'Lot's wife' in the pillars which atmospheric influences are constantly detaching from the great masses of mineral salt at the southern end of the Dead Sea, but these are all accidental and transient. The rock discovered by us does not fulfil the requirements of the Scriptural story, but there can be no doubt that it is the object which has served to keep alive for so many ages the local tradition of the event.

"The sun was just setting as we reached the spot; and the reddening orb sank down behind the western hills, throwing a bridge of sheeny light across the calm surface of the mysterious lake. As we gazed on the strange statue-like outline of the rock—at first brought out into strong relief against the soft yet glowing hues of the surrounding landscape, and then mingled with the deepening shadows, and lost amid the general gloom as night came quickly on, we yielded insensibly to the influence of the wild Arab tale, and could almost believe that we had seen the form of the prophet's wife peering sadly after her perished home in the unknown depths of that accursed sea."

H

6. *The Natural History of Palestine, as dependent on its Physical Geography.*

The gradual elevation of the countries of Egypt and Palestine, inferred by Professor Hull from the geological facts, appears to be borne out by a comparison of the fishes which inhabit respectively the Lake of Galilee and the lakes of south-eastern Africa.

Josephus, after describing in glowing language the beauty and fruitfulness of the country of Gennesaret, says, "For besides the good temperature of the air, it is also watered from a most fertile fountain. The people of the country call it Capharnaum. Some have thought it to be a vein of the Nile, because it produces the Coracin fish as well as that lake does which is near to Alexandria." * The truth turns out to be much stranger than Josephus imagined, for the Sea of Galilee can claim affinity by its fishes with the Victoria Nyanza. Rev. Canon Tristram, who more than any other traveller has studied the natural history of the Holy Land, has made the comparison in some detail, and made out the relationship of the fishes beyond doubt. He declares that of all the forms of life in Palestine the fishes are the most interesting. There are no fishes in the Dead Sea ; but there are fishes, chiefly Cyprinidæ, or of the perch tribe, in the little streams and rivers close to the Dead Sea. "I have seen the date palm absolutely dipping its fronds into the Dead Sea as it hung over—for on the east side the date palm is very luxuriant. On the eastern shores there is as wonderful an exuberance of vegetable life as will be found anywhere on the face of the earth. The plants are like hot-house plants growing wild. In the warm waters entering to the sea there are small fishes of various species. We found thirteen new kinds of fishes in the Jordan and its affluents. Dr Günther

---

* Josephus: "Wars," iii. 10. § 8.

of the British Museum kindly described them in a paper in the 'Proceedings of the Zoological Society of London,' and certainly such a discovery amply repaid our search.

"I wish now to point out the conclusions come to from these fishes, for they are really the climax of the physical geography of the Jordan Valley. The fishes found in the Sea of Galilee not only belong for the most part to species different from those found in any stream flowing into the Mediterranean, but they belong frequently to different genera. Some years before, I brought home the type specimen of a fish, the only species I could find in some salt lakes of the Sahara, and Dr Günther declared it to be not only a new species but a new genus. I remember Sir Charles Lyell observing, 'You have got there the last living representative of the Saharan ocean.' We found in the Sea of Galilee three more species of the same genus, but each distinct. Speke brought back two species of the same family from the Nyanza, and Dr Kirk has described several from the Zambezi and the neighbouring region.

"Now we may see what this amounts to. We have got the same genus of fishes represented in a variety of specific types from the Sea of Galilee and the Jordan that are found in the feeders of the Nile, and in the Central African lakes down to the Zambezi. The conclusion is natural that all these fishes come from a common origin, and that during the Tertiary period there was a chain of fresh-water lakes, extending to the lakes in Africa, similar to the chain of lakes in North America.

"We find in Palestine forty-three species of fishes, of which only eight belong to the ordinary ichthyological fauna of the Mediterranean rivers. But these belong to the rivers of the coast. In the Jordan system only one species out of thirty-six belongs to the ordinary Mediterranean fauna, viz., *Blennius lupulus.* Two others, *Chromis niloticus* and *Clarias macracanthus*, are Nilotic. Seven other species occur in other rivers of South-Western Asia, the Tigris, Euphrates, &c. Ten more are found in other parts of Syria, chiefly in the Damascus lakes, and the remaining sixteen species of the families *Chromidæ, Cyprinodontidæ,* and *Cyprinidæ,* are peculiar to the Jordan, its affluents, and its lakes. This analysis points at once to the close affinity of the Jordan with the rivers of Tropical Africa. The affinity is not only of species, but of genera, for *Chromis* and *Hemichromis* are peculiarly Ethiopian forms, while the other species are identical with, or very closely allied to, the fishes from other fresh waters of Syria. But the African forms are a very large proportion of the whole, and considering the difficulty of transportation in the case of fresh water fishes, the peculiarities of this portion of the fauna are of great significance.

"The fluviatile fishes claim special attention, dating, as they probably do, from the earliest time after the elevation of the country from the Eocene ocean. In the *Foraminifera,* mentioned above as found in the Dead Sea sand, such as *Gr. capreolus,* we have the relics of the inhabitants of that early sea. But of the living inhabitants we must place the Jordanic fishes as the very earliest, and these, we have seen, form a group far more distinct and divergent from that of the surrounding region than in any other class of existing life. During the epochs subsequent to the Eocene, owing to the unbroken isolation of the basin, there have been no opportunities for the introduction of new forms, nor for the further dispersion of the old ones. These forms, as we have seen, bear a striking affinity to those of the fresh-water lakes and rivers of Eastern Africa, even as far south as the Zambezi. But the affinity is in the identity of genera, *Chromis* and *Hemichromis* being exclusively African, while the species are rather representative than identical.

"The solution appears to be that during the Meiocene

and Pleiocene periods the Jordan basin formed the northernmost of a large system of fresh-water lakes, extending from north to south, of which, in the earlier part of the epoch, perhaps the Red Sea, and certainly the Nile Basin, the Nyanza, the Nyassa, and the Tanganyika lakes, and the feeders of the Zambezi, were members. During that warm period, a fluviatile ichthyological fauna was developed suitable to its then conditions, consisting of representative, and perhaps frequently identical species, throughout the area under consideration.

"The advent of the glacial period was, like its close, gradual. Many species must have perished under the change of conditions. The hardiest survived, and some perhaps have been gradually modified to meet those new conditions. Under this strict isolation it could hardly be otherwise; and however severe the climate may have been, that of the Lebanon, with its glaciers probably corresponding with the present temperature of the Alps at a proportional elevation (regard being had to the difference of latitude), the fissure of the Jordan being, as we certainly know, as much depressed below the level of the ocean as it is at present; there must have been an exceptionally warm temperature in its waters in which the existing ichthyological fauna could survive."

Such facts as these tell us that Palestine is not to be regarded as a European country, but rather as an African outlier, while it has also strong affinities with Asia, as proved by others of these fishes. In fact, it stands in the midst between three continents, and is, in a very important sense, the centre of the world. Dr Tristram, our best authority in this department, shows us how Palestine contains an epitome of the life of the world, and does so just because it includes almost every variety of climate.

Linnæus said that we know more of the botany and zoology of farther India than we do of those of Palestine.

It is pleasant to reflect that, to some extent, this reproach has been removed. It always entered into the plans of the Palestine Exploration Society to study the natural history of the Holy Land; and although they have not been able to equip and maintain a party of naturalists, charged with this business alone, some of their officers have gathered interesting facts incidentally. Other inquirers, like Rev. Wm. Houghton and Mr Thaddeus Mason, have been usefully engaged on the same work. Mr H. Chichester Hart, who accompanied Professor E. Hull through the Arabah and Southern Palestine, has written an interesting volume on "The Animals mentioned in the Bible." But it is to Rev. Dr Tristram we are chiefly indebted. The Memoirs of the Survey include a magnificent volume on the " Fauna and Flora of Western Palestine," in which he works out his valuable series of investigations, and besides giving facts and details, treats the subject in a large philosophical way, as he does also in his lectures. " You have on Lebanon and Hermon," he says, "a climate like that of the Alps, or two-thirds of the way up Mont Blanc. You have on the tops of Lebanon and Hermon an almost arctic climate, and you have a fauna and a flora (animals and plants) corresponding to that climate. You know that when you descend a coal-pit 1300 feet deep you get into a very warm temperature indeed. Now the Dead Sea is 1300 feet below the level of the Mediterranean, and the consequence is that you have around the Dead Sea a tropical or sub-tropical climate, and you have sub-tropical products.

"At the northern end of the Holy Land you find yourself at the starting point of the Jordan, which, being 1000 feet above the Mediterranean at the grotto of Banias, descends so rapidly that it is only a few feet above the sea level at Lake Huleh. Mount Hermon rises abruptly from its base near Lake Huleh (the ancient Waters of

Merom). Although Hermon is only 10,000 feet high, I am not aware of any mountain which rises so suddenly or so directly from its base. Take, for instance, Chamounix. If you want to go to the top of Mont Blanc, you know that Chamounix is many hundred feet above the platform of the Mediterranean. It is true that Mont Blanc is many thousand feet higher than Mount Hermon, but from its immediate base it is not so high. When you get up to the Grand Mulets you are not so far from the summit of Mont Blanc as you are at Lake Huleh from the summit of Hermon. The consequence of this is that you have brought together in that spot a greater contrast of produce, animal and vegetable, than I have found anywhere else. You have the arctic climate of the north on the tops of the mountains, and a tropical climate in the Jordan Valley, where, in the month of January, I have been glad to sleep in the open air, the thermometer never being below 80° at midnight. At the east and south you have the dry sandy desert; so that you have four distinct climates within view of each other. I can stand on any of the hills of Judea and see the snow-capped tops of Hermon and Lebanon, and look over this vast desert eastward and down to the seething tropical valley of the Dead Sea.

"Now, with all that, there is nothing in the physical character of that country which is striking or phenomenal, as people would call it. It is about the most commonplace and ordinary country in the world that I have ever seen. There are no startling features, but there is endless variety in it, and I cannot help thinking that there is something very providential in the extraordinary variety which is brought together within a district of the Holy Land, which is not so large as the six northern counties of England; because I remember that it was chosen as the country in which was written a Book, which was to be for the teaching and guidance of all mankind in every country and in every age ; and I know no spot in the world in which there could have been found brought together so many phenomena of Nature, maritime and desert, mountain and plain, hill and valley, tropical, temperate, and arctic, as are brought together there within the space of a few miles. And when I remember that that Book was to be for the teaching of all men, for all time, I feel that there is something providential in that ordering of circumstances which led to the selection of the only spot, as far as we know, in the whole world, in which there is such a great variety of objects for the illustration, comparison, and elucidation of Holy Writ as in that country of the Holy Land. Often, when I have been in that country, on one of its hills, and have noticed the variety of scenery brought into my view at one time, I have thought to myself, 'What would the Bible have been if its pages had been written by men who had lived only in the monotonous valley of the Nile ? What would they have been able to pen in the way of illustration which would have come home to the heart of the English peasant ?' Again, if that Book were written by men who were only familiar with the phenomena of Arabian deserts, how could it have come home to those who dwell on the sea ? Had it been written by inhabitants of tropical India, how would it have come home to those who are familiar with 'snow and frost and vapour, fulfilling His will ?' In fact, there are illustrations taken from every kind of natural phenomena, and yet none of them are very marked or startling."

[*Authorities and Sources :*—" Palestine in its Physical Aspects." Rev. Canon Tristram, F. R. S. Survey Memoirs : "The Fauna and Flora." Rev. Canon Tristram. " The Animals mentioned in the Bible." Henry Chichester Hart, B.A., F.L.S.]

7. *The Topographical Survey of Western Palestine.*

Before we can properly understand the history of any country we must have before us an accurate map, showing its physical features of mountain, plain, and river, and the relative positions of its cities and important places. This is true in an unusual degree in the case of Palestine, a country peculiar in its physical contrasts, and for more than a thousand years the home of a peculiar people. The sacred books of other religions—consisting greatly of rhapsodies, prayers, and devotions—might have been written as well in one country as another; but the Bible contains the history of a particular people, occupying a definite district of country, fighting their battles, making their journeys, and singing psalms oft suggested by their surroundings. It is absolutely necessary for the student of Hebrew history to make himself acquainted with Palestine geography and topography. " The history assumes everywhere a knowledge of the country, and the writer never stops to explain where the scene of every episode occurs, except to name it as a spot already known." Yet, until lately, no accurate map of the country could be obtained—because no scientific survey had been carried out. Bible towns and villages had disappeared, and their sites were not known. The visitor to Palestine, consulting Murray's "Handbook " as his best guide, found long columns of "places mentioned in Scripture, but not yet identified "—Admah, Adullun, Debir, Edrei, Gallim, &c., &c. In going up from Jaffa to Jerusalem he was shown a brook, and told that David there selected the five smooth stones before his combat with Goliath ; but the brook was in the wrong locality. Down by the Jordan he found the grave of Moses on the wrong side of the river. In Galilee he was perplexed how to decide between two rival sites for Cana, especially as the water-pots connected with the marriage feast were to be seen at both places. General uncertainty attended his footsteps throughout.

The people who did most to bring ·about this confusion in regard to the sacred sites were the Crusaders. Knights and priests of the twelfth century, arriving in Palestine, were strangers in the country, and although enthusiastic they were ignorant and illiterate. They used to land at Athlit, and journey thence to Nazareth or to Jerusalem, fixing as many places *en route* as they could. Athlit itself they regarded as the ancient Tyre! Meon, the home of Nabal, they fixed close by, because Mount Carmel was not far off, and Abigail came from Carmel. They did not recognise that the Carmel of Abigail and Nabal was a city in the south of Judah. Knowing that Capernaum was a fishing town, they placed it on the Mediterranean coast and identified it with a fortress of their day, now the village called Kefr Lam. These three places, which were shown to the religious devotee as soon as he landed, are in reality many days' journey apart. Caipha (Haifa) was shown as a place where Simon Peter used to fish. Shiloh was south of Bethel, and was in fact the mountain now called Nebi Samwil. Sychar and Shechem were one and the same place. "The Quarantania or Kuruntul mountain" (says Conder) "has, from the twelfth century down, been shown as the place where our Lord retired for the forty days of fasting in the desert. Near to it the Crusaders also looked for the 'exceeding high mountain' whence the Tempter showed our Lord 'all the kingdoms of the world and the glory of them' (Matt. iv. 8). Saewulf tells us that the site of this mountain was 3 miles from Jericho. Fetellus places it north of that town and 2 miles from Quarantania. The measurements bring us to the remarkable cone called the Raven's Nest. The story is wonderfully descriptive of the simplicity of men's minds in the twelfth century, for the summit of the 'exceeding high mountain,' whence all the kingdoms of the world were to have been seen, is actually lower than the surface of the Mediterranean, and it is surrounded on every side by mountains more than double its height."

Tradition having been shown to be untrustworthy, when unsupported by other evidence, a general uncertainty prevailed with regard to Scripture places. No traveller could believe what his guide or guide book told him, and no student could have confidence in his map. The labour of investigation was beyond the power of private individuals ; and no Government and no Society had ever sent out an organized expedition. But now happily this reproach is removed. The Committee of the Palestine Exploration Fund were able to send out Major Conder, R.E., and Colonel Kitchener, R.E., and these officers, with their little party, spent seven years in carrying out a triangulation survey of the entire country west of the river Jordan. As a result of their labours, followed up by much patient work at home, we are now presented with a magnificent map of Western Palestine, on the scale of one inch to the mile, as beautifully and accurately executed as the ordnance map of England, with every road and ruin marked, and every conspicuous object filled in ; with the hills and mountains correctly delineated and shaded, with the rivers and brooks all running in the right directions ; with every vineyard, every spring of water, and almost every clump of trees set down in its place, and with thousands of names that never appeared on a Palestine map before. Moreover, while there are six hundred and twenty-two Scripture names of places west of the Jordan, and out of these three hundred and sixty were missing, the surveyors have succeeded in finding one hundred and seventy-two of these. A reduced map, on the scale of three-eighths of an inch to the mile, has been prepared, and contains the Old Testament names and New Testament names conspicuously marked, while other forms of the map show the watershed and physical features of the country, or give the divisions of the land and the Arabic names of places in use to-day.

There could be no better aid in studying the Scriptures than to have such maps by our side; for whether we read of the marching and counter-marching of armies; of the positions taken up before a battle; of the direction taken by the retreating foe; the sites selected for places of worship; the journeys of prophets of the Old Testament, or of Jesus and his disciples in the New, so much depends upon the relative positions of places, and their distances one from another, that we necessarily lose a part of the meaning, and miss a portion of the enjoyment unless we have a correct map by our side.

The best modern map of the Holy Land, previous to that prepared by the Palestine Exploration Fund, was the work of Van de Velde, a careful and scientific traveller and scholar. Van de Velde not only took observations himself, but laid down on his map all the observations made by previous travellers. Yet, when at the annual meeting of the Palestine Exploration Fund in 1886, a portion of Van de Velde's map was shown on an enlarged scale, side by side with the same portion of the Society's map, similarly enlarged, the contrast was striking. The first, with its hills roughly sketched in, its valleys laid down roughly, and its inhabited places, villages, or ruins, 'gave all that was known of this piece of country before the Survey. It was on such a map as this, the best at the time, because the most faithful, that the geographical student had to work. There was little use, from a geographical point of view, in consulting previous books of travel, because Van de Velde had gleaned from them all their geographical facts. Yet hardly any single place was laid down correctly; none of the hill shading was accurate; the course of the rivers and valleys was not to be depended upon;

the depression of the Lake of Galilee was variously stated ; distances were estimated by the rough reckoning of time taken from place to place ; and the number of names was only about eighteen hundred, whereas the large map of the Palestine Exploration Society contains ten thousand.*

[*Authorities and Sources :*—" Tent-work in Palestine." Major Conder, R. E. " Twenty-one Years' Work in the Holy Land." P. E. Fund. " Quarterly Statements of the P. E. Fund."]

8. *Israel's Wars and Worship, considered in connection with the Physical Features of the Country.*

The Wars.

Now that we possess a detailed and accurate map of the Holy Land we are in a position to study with advantage the conquest of the country by Joshua, and to appreciate the motives of strategy and policy displayed in the successive phases of Israel's wars and worship.

The twelve tribes, coming out of the wilderness, encamped in the Plain of the Jordan, opposite Jericho. While they rested there, Balak, king of Moab, alarmed by their numbers, and uncertain as to their intentions, sent to Mesopotamia for Balaam, to come and curse them. Balaam ascended Mount Peor (sacred to Baal Peor, *i.e.,* Baal the Opener) and was constrained to bless them, and speak of them as "a people that dwell alone—not reckoned among the nations " (Num. xxiii. 9).

Under Moses the Israelites conquered the country east of Jordan. The gorge of the Arnon, 2000 feet deep, and with almost perpendicular sides, was a natural boundary

* " Twenty-one years' Work in the Holy Land."

for the Moabites. Sometimes, indeed, they possessed territory north of it; but since it would take a traveller several hours to cross at the easiest parts, it was a natural boundary. The district between the Arnon and the Jabbok, Moses wrested from Sihon, king of Heshbon. And then, with the aid of the Ammonites, he conquered the country north of the Jabbok, from Og, the king of Bashan. These lands were not divided among all the tribes of Israel, but were given to Reuben, Gad, and half the tribe of Manasseh as their portion, for it was planned and intended that the country west of the Jordan should be conquered and given to the rest.

The country west of Jordan was occupied by the Amorites and the Canaanites—that is, as some suppose, by the Highlanders of the central hills, and the Lowlanders of the plains around. But these peoples appear to have been subdivided, so that, together with the tribes of the Lebanon, we read of the Jebusite and the Girgashite, the Hivite, the Arkite, and the Sinite, the Arvadite, the Zemarite and the Hamathite, as well as Zidon and Heth (Gen. x. 15); and, in another place, of the Kenite, the Kenizzite, and the Kadmonite, the Hittite, the Perizzite, and the Rephaim (Gen. xv. 19). Of all these " nations" we are told by St Paul that seven were eventually destroyed, and Israel received their land for an inheritance (Acts xiii. 19).

It was not the object of Joshua in the first place to conquer the " nations" in the plains, but rather those in the hills. It is true that the hills were comparatively barren and infertile, while the plains were exceedingly fruitful; but the hill country offered counter-balancing advantages. Compared with the Egyptians, who sometimes invaded Syria, the Israelites were small and weak, and their greatest security would be in the hill fastnesses. More immediately also, they have to consider that they are but a nation of foot soldiers, while the Canaanites of the plains possess chariots and horses. In any case, if they can once gain possession of the hills, it may be easier thence to conquer the plains at their leisure, than it would be for them by-and-bye to conquer the hills, with the plains as their base of operations.

They approach the river opposite Jericho, and prepare to cross. The spot is very well known, and it is where the pilgrims now go to bathe. At this part the Jordan is ordinarily a brown, rapid, swirling stream, some 20 yards across, fringed with a jungle of tamarisk, cane, and willow, in which the leopard and the wolf find their hiding place. The stream often runs low and is easily fordable in two or three places hereabout. When we remember that the spies sent by Joshua had crossed and recrossed without difficulty a few days before, we might suppose that Joshua intended to march the entire army over at the fording places, at low water, were we not told that at this season the Jordan overflowed all its banks, it being the time of barley harvest. The Jordan, it is recorded, was divided—" The waters which came down from above stood and rose up in one heap a great way off from Adam, the city which is beside Zarethan : and those that went down toward the Sea of the Arabah, even the Salt Sea, were wholly cut off: and the people passed over right against Jericho " (Josh. iii. 16). Major Conder has discovered the name Zarethan, still in use, applied to a district 3 miles west of Bethshan ; and on examining the gorge of the Jordan at this part, a good way north of " Admah " or *Damieh*, he found that the lower cliffs approach in places so close to one another that a very little would dam up the river. In that event, in place of a shallow stream some 20 yards across, a lake would be formed nearly a mile in width, and the waters would have to rise to a height of 50 feet before they overflowed the barrier and

descended again to the south. But whether in this way
the bed of the Jordan was rendered dry while the Israelites
passed over, is a question upon which, of course, opinions
will differ.

When the tribes are safely across they encamp at a
place called Gilgal.

An important success in the way of identifying Scripture
sites has been the recovery of Gilgal. Robinson had heard
the name Jiljûlieh, but had not been able to fix the site.
In 1865 a German traveller (Herr Schokke), more fortunate,
was shown the place, at a mound about a mile east of the
modern Jericho; and Major Conder succeeded in fixing
the spot. Just west of the ruins grows a magnificent old
tamarisk tree, conspicuous from a distance. South-east of
the tamarisk is an oblong tank, measuring about 100 feet
by 80 feet; and near this about a dozen small mounds.
The mounds are called Tellcilât Jiljûlieh (the little hillocks
of Gilgal), and the tank is named Birket Jiljûlieh (the
Pool of Gilgal). " The Bedawin of the district," says Conder,
" have a well-known tradition regarding the site of Jiljûlieh.
Over the coffee and pipes in the evening, after the day's
work was done, they related it to us. By the old tamarisk
once stood the City of Brass, which was inhabited by
Pagans. When Mohammed's creed began to spread, Aly,
his son-in-law, 'the lion of God,' arrived at the city, and
rode seven times round it on his horse Maimûn. The
brazen walls fell down, destroyed by his breath, and the
Pagans fled, pursued by the Faithful toward Kŭrŭntŭl;
but the day drew to a close, and darkness threatened to
shield the infidels. Then Aly, standing on the hill which
lies due east of the Kŭrŭntŭl crag, called out to the sun,
' Come back, O blessed one!' And the sun returned in
heaven, so that the hill has ever since been called ' the Ridge
of the return.' Here stands the Mukâm, or sacred station
of Aly, and here also is the place where Belâl ibn Rubâh,

the Muedhen of the Prophet, called the Faithful to prayer after the victory."

Such is the legend, in which we see the fall of Jericho mixed up with the battle of Aijalon, and assigned to Mohammedan heroes instead of to Joshua.

Quite apart from the facilities of a ford, there was a good reason why the Israelites should cross the Jordan where they did. The hill country of Western Palestine is much broken by gorges, which serve not only as torrent beds after the rains, but as passes to the central plateau. The principal pass is by that great gorge, the continuation of the Wady Kelt, which runs to the north of Jericho and up to Ai and Bethel. Joshua intends to ascend by this pass. But there is an obstacle in the way. Just at the foot of the hills—where the springs issue forth and make a beautiful oasis—is the city of Jericho, "walled up to heaven." This is the key to the pass, and it would be bad generalship to rush past the place and leave it in the rear. So Jericho, "the city of palm trees," was besieged and taken.

Modern Jericho is not a city of palm trees, but a very poor village, of mud huts and black tents, standing amid low vineyards. For the convenience of travellers, indeed, an excellent hotel has lately been opened—the "Jordan Hotel"—but the proprietor has been disappointed in his neighbours ; the peasantry will not do a good day's work for good wages, he cannot even get fruit and garden stuff from them, and every requisite has to be brought down from Jerusalem.

The site of Jericho has shifted considerably since Scripture times, for the Bible city was near the Sultan's Spring —Elisha's Fountain—at the foot of the pass, the only natural position, whereas the present village is at a distance from the spring. Some Russian excavations in the neighbourhood have brought to light shafts, columns, and lintels, lamps, jars, rings, and weapons, some indication of former splendour.

The next city in the way of the invaders was Ai. We learn from the narrative that Ai had Bethel on the west of it, and a plain in the front or on the east, while there was a valley on the north side, and low ground on the west between Ai and Bethel. With these particulars it should be possible to identify the site. Sir Charles Wilson examined the district in 1865, and confirmed the opinion of Rev. Canon Williams that there is only one spot which answers to the description. " The description applies in a very complete manner" (says Conder) "to the neighbourhood of the modern village of Deir Diwan, and there are here remains of a large ancient town, bearing the name Haiyan, which approaches closely to Aina, the form under which Ai appears in the writings of Josephus. Rock-cut tombs and ancient cisterns, with three great reservoirs cut in the hard limestone, are sufficient to show this to have been a position of importance. To the west is an open valley called ' Valley of the City,' which, gradually curving round eastward, runs close to the old road from Jericho by which Joshua's army would probably advance. To the north of the site there is also a great valley, and the plain or plateau on which the modern village stands, close to the old site, expands from a narrow and rugged pass leading up towards Bethel, which is 2 miles distant on the watershed."

Ascending from Jericho the path at one point enters upon the plain in front of Ai, so that no army on its way to Bethel could afford to leave Ai behind. Joshua took the city by stratagem, and we can see every step of the proceeding. Marching troops up the northern valley, he placed an ambush in the depression west of the city. The main body of his troops attacked in front and presently feigned a retreat, drawing the men of Ai after them till

the city was empty. Then, at a given signal from Joshua
—who had posted himself on the hills to the north and
could be seen by both sections of his army—the ambush
rose up and fired the city, the men retreating turned back
to fight, and the men of Ai, caught "between two fires,"
became utterly demoralised.

Bethel itself is now called Beitin. The site is known,
but with the exception of a church of crusading date, and
a tower, there are no ruins of any importance. On a hill
to the east is a stone circle, consisting of large and small
boulders.

After the victory at Ai a rapid march was made to
Shechem, where, upon the mountains of Ebal and Gerizim,
the tribes assembled to hear the reading of the Law and to
pronounce their "amens" after the blessings and the curses.
It has been questioned whether they could hear one another
at the distance apart of these two mountain tops ; but they
would hardly be on the mountain summits, for there is a
natural recess in the hills, with natural benches in the
limestone rock, an amphitheatre which might seem to
have been formed for the purpose. Modern travellers
have stood in the midst of that valley and heard their
companions on either side reading the Law, and they
assure us that those who were reading could hear one
another's voices with sufficient distinctness to take up the
verse, each where the other left off.

Shechem is now called Nablous—a corruption of the
Roman Neapolis, by which name it was rebaptized—and is
a considerable city. The Samaritans, now reduced in
numbers to about one hundred and sixty individuals, all
told, live in this city, and none are found elsewhere. In
their synagogue they preserve several old copies of the
Pentateuch, and one of them, which is kept in a silver case
and jealously guarded, they declare to have been written
by Abishua, the great-grandson of Aaron. On a stone

built into a tower near the synagogue is an inscription—the oldest known in the Samaritan character—which it was formerly impossible to read, because the inscription is upside down in its place, and the investigator had to dangle on a rope and hold his head downwards. But here we see the advantage of photography : the picture was obtained in the camera, and the inscription when turned right way up was seen to be the Samaritan version of the Ten Commandments.

After the solemn ceremony of reading the Law at Shechem the Israelites under Joshua returned to the camp at Gilgal. But by this time the news of their victories had spread, the neighbouring cities became alarmed, and all the kings throughout an extensive district gathered together to fight against them. Meantime the wily Gibeonites, wearing " old shoes and clouted," and pretending to be ambassadors from a far country, came to Joshua and succeeded in making a treaty of alliance, offensive and defensive. After three days the deception was found out ; but it was held that the covenant must be kept, and when the kings of Jerusalem, Hebron, Jarmuth, Lachish, and Eglon—"the five kings of the Amorites"—went and encamped against Gibeon, Joshua went up from Gilgal all the night to raise the siege. He came upon them suddenly, and a terrible battle took place, which deserves to rank among the decisive battles of the world. The conflict raged before Gibeon, and the defeated kings were pursued, with continued slaughter, to higher ground (the ascent of Beth-horon) and then to lower ground (the going down of Beth-horon), as they vainly sought to escape down the Valley of Aijalon into the Plain of Philistia. According to the poetical book of Jasher,* quoted by the historian, " the sun stood still upon Gibeon and the moon in the valley of

---

* For an account of the " Book of Jasher," see the " Literary Remains of Emanuel Deutsch."

Aijalon," and lengthened out the day until Joshua had defeated his foes utterly. The five kings were found hidden in a cave at Makkedah, and were imprisoned there till the pursuit was over and Joshua had leisure to decide their fate.

Makkedah has been identified by Colonel Sir C. Warren as being *El Mughar*—" the cave"—a little south-west of Ekron. Conder tells us that this is a remarkable place, and one of the most conspicuous sites in the plain. A promontory of brown sandy rock juts out southwards, and at the end is the village climbing up the hillside. The huts are of mud, and stand in many cases in front of caves; and from these caves the modern name is derived. It is worthy of notice, he says, that this is the only village in the Philistine plain at which he found such caves.

Joshua made his victory complete, by overthrowing Libnah, Lachish, Eglon, Hebron, and other cities in succession, "utterly destroying all that breathed," until the centre and the south of the hill country were altogether in his power.

In the spring of 1890, a *firman* having been obtained, Mr Flinders Petrie went to excavate at *Umm Lakis* and *Ajlan*, the supposed sites of Lachish and Eglon, two of the five strongholds of the Amorites (Josh. x. 5). As soon as he arrived and could examine the ground, he saw, from his Egyptian experience, that the two sites named were only of Roman age and unimportant; while *Tell Hesy* and *Nejileh* in the same neighbourhood promised better results. *Tell Hesy* is a mound of ruins 60 feet high and about 200 feet square, and one side of it has been washed away by the stream, so that a clear section is afforded from top to base. The generally early age of it was evident from the fact that nothing later than good Greek pottery was found at the top of it, while near the middle, and from that to three-quarters of the height, was found Phœnician ware, which is known in Egypt to date from 1100 B.C. The foundation seems to date from about 1500 B.C., agreeing nearly with the beginning of the Egyptian raids under Thothmes I.

The actual remains of *Tell Hesy* consist of a mound which is formed of successive towns, one on the ruins of another, and an enclosure taking in an area to the south and west of it. This enclosure is nearly a quarter of a mile across in each direction, and is bounded by a clay rampart still 7 feet high in parts, and in one place by a brick wall. This area of about 30 acres would suffice to take in a large quantity of cattle in case of a sudden invasion ; and such was probably its purpose, as no buildings are found in it, and there is but little depth of soil. The city mound is about 200 feet square, and rests on natural ground 45 to 58 feet above the stream in the *wady* below. The earliest town here was of great strength and importance, the lowest wall of all being 28 feet 8 inches thick, of clay bricks, unburnt ; and over this are two successive patchings of later rebuilding, altogether 21 feet of height remaining. "Such massive work" (says Mr Petrie) "was certainly not that of the oppressed Israelites during the time of the Judges ; it cannot be as late as the Kings, since the pottery of about 1100 B. C. is found above its level. It must, therefore, be the Amorite city, and agrees with the account that 'the cities were walled and very great' (Num. xiii. 28), 'great and walled up to heaven' (Deut. i. 28), and also with the sculptures of the conquests of Rameses II. at Karnak, where the Amorite cities are all massively fortified."

Mr Petrie feels little doubt that *Tell Hesy* is Lachish and *Tell Nejileh*, 6 miles south of it, Eglon. There are no sites in the country around so suited to the importance of Lachish and Eglon as these two *tells* ; they command the only springs and water-course which exist in the whole district, and it is certain that the positions must have been of first-rate importance from the time of the earliest settlements.

Above the Amorite wall at *Tell Hesy* Mr. Petrie finds 5 feet of dust and rolled stones corresponding to the barbaric period of the Judges ; then a wall 13 feet thick, probably belonging to Rehoboam's fortifications of Lachish (2 Chron. xi. 9), and above this successive rebuildings until the city is finally destroyed about 500 B. C.   The mound is full of potsherds, and the good fortune of such a grand section as that of the east face from top to bottom, affords at one stroke a series of all the varieties of pottery extending through a thousand years.   "We now know for certain," Mr Petrie says, "the characteristics of Amorite pottery, of earlier Jewish, and later Jewish influenced by Greek trade, and we can trace the importation and the influence of Phœnician pottery.   In future all the *tells* and ruins of the country will at once reveal their age by the potsherds which cover them."

Lachish, with its wall 28 feet in thickness, is a specimen of the Amorite cities which Joshua overthrew in the south.

But now the kings of the north are alarmed, and Jabin king of Hazor gathers together the tribes of the Lebanon. He calls to his assistance the kings of the Jordan Valley, the kings of the Sharon Plain, with the Jebusites and all who are willing to come.   The battle takes place near the Waters of Merom.   The Canaanites are furnished with chariots and horses, and the Israelites, being without such helps, are prudently posted on the hills.   We read that Joshua "fell upon" the foe, down the slopes, and drove them before him, on the west as far as to Zidon, and on the east to the valley of Mizpeh : he burned their chariots, hamstrung their horses, and again "left none remaining."   So now the north as well as the south of the hill country is subdued ; Joshua settles four tribes in these northern districts, and the Sea of Galilee becomes a Hebrew lake,

There is no need any more to come back all the way to Gilgal, for no foe is left to dispute their occupation anywhere, and the armies only return as far as Shiloh, in the centre of the hills, and there set up " the Tent of Meeting." Nor is there need any longer to detain the two and a half tribes from the east of Jordan who have come across to assist in the conquest. So the soldiers of Reuben, Gad, and Manasseh are sent back to their homes. " And when they came to the region about Jordan that is in the land of Canaan " they built there an altar—" a great altar to see to," and which was afterwards called " Ed " or Witness. Their brethren were so indignant at this action—regarding it as heathen worship, and rebellion against the God of Israel—that they thought of going to war against them. However, they prudently sent envoys to demand an explanation, and the explanation was perfectly satisfactory.

Where was this altar of Ed, so conspicuous from afar? If we stand in the Jordan Valley near Jericho, and look northwards, we cannot fail to see, at a distance of 20 miles, a conical peak called *Kurn Surtabeh*, standing out like a bastion at the eastern end of a chain of blue hills. This peak is 1500 feet above the level of the Mediterranean, and 2500 feet above the Jordan, near to it. From the top of it one may see the Dead Sea to the south, the Sea of Galilee to the north, the mountains of Ebal and Gerizim in the centre. According to the Jewish Talmud this mountain was a beacon station, where the fires were lighted, in connection with fires on the Mount of Olives, to signify the advent of the new moon. Conder, some years ago, pointed out that this mountain would be in the path which the two and a half tribes should naturally take in going from Shiloh to their home in Gilead, the fords of the Jordan being a little way north of it. On the top of this almost inaccessible peak he found some huge masonry work of ancient character, which he was inclined at the time to regard as remnants of the altar. And when the identification seemed to be thus nearly complete, it appeared to be confirmed by the discovery that the north side of the mountain, the only accessible side, is called "the Ascent of Ed." But the identification was disputed.

It was pointed out that Josephus says the altar was on the east side of Jordan, and that the Scripture narrative makes the tribes to cross the river at "the passage of the Children of Israel," which is supposed to describe the Jericho ford and not the ford at Damieh. For these reasons Conder now regards his idea as "only a conjecture."

It may be reasonably questioned, however, whether the identification should be given up. We are told in Joshua xxii. 10, that the altar, so high to look to, was in "the region about Jordan that is in the land of Canaan"—"in the forefront of the land of Canaan, in the region about Jordan, on the side that pertaineth to the Children of Israel." The historian takes pains to distinguish between the two sides of the river, and if one side pertained to the Children of Israel more than the other, it was surely not the eastern side. Moreover, the altar was in the land of Canaan, and the eastern boundary of Canaan was the Jordan itself (see Gen. x. 19, and page 107 of this volume). The altar was "in the forefront of the land of Canaan," at the extreme of its eastern side, and therefore close by the Jordan. The Hebrew faced the rising sun, and spoke of the south as the right hand, the north as the left, so that his forehead or forefront was to the east. It was apparently because the supposed idolatrous altar was set up on territory belonging to the western tribes that those tribes felt so insulted. The east of Jordan was unclean, but the western country was "the possession of the Lord." "Come across," they said, "into the Lord's land, if you will ; but if you come, do not build rebel altars" (v. 19). Further, the

object of the two and a half tribes, according to their
apology and explanation, was to have a memorial in that
western land from which the Jordan seemed to cut them
off.

Two and a half tribes being settled east of Jordan, three
tribes north of the Plain of Esdraelon, and one in the
Plain itself, the remainder of the country is divided
between the remaining five tribes and a half.

In the Book of Joshua the boundaries of the tribes are
given with the greatest minuteness, but it was impossible
for us to trace them with any accuracy before the topographical survey was carried out. Many of the villages
by which the border lines passed were lost, in some cases
the sites were displaced ; but as soon as these things were
rectified the boundaries could again be drawn.

The blessing which Jacob pronounced upon his sons,
according to Gen. xlix., was true to the position of the
tribes in their several districts ; and their position determined in some degree their conduct and their fortunes.
When Joshua dismissed the two and a half tribes, they
went away to their tents : living on those green hills east
of Jordan, they remained for a long time a pastoral people.
Reuben, bordering on Arabia, and being "unstable as water,"
became hardly distinguishable from an Arab tribe. Gad,
of whom Jacob said, "a troop shall press upon him," was
subject to attacks from troops of Bedouin plunderers.
Divided from their brethren by the great gorge of the
Jordan, the eastern tribes were separated also in their
fortunes. The three northern tribes of Asher, Zebulon, and
Naphtali were also partially cut off by the great plain of
Esdraelon. They got into communication with the
northern nations from whom they were less separated
geographically, and they entered into alliance with
Phœnicia. Solomon gave away twenty of their cities to
Hiram, king of Tyre, apparently thinking that the allegi-

ance which was so nearly gone, might as well be parted
with altogether. These northern tribes, like those east of
Jordan, seldom came to the assistance of their brethren in
any great crisis. When Deborah required help from all
quarters she had to complain that Asher "sat still at the
haven of the sea," and Reuben "sat among the sheep-folds,
to hear the pipings for the flocks." In the south—in a
country half a desert, the lair of wild beasts—Judah
"couched as a lion," and it was dangerous to rouse him up.
Ephraim, the most powerful of the tribes, secured to himself the choicest portion of the hill country. Manasseh,
with territory on both sides of the Jordan, was "a fruitful
bough by a fountain, whose branches run over the wall."
Little Benjamin, situated between the two powerful tribes
of Ephraim and Judah, knew not which to be guided by,
and was at last torn asunder in the effort to follow both. Yet
Benjamin, on whose eastern border we still find a valley,
called the Wolf's Den, was "a wolf that ravineth" and
often "devoured the prey." Issachar "saw the land that
it was pleasant"—namely, the fruitful plain of Esdraelon,
—and "bowed his shoulder to bear, and became a servant
under task-work," cultivating the ground.

The tribe of Levi had no district of country assigned to
it, but in place thereof forty-eight cities, scattered throughout the tribes. Of these cities two have been identified by
the agents of the Palestine Exploration Fund.

The recovery of the site of *Gezer* we owe to M. Clermont
Ganneau. It is in the lowland district, and off the road to
the right as one goes up from Jaffa to Jerusalem, about
8 miles past Ramleh. The modern name, *Tell Jezer*,
represents the Hebrew exactly. Gezer had been a royal city
of the Canaanites; and it was in a position commanding
one of the important passes. The Levitical cities had
around them a margin of 1000 cubits. In 1874 M.
Ganneau was shown by the peasantry a rude inscription

deeply cut in the flat surface of the natural rock. It
appears to be in Hebrew letters, and to read " Boundary
of Gezer." He afterwards found a second, similar to it ;
and from their position he judges that the city lay four-
square, and had its angles directed to the cardinal points
of the compass. It was this city of Gezer which was re-
conquered from the Philistines by Pharaoh, and handed
over to Solomon as a dowry with his daughter.

We owe to Major Conder the discovery of another of
these Levitical cities, namely, the royal city of Debir, south-
west of Hebron, together with the "upper and nether
springs of water" (at a distance), which Caleb gave to his
daughter, on the occasion of her marriage (Judges i. 15).
The modern name is Dhâberuyeh, and the place is evidently an ancient site of importance, to which several old
roads lead from all sides. Another name for this place
was Kirjath-Sepher, which means Book-Town ; so that it
must have been noted for books or writings of some kind.

In tracing the boundaries of the tribes the surveyors
found reason to look upon the Book of Joshua as "the
Domesday Book of Palestine." The towns in a district
are all mentioned together, and in such consecutive topographical order that many Scripture sites could be identified
from this very circumstance. The tribal boundaries are
shown to be almost entirely natural, namely, rivers, ravines,
ridges, and the water-shed lines of the country. It is a
remarkable fact, however, that while the descriptions of
tribal boundaries and cities are full and minute in the
territory of Judea, and scarcely less so in Galilee, they are
fragmentary and meagre within the bounds of Samaria.
There is no account of the conquest of Samaria, nor does
the list of royal cities include the famous Samaritan towns
of Shechem, Thebez, Acrabbi, and others. No list of the
cities of Ephraim and Manasseh is included in the topographical chapters of the Book of Joshua, nor any descrip-

tion of the northern limits of Manasseh, and only a very slight one of the southern border, where that tribe marched with Ephraim.

Thus far, in our description of Joshua's conquest, we have seen how his good generalship secured possession of the hills—the central hills only, and not the plains. The Canaanites still dwelt in the plains round about. The Philistines held the south-west. The Phœnicians were secure in the north. The outlying nations of Edom and Moab were undisturbed. In this condition things remained for a long time; and the Israelites, occupying the hills only, were not likely to become a race of sailors. Nor did they desire it, if we may judge from such notices of the sea as occur in the Bible, for they seem to show the awe with which the writers regarded its rolling waves. And besides, the coast was not suited for it. The principal harbour was Tyre; but that was in Phœnicia, which was hardly to be included in Palestine. South of Tyre we have Accho, Caipha, and Joppa; but these are by no means good and convenient as ports. Accho is the best, but has been the least used, although Napoleon considered it "the key of Palestine." It was to Joppa that the Phœnicians brought timber in rafts for the building of Solomon's Temple; and thence it was carried by road to Jerusalem. It was at Joppa that Jonah found a ship going to Tarshish, and took his passage.

If the sea coast was little available for the Israelites, the Jordan was still worse: a narrow, shallow, rocky stream, ending in the Dead Sea, it led to nowhere, and was useless for purposes of commerce.

Naturally the capitals of the country were inland— Jerusalem in the centre of the hills, and afterwards Shechem. The main road of the country ran from south to north, along the water-shed, the backbone of highest ground. But since the hills were comparatively unfruitful, the dwellers there suffered more in times of famine than the dwellers in the plains. In times of war they had some advantage, and preferred to fight from the hillsides, as they did not possess chariots and horses, and could have found no use for them. Their enemies said of them,—"their God is a God of the hills ; He is not a God of the plains !"

Accordingly, the enemies of Israel sought to entice them to fight in the plains, and sometimes partially succeeded. The Plain of Esdraelon became a great battle field. The Great Plain, as distinguished from the Plain of Acre, the Valley of Jezreel, and others which are continuous with it, measures about 14 miles by 9. It is described by Conder as one of the richest natural fields of cultivation in Palestine, or perhaps in all the world. " The elevation," he says, " is about 200 to 250 feet above the sea, and a Y-shaped double range of hills bounds it east and west, with an average elevation of 1500 feet above the plain on the north-east. On the north-east are the two detached blocks of Neby Duhy (Little Hermon) and Tabor, and on the north-west a narrow gorge is formed by the river Kishon, which springs from beneath Tabor, and, collecting the whole drainage of this large basin, passes from the Great Plain to that of Acre. On the east of the plain the broad Valley of Jezreel gradually slopes down towards Jordan, and Jezreel itself (the modern Zerin) stands on the side of Gilboa above it. On the west are the scarcely less famous sites of Legis, Taanach, and Joknean, while the picturesque conical hill of Duhy, just north of the Jezreel Valley, has Shunem on its south slope, and Nain and Endor on the north. Thus seven places of interest lie at the foot of the hills east and west ; but no important town was ever situated in the plain itself.

The first great struggle in this plain was against Sisera, captain of the host of Jabin, king of Canaan, who came with nine hundred chariots, and threatened the Israelites near the sources of the Kishon. The topography of the Scriptural episode of the defeat and death of Sisera has been hitherto very little understood. The scene of the battle has often been placed in the south-west of the great Esdraelon plain, and the defeated general has been supposed to have fled a distance of 35 miles over the high mountains of Upper Galilee. But this is contrary to what we know of the general character of the Biblical stories, the scenes of which are always laid in a very confined area. The kings of Canaan assembled in Taanach and by the waters of Megiddo, but it was not at either of these places that the battle was fought. Sisera was drawn to the river Kishon (Judges iv. 7), and the conflict took place in the plain south-west of Mount Tabor.

The forces of the Israelites were posted on the side of Mount Tabor. At a signal from Deborah they rushed down the slope and attacked the foe. At that moment a terrible storm from the east sent sleet and hail full into the face of the enemy. They turned and fled along a line at the base of the northern hills, where a chain of pools and springs, fringed with reeds and rushes, marks, even in the dry season, the course of the Kishon. The rain converted the volcanic dust of the plain into mud, and clogged the wheels of the chariots. The water pouring down from the hills swelled the stream, and "the river of Kishon swept them away, that ancient river the river Kishon." The remainder fled to Harosheth, now only a miserable village (*El Harathiyeh*), named from the beautiful woods above the Kishon at the point where, through a narrow gorge the stream, hidden among oleander bushes, enters the Plain of Acre.

The flight of Sisera himself was in an opposite direction —to the Plain of Zaanaim, or rather Bitzaanaim, "the marshes," *i.e.*, the marshy springs east of Tabor — the neighbourhood of *Bessum*. The Kedesh of the passage is probably a site so called south of Tiberias ; and the tent of Heber the Kenite would thus have been spread on the open plateau within 10 miles of the site of the battle.

The next great struggle in this plain was one upon which the Survey of Palestine has thrown some new light, enabling us to follow the fugitives in their retreat, and to fix some sites which are named in the narrative. The fruitfulness of the Great Plain has been, in our own times and all through the ages, an irresistible attraction to the Bedouin from the east of Jordan. Pressed by war or famine, they have crossed the Jordan at the fords near Beisan, poured up the Valley of Jezreel, and covered the plain with their tents and camels. The peaceful husbandmen have laboured, only to be periodically plundered and oppressed. Thus in 1870 only about a sixth part of the beautiful corn land was tilled, and the plain was black with Arab "houses of hair." But the Turks wrought a great and sudden change ; they armed their cavalry with the Remington breech-loading rifle, and the Bedouin disappeared as if by magic. In 1872 nine-tenths of the plain was cultivated, nearly half with corn, the rest with millet, sesame, cotton, tobacco, and the castor-oil plant. It was, of course, to be expected that when external troubles had weakened the Government, the lawless Nomads would again encroach and levy toll as before. Accordingly, in 1877, Fendi el Fais and the Sukr Arabs once more invaded the plain and levied blackmail on the luckless peasantry. Thus it has ever been ; for the history of Palestine seems constantly to repeat itself from the earliest period recorded, in a recurring struggle between the settled population and the Nomads.

Some time after the days of Barak and Deborah,' the historian tells us, "the children of Israel did that which was evil in the sight of the Lord, and the Lord delivered them into the hand of Midian seven years." These marauders from the east came across the Jordan, bringing their cattle and their camels, and pitching their black tents. They came as locusts for multitude, eating up the fruitful country and levying tribute on the villages, all the way round to Gaza. The Israelites fled in alarm, taking refuge in the mountains, and existing in dens and caves. No sustenance was left them, either for sheep, or ox, or ass ; and " Israel was brought very low because of Midian." Perhaps they might have borne the oppression longer, only that their lives were not safe from the sword, and they smarted under losses inflicted on their families. In some petty struggle, perhaps it was, in which one brother came to the assistance of another, that seven fine young men, sons of Joash of Abiezer, were put to death by Zeba and Zalmunna the Chiefs of Midian. But there was one son left, whose name was Gideon, and he was a man of valour. He felt this oppression to be insupportable: the spirit of the Lord came upon him, and after destroying the altar of Baal in his native place, he blew a trumpet, and raised a revolt. His own tribesmen (the men of Menasseh) gathered to his standard, and the men of the northern tribes also, even Asher assisting on this occasion.

Gideon "pitched beside the Spring of Harod, and the camp of Midian was on the north side of them, in the valley." The Bible narrative appears to show that the spring was in the neighbourhood of Gilboa, being towards the south of the Valley of Jezreel. "It is very striking," says Conder, "to find in this position a large spring with the name '*Ain el Jem'ain,*' or 'fountain of the two troops' and there seems no valid objection to the view that this is the Spring of Harod."

Gideon went down upon the enemy in the midnight darkness, leading three hundred men, who carried concealed torches, as well as trumpets. The sudden sounding

of trumpets and flashing of lights spread consternation
among the Midianites ; they fought suicidally, every man's
hand was against his brother, and they fled down the
Valley of Jezreel.   It was some 10 miles or more to
the fords of the Jordan.   At the fords they divided,
Zeba and Zalmunna, the sheikhs, passing over, while
Oreb and Zeeb, the lesser chiefs, continued their journey on the western side.   Presumably they were hoping
to get across at the great ford opposite Jericho ; but
Gideon sent word to the men of Ephraim to intercept
them, and they did so.   Gideon himself crossed at the
northern fords, pursuing Zeba and Zalmunna, as far as
Karkor, and when he had captured them he brought
them back to Penuel.   "Then said he to them, 'What
manner of men were they whom ye slew at Tabor ?'
And they answered, 'As thou art, so were they ; each
one resembled the children of a king.'   And he said,
'They were my brethren, the sons of my mother : as
the Lord liveth, if ye had saved them alive, I would
not slay you.'"

The men of Ephraim "slew Oreb at the rock of Oreb,
and Zeeb at the winepress of Zeeb."   These two names
signify the *Raven* and the *Wolf*—not unnatural names
for the chiefs of Nomad tribes—and Conder has discovered these names in the Jordan valley, a little north
of Jericho.   There is a curious conical chalk hill called
'*Osh el Ghurab*, the "Raven's Peak," and near to it a
lesser hill with a valley, know as *Tuweil edh Dhiab*, the
"Wolf's Den."   The executions, if they took place on
these elevations, would be in sight of all the people in
the plain ; and afterwards the heads were carried across
to Gideon, who was now beyond Jordan.

But victory was not always given to the Israelites in the
Plain of Esdraelon.   In the days of King Saul the Philistines, having been twice beaten in the hills, determined to

try their fortune in the plains. Under the leadership of
Achish, king of Gath, they marched northward, round
the promontory of Carmel, and took up their position at
Shunem, under "Little Hermon."* Saul was posted on
Mount Gilboa, but had no confidence in his strength. In
his distress, indeed, he actually paid a night visit to the
witch of Endor, although Endor was north of "Little
Hermon," and he had to go past the Philistine camp
to reach it. The next morning the battle went against
him: the Israelites were positively driven up the slope
of Gilboa and slaughtered on the heights, which should
have been their natural battle-ground. David, when he
heard of it, felt the humiliation of it, or at least the
depth of the misfortune, and his dirge for Saul and his
son opens with the words, "Thy glory, O Israel, is slain
upon thy high places! How are the mighty fallen! Tell
it not in Gath" (2 Sam. i.).

The head of Saul was sent round to Ashdod, to the
temple of Dagon, the Philistine Fish-god. The armour
of Saul was dedicated to the goddess Ashtoreth, in the
city of Bethshan, not very far from the scene of the
battle. We may judge that Bethshan was still in possession of the Canaanites. The bodies of Saul and his
sons were fastened to the wall of Bethshan. But the
men of Jabesh Gilead, east of Jordan, a city which Saul
had once befriended (1 Sam. xi.), came across in the
night and took them away. After burning them in
Jabesh, they buried the bones under a tamarisk tree;
and thence, at a later opportunity, David fetched them
away and buried them in the family tomb in Benjamin.

We read in Scripture of "Bethshan and her daughter

* Little Hermon is really a misnomer for the conical hill of Duhy just north
of the Valley of Jezreel. The mention of Tabor and Hermon together in
Psalm lxxxix. 12, has misled those who did not realize that Tabor would
be in the same line of vision with Mount Hermon, for many observers in
the south.

towns" as belonging to the tribe of Manasseh (1 Chron. vii. 29). A black mound at the modern Beisan represents the Bethshan or Bethshean of the text. On this natural fortress stood the citadel. The ruins have been planned by Conder ; and his drawings will be found in the Memoirs of the Survey. Not far from Beisan are the ruins of a Roman bridge across the Jordan—the highway to Gadara. In the plain of Beisan, as we learn from Mr Trelawney Saunders, are twenty-four *tells*, scattered all over the upper and lower terraces. They still bear distinctive names ; and Mr Saunders feels no doubt that they are the sites of former habitations, scenes of domestic happiness and abundant wealth. Moreover, he surmises that the life and happiness of the district may be restored almost as rapidly as they were obliterated, when once the civilisation and power of the West becomes conscious of the connection between Oriental prosperity and that of its own manufacturing populations. " These *tells*," he says, " probably mark the substantial and lordly centres of villages, the latter more or less extensive, and readily levelled with the ground. They denote the populous character of the region, when a strong government restrained the plundering Ishmaelites, and protected instead of robbed people. The *tells* are more indicative of a large population than the remains of such a ' splendid ' and ' noble' city as Beisan, when it was either Jewish Bethshan or heathen Scythopolis ; with its dominating citadel, temples, hippodrome, theatre, baths, monument, and bridge." If there be any truth in this view of the matter we may expect interesting results from an exploration of these *tells*. Conder describes the locality as one of the best watered in Palestine, and (in April) literally streaming with rivulets from some fifty springs.

The death of Saul brought David to the throne. But David had previously gone through an adventurous experience, the story of which is intimately connected with localities that are mentioned, and requires a knowledge of the topography fully to appreciate. "The desert of Judah," says Conder, "was no doubt as much a desert in David's time as it is now. Here he wandered with his brigand companions as 'a partridge on the mountains.' Here he may have learned that the coney makes its dwelling in the hard rocks. Here, in earlier days, he tended the sheep, descending from Bethlehem, as the village shepherds of the present day still come down, by virtue of a compact with the lawless Nomads, and just as Nabal's sheep came down from the highlands under agreement with the wild followers of the outlaw born to be a king. I do not know any part of the Old Testament more instinct with life than are the early chapters of Samuel which recount the wanderings of David. His life should only be written by one who has followed those wanderings on the spot ; and the critic who would imbue himself with a right understanding of that ancient chronicle should first with his own eyes gaze on the 'rocks of the wild goats' and the 'junipers' of the desert."

Conder declares that we have now so recovered the topography of David's wanderings that the various scenes seem as vivid as if they had occurred only yesterday. First, we have the stronghold of Adullam, guarding the rich corn valley of Elah ; then Keilah, a few miles south, perched on its steep hill above the same valley. The forest of Hareth lay close by, on the edge of the mountain chain where Kharas now stands, surrounded by the "thickets" which properly represent the Hebrew "Yar "— a word wrongly supposed to mean a woodland of timber trees.

Driven from all these lairs, David went yet further south to the neighbourhood of Ziph. . . . The treachery of the inhabitants of Ziph, like that of the men of Keilah, appears to have driven David to a yet more desolate district, that of the Jeshimon, or "Solitude," by which is apparently intended the great desert above the western shores of the Dead Sea, on which the Ziph plateau looks down.   As a shepherd-boy at Bethlehem, David may probably have been already familiar with this part of the country, and the caves, still used as sheep-cotes by the peasant herdsmen, extend all along the slopes at the edge of the desert.

East of Ziph is a prominent hill on which is the ruined town called Cain in the Bible.   Hence the eye ranges over the theatre of David's wanderings : the whole scenery of the flight of David, and of Saul's pursuit, can be viewed from this one hill.

The stronghold chosen by the fugitive was the hill Hachilah, in the wilderness of Ziph, south of Jeshimon. "This, I would propose" (says Conder) "to recognise in the long ridge called El Kôlah. . . . On the north side of the hill are the 'Caves of the Dreamers,' perhaps the actual scene of David's descent on Saul's sleeping guards."

Pursued even to Hachilah, David descended farther south, to a rock or cliff in the wilderness of Maon, which was named "Cliff of Division" (1 Sam. xxiii. 2-8).   Here he is represented as being on one side of the mountain, while Saul was on the other.   Now, between the ridge of El Kôlah and the neighbourhood of Maon there is a great gorge called "the Valley of Rocks," a narrow, but deep chasm, impassable except by a detour of many miles, so that Saul might have stood within sight of David, yet quite unable to overtake his enemy ; and to this "Cliff of Division" the name *Malâky* now applies, a word closely approaching the Hebrew Mahlekoth.   The neighbourhood is seamed with many torrent-beds, but there is no other place near Maon where cliffs, such as are to be inferred from the word Sela, can be found.   "It seems to me pretty safe, therefore" (says Conder) "to look on this gorge as the scene of the wonderful escape of David, due to a sudden Philistine invasion, which terminated the history of his hair-breadth escapes in the South Country."

To return to Adullam. The famous hold where David collected "every one that was in distress and every one that was in debt, and every one that was discontented," was, according to Josephus, at the city called Adullam (Ant. vi. 12, 3). This city was one of the group of fifteen situated in the Shephelah or Lowlands (Josh. xv. 35). The term Shephelah is applied to the low hills of soft limestone which form a distinct district between the maritime plain and the central line of mountains. M. Clermont Ganneau was the first explorer who found the name Adullam still in use; but Major Conder also, on finding it among the names which Corporal Brophy had collected, set out to examine the site.

The great Valley of Elah (Wâdy es Sunt) is the highway from Philistia to Hebron ; and divides the low hills of the Shephelah from the rocky mountains of Judah. Eight miles from the valley-head stands Shochoh, and Wâdy es Sunt is here a quarter of a mile across : just north of this ruin it turns round westward, and so runs, growing deeper and deeper, between the rocky hills covered with brushwood, becoming an open vale of rich corn land, flanked by ancient fortresses, and finally debouching at the cliff of *Tell es Safi.* About 2½ miles south of the great angle near Shochoh there is a very large and ancient terebinth—it is from *elah* the "terebinth" tree that the valley gets its name—and near it are two ancient wells, with stone water-troughs round them. South of the ravine is a high rounded hill, almost isolated by valleys, and covered with ruins, a natural fortress, not unlike the well-known *tells* which occur lower down the valley of Elah. "This site seems to be ancient" (says Conder), "not only because of the wells, but judging from the caves, the tombs, and the rock quarryings which exist near it."

Below the hill, and near the well, there are ruins which are called *'Aid el Ma*, and this is radically identical with the Hebrew Adullam. " But if this ruined fortress be, as there seems no good reason to doubt it is, the royal city of Adullam, where, we should naturally ask, is the famous cave ? The answer is easy, for the cave is on the hill. We must not look for one of the greater caverns, such as the Crusaders fixed upon in the romantic gorge east of Bethlehem, for such caverns are never inhabited in Palestine ; we should expect, rather, a moderate-sized cave, or (considering the strength of the band) a succession of ' hollow-places.' The site of Adullam is ruinous, but not deserted. The sides of the tributary valley are lined with rows of caves, and these we found inhabited, and full of flocks and herds. But still more interesting was the discovery of a separate cave on the hill itself, a low, smoke-blackened burrow, which was the home of a single family. We could not but suppose, as we entered this gloomy abode, that our feet were standing on the very foot-prints of the Shepherd King, who here, encamped between the Philistines and the Jews, covered the line of advance on the corn fields of Keilah, and was but 3 miles distant from the thickets of Hareth.

" The hill is about 500 feet high. . . . There is ample room to have accommodated David's four hundred men in the caves, and they are, as we have seen, still inhabited.

" It is interesting to observe that the scene of David's victory over Goliath is distant only 8 miles from the cave at *'Aid el Ma*."

When David became king of all Israel, he made it his first great object to capture Jerusalem. There might be several reasons for this. In the first place, his capital hitherto had been Hebron, a city which was not sufficiently central. Secondly, the border line between Judah and Benjamin ran right through Jerusalem; the city was partly in the territory of one tribe, partly in the other; Saul was a man of Benjamin, while David belonged to Judah; so that there were jealousies between these two tribes, which might be healed if David could make the city his capital. Thirdly, Jerusalem had proved itself to be a strong city, well-nigh impregnable. Joshua had not taken it, as he took the other cities of the Gibeonite league—it has defied the arms of Israel for four or five centuries—and therefore, if David can capture it, he will possess a redoubtable stronghold. Jerusalem, therefore, was besieged and taken. Secure in Jerusalem, David extended his conquests on every side, subduing Philistines, Moabites, Edomites, Ammonites, and Midianites; placing garrisons in the towns of Syria, and even extending his rule as far as the river Euphrates. Of all these countries Philistia alone comes into the survey of Western Palestine.

Gaza, the capital of Philistia, still exists as an inhabited city, and is very picturesquely situated, having a fine approach down a broad avenue from the north. It rises on an isolated hill, about 100 feet above the plain, and bristles with minarets. The population is given by Conder as eighteen thousand, including sixty or seventy houses of Greek Christians. The town is not walled, but the green mounds traceable round the hill are probably remains of the ancient enclosure. The new mosque, built some forty or fifty years ago, is full of marble fragments, from ancient buildings which were principally found near the sea-shore. East of the Serai is the reputed tomb of Samson; and south-east of the city is a hill called the Watch-tower, to which place, according to tradition, Samson carried the gates of Gaza. A yearly festival of the Moslems is held there.

North-east of Makkedah, Ekron still stands, on low

rising ground—a mud hamlet, with gardens fenced with prickly pears.   Conder says there is nothing ancient here.

At Azotus, or Ashdod, one of the Philistine cities, is a large mound, with columns cropping up out of the ground on the outskirts of it.   Mr Trelawney Saunders, the geographer, has described the site in his "Introduction to the Survey of Western Palestine."   Ashdod, on a hillock (alt. 140 feet), at the western end of the plain of Zeita, is now separated from all that remains of its port, by sand-downs 3 miles in breadth.   The site is occupied by the present village

TELL ES SAFI.   (Site of Gath?)   (*By favour of the Palestine Exploration Fund.*)

of Esdud, with eighteen hundred people, but the remains of this primeval city, once so strong and mighty, are so few and insignificant that one is tempted to suppose the greater part of the city may be buried beneath the sands.   If so, they may be in a superior state of preservation, and would perhaps repay for digging out.

Gath, the birth-place of Goliath, has long been a lost city, but is now reasonably identified with *Tell es Sufi* at the mouth of the *Wady* or water-course which runs from near Hebron, past Adullam and Shochoh, and westward towards Ashdod. It is the site of the Crusading fortress of Blanche Garde, which was built in 1144 A.D. as an out-post for defence against the people of Ascalon. It is now a mud village with olives beneath it, standing on a cliff 300 feet high, which is burrowed with caves. The Rev. Henry George Tomkins takes *Tell es Sufi* to be the "mound of Safi," and regards Safi as a personal name. In a learned paper in the *Quarterly Statement*, October 1886, he argues that Safi was a brother of Goliath's, and if so this is an additional reason for regarding *Tell es Sufi* as Gath.

Ascalon, "the bride of Syria," is still called Askalon. The fortifications and walls are in ruins, and the site of the city is a garden planted with fruit trees and vegetables. The walls are the ruins of battlements, erected by Richard Lionheart in 1191 A.D., in place of those destroyed by Saladin, and doubtless with the same materials. They are half buried by the great dunes of rolling sand which are ever being blown up by the sea breeze from the southward. The whole interior of the site is covered with rich soil, to a depth of about 10 feet, and the natives find fragments of fine masonry, shafts, capitals, and other remains of the old city, by digging into it. Of Herod's beautiful colonnades nothing now remains. The Crusaders had little respect for antiquities, and the innumerable granite pillar shafts which are built horizontally into the walls are no doubt those originally brought to the town by Herod.

Conder says, " We heard a curious tradition at Ascalon. A tomb had been opened by the peasantry, near the ruin, some thirty years ago. Under a great slab, in the eastern cemetery, they found a perfectly preserved body, with a sword by its side, and a ring on its finger. The dead eyes glared so fiercely on the intruders that they let fall the slab ; and as one of the party soon after died, they came to the conclusion that it was a *Nebi* or Prophet whom they had disturbed, and the place has thus become surrounded with a mysterious sanctity."

In the days of David's grandson the kingdom of the Israelites divided in two, and began the new phase of its existence as the parallel monarchies of Israel and Judah. The disruption, it may be said, was owing to the fact that Ephraim envied Judah, and Judah vexed Ephraim. Naturally, the split, when it came, took place along a line between these two powerful tribes and right athwart the tribe of Benjamin. Benjamin was torn asunder—Jericho and Bethel going to the northern kingdom, while other towns went to the south. Jerusalem continued to be a capital, but it was now the capital of the kingdom of Judah only ; and Shechem was chosen as the capital of the northern kingdom, which was called Israel.

But these northern monarchs had their pleasant summer residences as well, corresponding to Windsor or Versailles. One of these was Samaria, another was Tirzah, a third was Jezreel.

The Samaria of the present day is a large and flourishing village of stone and mud houses, standing on the hill of the ancient Samaria. The most interesting ruins now to be seen there are those of Herod's colonnade to the west of the modern village. The colonnade seems to have surrounded the whole city with a kind of cloister, which was 60 feet wide, and the pillars 16 feet high. The city of Samaria of the Old Testament has disappeared. But the kings of Israel were buried here, and the ancient tombs may yet perhaps come to light.

Tirzah, famous for its beauty, is the only Samaritan town mentioned among the royal cities taken by Joshua. Conder finds it in the present mud hamlet of Teiasir. It was delightfully situated on a plateau where the valleys begin to dip suddenly towards Jordan.

Conder found numerous rock-cut sepulchres burrowing under the houses; and he thinks that some of them are probably those of the early kings of Israel, before the royal family began to be buried in Samaria.

Jezreel is now called Zerin, and the site of Ahab's palace is now a village, surrounded by heaps of rubbish. The position of Zerin is remarkable. On the south the ground slopes gently upwards towards the site, and on the west also the place is accessible. But on the north the ground is extremely rugged and falls rapidly, and on the east occurs a saddle separating the high point on which the town stands from the Gilboa chain, the road ascending from the valley and the neighbourhood of 'Ain Jalud. The top of the hill is 284 feet above this spring, which is visible beneath. Thus the site is naturally strong, except on the south-west. It is conspicuous from the plain, and it commands a view down the valley to Beisan and the trans-Jordanic ranges. Major Conder, climbing up to the village, was struck by the absence of any traces of antiquity. But the houses stand on a mound of rubbish, and in this a great number of ruined cisterns exist.

Ahab from his palace in Jezreel looked down upon Naboth's vineyard. There seem to be no vineyards in the neighbourhood now; but on the east and south-east there are rock-cut wine-presses on the rugged hills, where no doubt the "portion of the field of Naboth" and his vine-yard are to be placed. The commanding position of the place would also enable Joram's watchmen, looking down the Valley of Jezreel, to observe the two horsemen sent forward by Jehu coming up from Bethshan—the dust raised, the gleam of their armour—and Jehu himself following and "driving furiously." It was by "the fountain which is in Jezreel" that Saul had pitched before the fatal battle of Gilboa.

Here at Jezreel, with Mount Carmel in the distance,

we are reminded that the sacrifice which Elijah offered did not take place on the point of Mount Carmel nearest the sea, as commonly imagined, but much nearer to Jezreel, on a part of the range where our explorers discovered a perennial spring, that would supply the prophet with water when the rest of the country was dry. Stationed at this spot, he might see the palace of Jezebel in the city of Jezreel. From this position he sent his servant a few minutes' distance, to the highest point of the range, where he could overlook the sea and perceive the little cloud rising. Then said Elijah, " Get thee down, Ahab, there is a sound of abundance of rain "—get thee down Ahab, or the river of Kishon will sweep thee away ! Elijah himself, amidst the rushing storm, ran before the chariot of the monarch, down the slope, and as far as the entrance of Jezreel. And soon thereafter, fearing Jezebel's threats, he journeyed swiftly by the north and south road, nor stopped till he got to Beersheba. This is the extremity of Judah, and here he leaves his servant behind him and plunges into the wilderness, for he is going to " Horeb, the Mount of God," to seek a revelation.

Elijah was commissioned to call Elisha to be his successor; and Elisha in his turn made frequent resort to Mount Carmel. When the Shunamite woman came to him there, her journey lay across the plain, and he could see her approaching (2 Kings iv. 24). Shunem, now called *Sulem*, stands on the southern slope of *Neby Duhy* (Little Hermon), and is only a mud hamlet, with cactus hedges and a spring. West of the houses there is a beautiful garden, cool and shady, of lemon trees, watered by a little rivulet, and in the village is a fountain and trough. Westward the view extends as far as Carmel, 15 miles away. Thus the whole extent of the ride of the Shunamite woman, under the burning noon-tide sun of harvest-time, is visible. Conder remarks that if the houses of that time were no larger than the mud-cabins of the modern village, it was not a great architectural undertaking to build a little chamber for the prophet; and the enumeration of the simple furniture of that chamber—the bed (perhaps only a straw mat), the table, the stool, and the lamp—seems to indicate that it was only a little hut that was intended. Another point may be noted : how came it that Elisha so constantly passed by Shunem? The answer seems simple ; he lived habitually on Carmel, but he was a native of Abel Meholah, "the Meadow of Circles," a place now called *'Ain Helweh*, in the Jordan Valley, to which the direct road led past Shunem down the Valley of Jezreel.

Before we leave the Plain of Esdraelon, which is also called the Plain of Megiddo—and because of its typical character as the field of great battles, is used in the Apocalypse as the scene of the great final struggle, *Ar-Mageddon*—let us glance at the fruitless effort of Josiah, king of Judah, to stop the march of Pharaoh Necho. It was in the last days of the Jewish monarchy, when the northern kingdom had been already destroyed, that Palestine was first exposed to the disastrous fate which involved her in so long a series of troubles from this time forward —that of being the debatable ground between Egypt and the further East ; first under the Pharaohs and the rulers of Babylon ; then under the Ptolemies and Seleucidae. "In the days of Josiah, Pharaoh Necho, king of Egypt, went up against the king of Assyria to the river Euphrates" (2 Kings xxiii. 29), possibly landing his army at Accho (says Dean Stanley), more probably, as the expression seems to indicate, following the track of his predecessor Psammetichus, and advancing up the maritime plain till he turned into the plain of Esdraelon, thence to penetrate into the passes of the Lebanon. King Josiah, in self-defence, and perhaps as an ally of the Assyrian king, went against him. Josiah would march by the watershed road, northward from Jerusalem, and descend into the plain, perhaps by Dothan. The engagement took place in "the Valley of Megiddo" (2 Chron. xxxv. 22). The Egyptian archers in their long array, so well known from their sculptured monuments, shot at King Josiah, as he rode in state in his royal chariot, and he was sore wounded, and placed in his reserve chariot, and carried to Jerusalem to die. Dean Stanley remarks that all other notices of the battle are absorbed in this one tragical event, and the exact scene of the encounter is not known.

The position of Megiddo is not fixed very definitely in the Bible narrative. But a broad valley (as we see above) was named from the city, and the "waters of Megiddo" are also spoken of. Major Conder believes he has found the place and the name, in the large ruined site of Mujedda, at the foot of Gilboa—a mound from which fine springs burst out, with the broad valley of the Jalud river to the north. Otherwise Megiddo has been located on the *Mukuttà*, near *Lejjun*. Mr Trelawney Saunders considers it an objection to Conder's site that it is separated from the river Kishon and the town of Taanach, and cannot be made to fit in with the account of Ahaziah's flight from Jezreel (2 Kings ix. 27). The king, having been smitten at "the going up to Gur," near Ibleam, fled to Megiddo, where he died. But if Megiddo were in the Plain of Bethshean he would hardly be likely to do this, seeing that Jehu his enemy made his furious advance upon Jezreel through that plain. Besides, he fled by the way of the "garden house," En-gannim (the modern *Jenin*), the garden-like character of which spot is still perserved—and *Jenin* would not be on the route between *Zerin* and *Mujedda*.

[*Authorities and Sources* :—"Tent-Work in Palestine." Major Conder. "**Introduction to the Survey of**

Western Palestine." By Trelawney Saunders. "Survey of Western Palestine." P. E. Fund. "Twenty-one Years' Work in the Holy Land." P. E. Fund.]

9. *Sacred Sites of the Hebrews.*

In order to pass in review the sites selected by the Israelites for places of worship, it will be convenient to go back to the time when we find the tribes encamped at Gilgal, on their first entrance into the country.

That Mount Sinai should remain sacred after the giving of the Law was to be expected ; and we have just now seen that its sacredness could attract Elijah after many centuries. The Israelites, when they left the wilderness, and came to sojourn in the outskirts of Moab, were attracted by the shrine of Baal-Peor ; but they were made to feel that this was wrong, and the ambassadors of the western tribes refer to it as a warning when they expostulate with their brethren about the altar called Ed (Joshua xxii. 17). In passing over into Canaan, they carried the Lord's tabernacle with them ; where that rested was holy ground, and it was not intended that any rival site should be tolerated.

The ark of the covenant—the chest which contained the agreement or treaty between Jehovah and his people —was set down at Gilgal, the tabernacle or holy tent was erected over it, and Gilgal became a sacred place. Afterwards, when the hill country had been conquered, the ark and tabernacle were brought to Shiloh, and then Shiloh became a sacred place. Shiloh is now called *Seilun*, and here the ruins of a modern village occupy a sort of *tell* or mound. The position of the place is remarkably retired, shut in between high, bare mountains. A deep valley runs behind the town on the north, and in its sides are many rock-cut sepulchres. " The site being so certainly known," says Conder, " it becomes of interest to speculate as to the exact position of the tabernacle. Below the top of the hill, on the north of the ruins, there is a sort of irregular quadrangle, sloping rather to the west, and perched above terraces made for agricultural purposes. The rock has here been rudely hewn in two parallel scarps for over 400 feet, with a court between, 77 feet wide and sunk 5 feet below the outer surface. Thus there would be sufficient room for the court of the tabernacle in this area. From the Mishna we learn that the lower part of the tabernacle erected at Shiloh was of stone, with a tent above. There are, however, two other places which demand attention as possible sites, one being, perhaps, a synagogue, the other a little building called the 'Mosque of the Servants of God.' "

According to the Jews, the ark and tabernacle remained at Shiloh three hundred and sixty-nine years— so long that Shiloh was regarded as only second to Jerusalem in sanctity. In the disastrous days of Eli the ark was sent into the battlefield and captured by the Philistines, who carried it to Ashdod, to the temple of Dagon. When Dagon fell down before it they sent it away again, and it was, after some adventures, recovered by the men of Kirjath Jearim. Eventually David brought it to Mount Zion, and then Zion became a sacred place. Solomon said, " the places are holy whereunto the ark of the Lord hath come" (2 Chron. viii. 11), and on that account he brought up the daughter of Pharaoh out of the City of David (which is Zion, 1 Kings viii 1), unto the house that he had built for her. The ark never went back to Shiloh after Eli sent it away. The tabernacle, however, appears to have remained there for some time, and so Shiloh remained sacred in some degree.

Soon, however, even the tabernacle would appear to have been removed from Shiloh, for although we have no direct mention of its removal, we seem to find it in other places. Samuel, the successor of Eli, judged the people, and on important occasions called the solemn assembly and offered sacrifices. He was accustomed to do this at three different places, which in his day were revered as sacred. One of these was Gilgal, rendered sacred by the first resting of the ark : and although the ark and tabernacle had been removed, and sanctity was to be transferred along with them, yet it is not easy to obliterate the sanctity of a place from the tradition and practice of the people. Another of these three places was Bethel, where Jacob had seen his vision of the ladder with angels ascending and descending, and had been constrained to say, " This is the house of God and the gate of Heaven." The third place at which Samuel called assemblies and offered sacrifices was not Shiloh, as we might suppose it would be, but one of the many places called Mizpeh. We do not know where this Mizpeh was. Conder is inclined to identify it with *Neby Samwil*—the Mount of the Prophet Samuel, a conspicuous conical hill, 4 or 5 miles north of Jerusalem ; and as Mizpeh means a watch-tower, there is plausibility in this suggestion. We do not know whether the tabernacle was pitched at either of these three places in Samuel's day : we do not know why Samuel should be content to regard three different places as holy ; but it is not altogether impossible that the tabernacle was carried from one meeting-place to another, and made each one holy in turn.

A little later we seem to find the tabernacle nearer to Jerusalem. When David is fleeing from King Saul, and taking the road from Rama in Benjamin to Gath in the land of the Philistines, he comes to Nob, to Ahimelech the priest, and is permitted to eat the shewbread (the holy bread exhibited before the Lord in the sanctuary), and to carry off the sword of Goliath, which had been laid up as

a trophy.   So here we have the priests, the shewbread, and
the tabernacle at Nob.   As to the locality of Nob, Dean
Stanley follows Mr Thrupp in fixing it on the northern
summit of the Mount of Olives, and Mr Thrupp reminds
us that David brought the head of Goliath to Jerusalem,
before the city itself was captured (1 Sam. xvii. 54).
David, in fleeing from Rama to Gath, could hardly find a
shorter or more convenient route than that which took him
past Jerusalem.

This position for Nob is confirmed by Isaiah's graphic
and detailed description of the advance of the Assyrian
invader (Isaiah x. 28) :—

> He comes to Ai, passes through Migron,
> At Michmash deposits his baggage ;
> They cross the pass, Geba is our night station :
> Terrified is Ramah, Gibeah of Saul flees.
> Shriek with thy voice, daughter of Gallim ;
> Listen, O Laish ! Ah ! poor Anathoth !
> Madmeneh escapes, dwellers in Gebim take flight.
> Yet this day he halts at Nob :
> He shakes his hand against the mount, daughter of Sion,
> The hill of Jerusalem.

" In this passage " (says Sir Charles Wilson), " if it has a
meaning—and I cannot suppose that it has not—the prophet
describes, in such detail that it is difficult to believe he is
not describing an actual event, the march of an Assyrian
army upon Jerusalem ; and we may be quite certain that,
with his knowledge of the country, and writing as he did
for those who were equally well acquainted with it, he would
describe a line of march, which, under certain conditions,
an army would naturally follow if its special object were
the capture of Jerusalem.   The conditions to which I
allude are the passage of the great ravine at Michmash,
and encampment for the night at Geba ; why this route
was selected in preference to the easier road along the line

of water-parting we have no means of ascertaining, and it does not affect the question.

Of the places mentioned by Isaiah, we know, with a considerable degree of certainty, the positions of Michmash, Geba, Ramah, Gibeah, and Anathoth; of the others nothing is known. From Geba to Nob was evidently a day's march in the progress of the army; and the order in which the villages are mentioned leads us in the direction of Jerusalem. If, as I believe, the passage means that the Assyrian warrior was leading an army from Geba against Jerusalem, and that his progress was suddenly arrested at Nob, we must seek a site for Nob on the road between these two places, and I cannot imagine a more natural one than some place in the vicinity of that Scopus whence, in later years, Titus and his legions looked down upon the Holy City."

Doeg, the Edomite, who happened to be present when Ahimelech gave David the sword, informed Saul, and Saul, who was mad with suspicion, slew all the priests and utterly destroyed all the inhabitants of Nob. But even after the destruction of the sanctuary by his violence the sanctity of the summit of Olivet was still respected. It was necessary, however, to remove the tabernacle from the scene of so much bloodshed, and perhaps it was immediately removed to the high-place of Gibeon, where we find it in the early part of Solomon's reign.

The state of things at the beginning of the reign of Solomon is described in 1 Kings iii.—" The people sacrificed in the high places, because there was no house built for the name of the Lord until those days. And the king went to Gibeon to sacrifice there, for that was the great high place." We learn from 2 Chron. i. that at Gibeon was the Tent of Meeting (the tabernacle) which Moses had made in the wilderness. Moreover, the brazen altar made by the inspired artist in the wilderness was there before the tabernacle, and Solomon and the congregation sought unto it, and offered a thousand burnt offerings upon it.

Thus far, then, we have at least half a dozen sacred places, venerated in turn, and more or less acknowledged simultaneously,—namely, Gilgal, Bethel, Shiloh, Mizpeh, Nob, and Gibeon. To these we must add Zion, to which David brought the ark, setting it up in the tent which he had prepared for it, though *the* tent, time-honoured and sacred, was at Gibeon (2 Sam. vi. 17; 1 Chron. i. 4-6).

The ark, however, did not remain in "the city of David, which is Zion;" for when the temple was built upon Mount Moriah, the ark was brought up into the oracle of the house, with much sacrificing of sheep and oxen, and the Tent of Meeting was brought along with it (1 Kings viii.). Mount Moriah was now God's holy mountain, and it was intended to concentrate all public worship at the Temple. Even previously it had been the law that the high places of the heathen should be discarded, and irresponsible sacrifice in the open field should be discountenanced, and that every man who had sacrifices to offer should bring them to the tabernacle, wherever the tabernacle might be located at the time (Levit. xvii. 1-6; Deut. xii. 1-6). So, now that the permanent temple had superseded the wandering tent, it was ordered, of course, that all sacrifices and public worship should take place on Mount Moriah. "For in my holy mountain, in the mountain of the height of Israel, saith the Lord God, there shall all the house of Israel, all of them, serve Me in the land: there will I accept them, and there will I require your offerings, and the first fruits of your oblations, with all your holy things" (Ezek. xx. 40).

Nevertheless, during the years of David's reign, and until the temple was built, the ark resting on Zion conferred sanctity on that mountain. Psalms of David, and others written at that time, would of course make reference to Zion and not yet to Moriah.

> "In Salem also is his tabernacle,
> And his dwelling-place in Zion."
>
> Psalm lxxvi. 2.

And even after the ark had been carried up to the Temple, Mount Zion would retain its sanctity by tradition ; or perhaps the name Zion would be extended so as to include Moriah, as they may in truth be related as the slope and the summit of the same hill.*

His foundation is in the holy mountains,

> "The Lord loveth the gates of Zion
> More than all the dwellings of Jacob."
>
> Psalm lxxxvii. 1.

So shall ye know that I am the Lord your God dwelling in Zion, my holy mountain. (Joel iii. 17 and Zech. viii. 3).

Human nature would not be what it is if theory and practice always went hand in hand. Laws may be good, but universal obedience to them cannot always be secured. Solomon himself, who had built the temple, and by bringing the Tent of Meeting into it, had disestablished Gibeon, set the example, in his later years, of recognising afresh other high places and the gods of the heathen. Having married "women of the Moabites, Ammonites, Edomites, Zidonians, and Hittites," besides the daughter of Pharaoh, he doubtless thought it only an enlightened toleration to let them worship in their own way, and as a logical consequence he supplied them with the means, and perhaps occasionally accompanied them to their respective places of worship. "For Solomon went after Ashtoreth the goddess of the

---

* See the chapter on Jerusalem,

Zidonians," and " did build a high place for Chemosh, the abomination of Moab, in the mount that is before Jerusalem, and for Molech, the abomination of the children of Ammon. And so did he for all his strange wives, which burnt incense and sacrificed unto their gods " (1 Kings xi.).

We see in this passage that the site selected as the high place for Chemosh was on the Mount of Olives—perhaps the place where Nob had stood, a site which had the tradition of sanctity already.

Many later kings imitated Solomon, and declined to regard Jehovah as the only God, or the holy mountain at Jerusalem as the only high place possessing sanctity. It was hardly to be expected that the people should be more faithful than their kings ; and the after history furnishes many examples of lapses into heathen worship, and periodical reforms attempted by such kings as Josiah and Hezekiah.   It was not convenient for the more distant tribes north of Esdraelon or east of Jordan to come up to Jerusalem to worship. Added to this consideration there was the local shrine, and time-honoured tradition in its favour.   Just as in our own country Ripon cathedral is built over St Wilfrid's Saxon church, and St Paul's cathedral on the site of a heathen temple, so on the part of the Israelites there was a disposition to keep to the old spots. What wonder if there was, besides, a frequent adherence to the old forms of worship ?

The tribes east of Jordan worshipped eastern gods— Peor, Chemosh, Milcom. Gad worshipped the god of Fortune (Isaiah lxv. 11), and was named after that deity. Josephus spells the name of Reuben as *Reubel* (Ρουβελος), and Bel was one of the eastern gods. Manasseh had a sanctuary in the city of Golan. From the east of Jordan came Jephthah, who made a rash vow like a heathen, and kept it, although it involved human sacrifice.

Beyond Esdraelon we have Kadesh Naphtali, a heathen

sanctuary adopted by the Israelites as a city of refuge, but apparently without any entire suppression of the original worship. The place is now called *Kedes*, and among the ruins found by the explorers are those of a temple with a figure of an eagle on the lintel, besides richly executed scroll-work of vine-leaves, bunches of grapes, a stag, and a bust (possibly of Baal). There were also places called Beth-shemesh (House of the Sun) scattered up and down the country.

At the disruption of the kingdom, Jeroboam, fearing that his subjects would be attracted to the religious festivals at Jerusalem, established two other centres. One of these was Bethel, convenient for the southern part of his kingdom, and sacred already, because there Abram had builded an altar, and Jacob had seen his vision, and Samuel had called solemn assemblies. The other was Dan, convenient for the northern part of his kingdom, and sacred again, already, for here, in the time of the Judges some colonists from the tribe of Dan had set up a graven image and established a priesthood. Besides, it was probably a sanctuary of the Phœnician inhabitants whom the Danites displaced; and, as we have seen in a previous chapter, the heathen god Pan came to be worshipped here. Thus we see that Jeroboam selected religious centres which combined traditional sanctity with geographical convenience.

When the tribes of the northern kingdom were carried into captivity, and the Assyrian conquerors brought people from Babylon, from Cuthah, and from Avva, and from Hamath, and Sepharvaim, and placed them in the cities of Samaria (2 Kings xvii. 24), the foreigners, or the mixed population which sprung up, fixed upon Mount Gerizim as their sacred high place. But Mount Gerizim already possessed a traditional sanctity, for the ark and tabernacle had accompanied Joshua to Shechem; the tribes had assembled on the twin mountains to hear the reading of the Law ; and in earlier time Abram had builded an altar hereabout, the first altar to Jehovah in all the Holy Land.

Thus there were many high places in Palestine, and there was much disputing as to which should have the pre-eminence, the jealousy reaching its height in the later centuries in the rival claims of Gerizim and Jerusalem. No final solution was possible excepting that which Jesus Christ gave to the woman of Samaria. "The hour cometh, and now is, when the true worshippers shall worship the Father in spirit and truth : for such doth the Father seek to be his worshippers. God is a Spirit : and they that worship Him must worship in spirit and truth." (John iv. 23). Local centres lose their special sanctity because "every place is holy ground." The Temple at Jerusalem might be destroyed—probably soon would be—but within a marvellously short period the spiritual temple would take form. For such true teaching Jesus Christ was crucified and Stephen stoned.

It was a matter of much interest to Major Conder to find out if possible where the mountain of the scape-goat was situated. According to the Law of Moses the scape-goat was led to the wilderness, and there set free. "This was not, however, the practice of the later Jews. A scape-goat had once come back to Jerusalem, and the omen was thought so bad that the ordinary custom was modified, to prevent the recurrence of such a calamity. The man who led the goat arrived at a high mountain called Sook, and there was at this place a rolling slope, down which he pushed the unhappy animal, which was shattered to atoms in the fall." The district where this was done was called Hidoodim, and the high mountain Sook. Sook was 6½ English miles from Jerusalem, as reckoned by the ten tabernacles which divided the messenger's path into stages of 2000 cubits. Conder identifies the place in the neighbourhood of the convent of St Saba. At the required distance from Jerusalem is the great hill of *El Muntâr*, the highest point of a ridge of mountains running north and south. The rest of the ridge is called *El Hadeidûn;* and beside the ancient road from Jerusalem is a well called *Sûk*. From this high ridge the victim was yearly rolled down into the narrow valley beneath, at the entrance of the great desert, which first unfolded itself before the eyes of the messenger as he gained the summit half a mile beyond the well of Sûk.

[*Authorities and Sources* :—Colonel Warren, Colonel Wilson, &c., in the *Quarterly Statements*, P. E. Fund. "Tent-Work in Palestine." Major Conder. "Sinai and Palestine." Dean Stanley.]

10. *The Method of the Survey, and Incidents of the Work.*

At the commencement of the Triangulation Survey a base line was measured, near Ramleh, on the Jaffa plain, and this was afterwards checked by a second line measured on the Plain of Esdraelon. The method of work employed is described by Major Conder, both in his "Tent-Work" and in his volume called "Palestine." The camp, consisting of three or four tents, was pitched in some convenient central position, by a town or village. Thence the surveyors were able to ride 8 or 10 miles all round; and first visited a few of the highest hill-tops. As each was found satisfactory, or one near it preferred, they built great cairns of stones, 8 or 10 feet high, and white-washed them to make them more conspicuous. This work took about five days. When the points were chosen, five more days were consumed in revisiting them with the theodolite, which travelled in its box bound to the back of

a mule, the muleteer perched behind it ; and with it went
the saddle bags, holding lunch, the chisel and hammer for
cutting the broad arrow on the summits of the hills, the
hatchet for hewing down trees and copses. From two to
four hours were spent at each point, fixing the position of
every prominent object, tree, village, white dome or min-
aret visible within 10 miles. " The names were collected "
(says Conder) "from the peasant who accompanied the party,
and as the afternoon shadows began to lengthen, we slowly
wound down the hill-side, a rough-looking cavalcade, preceded by our Bashi-bazouk in his red boots, armed to the
teeth, and followed by the non-commissioned officers, who
had become well accustomed to their stout little Syrian
ponies, whilst the pack-mule and guide came last. We all
wore revolvers and the native head-dress, the Bedawin
Kufeyeh or shawl, a sure protection from sun-stroke and
substitute for an umbrella. Our appearance was therefore
an extraordinary compound of European and Bedawin,
which is often, however, assumed by the Turkish officials
in travelling, and thus attracted less attention."

The theodolite work over, and the fixed points laid down,
the filling in of the detail followed. The two non-commissioned officers divided the work between them, and Major
Conder took alternate days with each, to enable him to do
the hill sketching and examine the geology. In open
country they found the daily riding pleasant, but when the
hills were precipitous and the valleys deep and stony, the
labour was very severe. Starting at eight, resting at noon,
returning at sunset, and sleeping immediately after dinner,
the days sped by with wonderful rapidity, and the Survey
spread gradually over the country.

The old cultivation was traced by the wine-presses, olive-
presses, ruined terraces, and rude garden watch-towers.
Ancient sites were recognised by their tombs, cisterns,
and rocky scarps. In seeking to identify sites the greatest

care was exercised : it was laid down that the site must show traces of antiquity ; it must be known to the natives under its original name, or a modification of that name ; its position must suit the known accounts of the place ; and the measured distances must lend confirmation.

The new map was to include every object that has a name, and the name itself was to be correctly given. But here was a difficulty. How are names to be accurately ascertained in Palestine ? The natives are perverse, or they suspect you of designs against their country, and they purposely mislead you. On the other hand, they are obliging, and if you express a hope that you have found a Scripture site, which you name, they will confirm your impression that it is so. Or it may be that you yourself are deficient in Arabic, and after being at the greatest pains to inquire the name of a site, find that the name you have noted down signifies " a heap of stones." A story is told of a European traveller who asked his guide the name of a place, and received the reply—*Mabarafsh.* Carefully marking it on the sketch-map of his route, he by-and-bye inquired concerning a second site which he did not recognise, and received the same reply—*Mabarafsh !* Of course it is possible that names should be repeated, as in England we have several Newports, Nortons, and Hamptons; but *Mabarafsh* actually means, " I don't know ! " A wise suggestion was made that travellers and surveyors should always get the sheikh of the village to write down the name correctly in Arabic; but, unfortunately, only one sheikh in ten can write at all, and he cannot spell correctly.

The plan adopted by the Survey party was one which guarded as far as possible against all mistakes. It is described by Major Conder in " Tent Work," where he speaks as follows of his inquiries in the neighbourhood of Hebron. " My party now consisted of three non-commissioned officers; and Lieutenant Kitchener was expected to join me in about a month.   We had with us eleven natives, including Habib the head man, a scribe, a second valet, two grooms, the cook (a villain who only sat and watched his boy cooking), two muleteers, and two Bashi-bazouks ; the party was thus at its full strength composed of only sixteen persons, with nine horses and seven mules. . . . By night a guard was provided by the sheikh of the village.   Four guides were hired, who received a shilling a day, a mule to ride, and breakfast. The information which they gave the Surveyors was written down from their mouths by the scribe, an intelligent young Damascene recommended by Mr Wright.   Thus correctness, both of pronunciation and of locality, was ensured, and the names were checked by every means in our power.   Besides obtaining names from the local guides, inquiry was made of peasants, and generally of several peasants separately.   No leading questions were put, nor were either guides or peasants allowed to suppose that one name would be more acceptable than another.   Such was the daily routine.   The parties left by eight a.m. and returned by five p.m. ; dinner was at sunset, and from about eight to eleven, or even until midnight, I studied, after the day's work, the topography of the district.   This labour was not unrewarded, for one might easily have passed over many places of interest had one not known the points to which Mr Grove and other scholars required special attention to be directed."

Fortunately in Palestine the ancient names retain their hold very tenaciously, and reassert themselves after all the efforts of conquerors to displace them.   Thus the town of Bethshan (or Bethshean) which in Greek and Roman times became Scythopolis, is to-day again known to the natives as *Beisan. Tell-el-Kadi*, at the foot of Mount Hermon, signifies in Arabic the "heap of the Judge ; " but in Hebrew the word for judge is *Dan*, and this is the mound of Dan, the northern extremity of the land whose length was measured "from Dan to Beersheba."   Shiloh is now called

Seilun, and no site is more certain. Almost every important site retains its Biblical name. The pretentious titles, Eleutheropolis, Nicopolis, &c., have quite vanished, and the old native names of these cities, *Beth Gubrin, Emmaus,* &c., are those by which they are now again known. An important exception, however, is *Nablous* (corrupted from Neapolis) for the ancient Shechem—a change which may perhaps be traced to Jewish hatred of the name of Shechem.

Tradition also is valuable as confirming the identification of sites, although it might be insufficient if it stood alone. In the case of Jacob's Well, near Nablous (Shechem), the Hebrew and Samaritan traditions, the Mohammedan and Christian traditions, all agree. There is agreement also about the grotto at Bethlehem, under the Church of the Nativity, as the place of Christ's birth. There can be no question that the cave of the field of Machpelah, which Abraham bought for a burial place, is that which is now covered by the great mosque at Hebron. And here again we have that valuable consent of traditions—Jewish, Christian, and Moslem—which seems to distinguish the true sites from those less genuine concerning which two or more discordant traditions have arisen. The Prince of Wales, Dean Stanley, and a few other Europeans have been admitted into the mosque; but it seems very doubtful if any living being has ever descended into the mysterious cavern beneath the floor since the Moslem conquest of Palestine. The surrounding wall of the mosque is also one of the mysteries of Palestine, and a monument inferior only to the Temple Enclosure at Jerusalem, which it resembles in style.

The Temple Area at Jerusalem is still a sanctuary; and the Tower of Antonia maintains its military character in the present Turkish barracks. In Palestine we find a Mohammedan mosque where a Christian church used to be—and built from the same materials. The church in its time had followed a Jewish synagogue. Throughout the country for thousands of years the people have gone on living in the same way and in the same place, and calling the places by the same names. The name of almost every village is Hebrew, and each stands on the great dust-heap into which the ancient buildings have crumbled. The Hebrew names are retained, and are scarcely changed since the days of Abraham, because the peasantry are really Semitic in descent.

In those parts of the country which are seldom visited by Europeans the natives were much astonished to see the Survey party at work. At one place called *Baka* (in the Sharon district) the great gig umbrella over the theodolite attracted much attention, and the chief delight to elderly men was a peep through the theodolite telescope. "What do you see, O father?" cried the less fortunate who crowded round the observer. "I see Hammad and his cows, two hours off, as if he were close here!" replied the delighted elder.

It was a common notion that the English intended to take the country, the Survey being only preparatory to that step. The land was being parcelled out, and cairns erected on the high mountains where the chief men would build their houses. The surveyors were looking for crosses cut on the ruins, and intended to claim ownership of all such places. Most of the peasantry believed they were seeking for hid treasure, which by incantation would be wafted to England. Sometimes they dug for gold under the cairns; often they pulled them down, and had in consequence to be imprisoned. A shepherd saw the party levelling, and had a vague idea they were making a railway, "Will you let the sea into Jordan?" he asked, "or will the steamships go on wheels?" "The best idea" (says Conder) "was that we were sent by the Sultan to see what villages had become ruinous, and to remit their taxes. We were favourites then!"

The work of the Survey was not carried out without frequent discomforts. For instance, the Bukei'a plain is good corn land, "but seems to have a bad natural drainage, and our mules floundered in deep bogs, sometimes up to their girths. Farther north we began to descend a long valley, and came on a different kind of country; a basaltic outbreak appeared, and cliffs tilted in every direction; the valley bed was strewn with fragments of hard basalt. Passing over a bare ridge we descended into a most desolate valley where a muddy stream was flowing. We had ridden 15 miles, and it now began to rain again. We found to our dismay that this was where we had to camp, as no other supply of water existed in a position central to the new work. We soon made a still more unpleasant discovery. The valley was full of clear springs, but they were all tepid and salt. If the Survey was to be done at all, it appeared that we should have to drink brackish water for ten days or more. Here, then, we sat down on the wet grass, in a driving drizzle of rain, by the brackish stream: not a soul was to be seen, either Bedawi or peasant, and it was evident that food would have to be brought from a distance. The mules soon arrived with our tents and beds, which though soaked with rain, we set up on the bare ground. Of course all the party were cross, and thought themselves injured. I had a very bad cold and rheumatism, and Habib had tic-douloureux. The Arabs looked wretched; but I was glad they should have their share of the hardships, for, unlike our Abu Nuseir friends at Jericho, they were the most lazy and good-for-nothing tribe we had come across."

Again, at the miserable little hamlet of *El B'aineh*—be

tween Lake Tiberias and the Mediterranean—they found the inhabitants all fever-stricken from the malarious exhalations of the great swamp, which even as late as July extended over half the plain.   The place was evidently unhealthy, and they were tortured by armies of huge mosquitoes, rendering sleep impossible at night.   Attacks of fever were frequent.   " Once or twice " (says Conder) " the fit came on while I was riding, and I can imagine nothing more disagreeable than to be 10 miles from home, on a rough road, with a fever headache."

One night the Sukr Arabs tried to steal the horses, but the big dog gave a sharp bark, and the thieves were seen and fired on just as they reached the tethering rope.   In another place, when the dog had been left behind, a thief came into the tents, ripped up the saddle-bag containing the provisions and took them all with him, besides the tin washing-basin, and the plates, bread, chickens, and barley from the servants' tents—all being noiselessly and neatly accomplished in about ten minutes.   The next morning the party were without food.

But there were worse things than these to endure.   In the district of David's wanderings Corporal Brophy was attacked by four cowherds, who abused him as a " pig," and threatened to stone him.   He had, indeed, some difficulty in escaping.   " The first really serious attack on the party " (says Conder), " though not the last nor the worst, was made near Mount Carmel.   Sergeant Black was quietly surveying near the village of *El Harithiyeh*, where, as it appeared afterwards in evidence, a fete or ' fantasia ' was being held.   The young men were firing at a mark, and one or more turning at right angles, deliberately fired at the sergeant on the neighbouring hill.   He must have been in no little danger, as he brought home two bullets which had fallen near him."

On the 10th July 1875 a very serious attack was made

upon the whole party, and it is a marvel that any of them escaped with their lives. Fatigued with a long and arduous march, and a final ascent of 2000 feet, they chose a camping ground north of *Safed*, a town which lies in a saddle of the high mountains of Upper Galilee and looks down on the lake. The tents were about half way up when Major Conder, resting on his bed, in shirt-sleeves and slippers, heard angry voices in altercation. Looking out, he saw to his astonishment a sheikh, evidently a man of good position, engaged in throwing stones at Habib, who, with his hands spread out, was calling the bystanders to witness the treatment he underwent. Conder advanced to demand an explanation; but the shiekh, who was mad with passion, strode up to him, seized him by the throat and shook him, meantime pouring out unintelligible words. Major Conder had been accustomed to be treated with respect, even by the highest officials in the country; and he felt that if he submitted to this insult he would lose his influence with the natives for ever, so he knocked the man down. He got up and returned to the attack, with one arm behind him. Conder knocked him down a second time, and as he fell observed in his hand a knife with a blade a foot long. Conder's party consisted of five Europeans and ten Maronites, and when the latter heard news of the insult received by their "Kabtân," they came running up, quite beside themselves, and soon seized the sheikh, took his knife away, and bound his arms behind his back. The sheikh cried out, " Where are my people ? " and the Moslem bystanders began to throw stones. Conder's servants were running to the tents for arms, for they had eight revolvers ready for use, besides three shot-guns and a rifle. Their "captain," however, was wiser ; he had the sheikh immediately released, and sent Habib at once to the Governor of the town. But the crowd presently numbered about three hundred, and all the more violent engaged in hurling stones. Lieutenant Kitchener was struck more than once, and a muleteer was knocked over. The cries which Christians in Palestine have good reason to dread, associated as they are with memories of bloodshed, were now raised by the mob—" Allah! Allah!" and "Din! Din! Mohammed!" the cry of the Damascus massacres. Presently a number of fully-armed men came running down the hill-side, all relatives and retainers of the sheikh, who indeed, it afterwards appeared, was no less a person than 'Aly Agha 'Allân, a near relative of 'Abd el Kâder himself. "I advanced at once" (says Conder) "to meet these assailants, and singled out two men, one a white-bearded elder with a battle-axe, the other a tall man with a club. They addressed me with many curses, and the old man thrust the battle-axe against my ribs ; but it was a wonderful instance of the influence which a European may always possess over Arabs, that they allowed me to take them by the arms and turn them round, and that on my telling them to go home, with a slight push in that direction, they actually retreated some little way. Meantime a most extraordinary figure appeared—a black man with pistols in his belt, brandishing a scimitar over his head, and bellowing like a bull. He was the Agha's slave, and bent on revenge ; seeing him so near, and seeing also a gun pointed at my head, I retreated to the tents. I could not help laughing, even at so serious a juncture, when I found myself supported by Sergeant Armstrong, who stood at 'the charge' armed with the legs of the camera-obscura ! I now saw that Lieutenant Kitchener was opposing another group to my right front, and went forward to him, when I was greeted with a blow on the forehead from a club with nails in it, which brought the blood in a stream down my face. The man who wielded it raised it once more, in order to bring it down on the top of my skull, but luckily I was too quick for him, and ducked my head close to his chest. The blow fell short upon my neck, but even then it stunned me for the moment, and I staggered."

All the party were wounded, and as they were averse to using fire-arms, they at last " bolted over thistles and stone-walls to a hillside some hundred yards away, and stood there in suspense and anxiety." They were much surprised to hear no more the cries of the crowd ; but soon learned that the Governor had sent a body of soldiers, and they were safe, at least for the moment. They returned to camp, and held their ground for the night, in spite of the threat of 'Aly Agha that he would come back and cut their throats. Next morning they marched out in good order, with four mounted guards, and made for the coast. Arriving at Acre they laid the affair before the Pacha, and telegraphed to Constantinople ; for it would have been unsafe to attempt to continue their work until the assailants had been punished. Such was the attack at Safed. It was due to the insolence of one man, accustomed to over-bear and bully the few Christians who pass through the town, and to the fanaticism of the Moslem population.

The strain upon the Europeans had been too much for health. Excitement, fatigue, pain, and anxiety, added to malarious poison imbibed in the swamps, brought on a severe attack of fever. For twenty-four hours Major Conder was not expected to recover. Lieutenant Kitchener also soon succumbed, and the rest followed. They lay in their beds in the Carmel convent, and Sergeant Armstrong nursed them. Truly, as Conder remarks, the Survey of Palestine was no holiday work.

The Committee who organized the Survey and the officers who carried it out deserve our gratitude, for they have conferred a lasting benefit upon Palestine travellers and upon all students of the Bible. We have now a map by which a traveller can find his way. Dr Robinson and other explorers of that day used to describe the position of a place by saying it was two hours east from the last, and then one and a quarter hours northwest ; but we now have exact distances. We have a map which helps us to understand Bible narratives of personal journeys or the march of armies. We can now see which route *must* have been followed ; we can pursue step by step the Scripture events. We are certain now that the Bible could not have been written in any other country under heaven.

Before the Survey the Sea of Galilee was variously computed as being from 300 feet to 600 feet below the Mediterranean : it is now fixed at 682. The courses of the affluents of the Jordan are found to be entirely different from those previously shown. Only four fords of the Jordan were known and marked on the maps, whereas we now have more than forty. Villages have had to be transferred from one side to the other of the great boundary valleys. Scores and scores of Scripture sites, wrongly placed or altogether lost, have been found and fixed. And the finding of the sites has enabled the surveyors to trace accurately the boundaries of tribes and provinces. How was it possible to understand the Bible history unless we knew the situation of towns, the boundaries of tribes, the fords and passes and valleys which were open to foreign invaders ? How could we understand it unless we knew the routes of wayfarers and the way of commerce ? These things have now at last been ascertained, and with accuracy. When the base line which was measured on the Jaffa plain was checked by a line measured on the plain of Esdraelon, it was found to be perfectly satisfactory ; and the closing line when calculated in 1876 at Southampton had a margin of only 20 feet, which is an invisible distance on the one inch scale. It may be claimed for the Survey that the new discoveries are almost as numerous as all those of former travellers put together ; and nothing so great has been done for the right understanding of the Old and New Testaments since the translation of the Scriptures into the vulgar tongue.

[*Authorities and Sources (Western Palestine)* :—" Survey Memoirs of Palestine Exploration Fund." "Tent Work in Palestine." By Major Conder. "Palestine in its Physical Aspects." Rev. Canon Tristram. "Sinai and Palestine." By Dean Stanley. "Twenty-One Years' Work in the Holy Land." Published by the P. E. Fund. "Memoir on the Geology." Dr Ed. Hull. "Mount Seir." Dr Ed. Hull. "Introduction to the Survey." Trelawney Saunders. "Quarterly Statements of P. E. Fund." Smith's "Dictionary of the Bible." "*Rob Roy* on the Jordan." John Macgregor.]

11. *The East of Jordan.*

It would be well if the topographical survey could be extended so as to cover all the ground occupied by the tribes of Reuben and Gad, and the half tribe of Manasseh. It is true indeed that the East of Jordan is less intimately bound up with the Scripture narrative than the West, yet still there are ninety-six places east of Jordan mentioned in the Bible—Dr Selah Merrill estimates that there are two hundred and forty—and it would be an advantage to have them all identified. On the east side, also, the country is much more thickly strewn with ruins than on the west; and although the so-called "giant cities" of Bashan may not deserve that name, yet is the region full of Roman towns, of Nabathean and Arab texts scrawled on the rocks, of Greek temples and Greek inscriptions, and of dolmen groups yet older.

In the absence of detailed trigonometrical survey of the whole region, the map published by the Palestine Exploration Society in 1890 is the best that could be compiled from all sources. The sources available were—Van de Velde's map as a general basis; the route maps of later travellers; the work of the American Palestine Exploration Society as reported in their "Statements;" Major Conder's survey of 500 square miles in the land of Moab in 1881 and 1882; and lastly, surveys made by Herr Schumacher in the Hauran and the Janlan.

Bashan: the territory of the half tribe of Manasseh. As an illustration of the abundance of the ancient remains east of Jordan, Dr Selah Merrill, the archæologist of the American Exploring Expedition, says that every one who has visited *Kanawat* is amazed at the number and variety of the ruined buildings, castles, temples, churches, convents, theatre, bath, palaces, reservoirs, underground apartments or vaults, costly tombs, and still others which have never been fully examined. Dr J. L. Porter found here what he calls a colossal head of Astarte, sadly broken . . . with the crescent moon (which gave to this goddess the name *Karnaim* or two-horned) still on her brow. Mr Tyrwhitt Drake secured a stone at this place which was thought to be part of an altar, upon two opposite sides of which were the features of Baal and Astarte, boldly cut in high relief upon the closest basalt, with foliage, showing the artistic hand.

One's first impression is that all the antiquities are of Roman times and date only from the early centuries of the Christian era. This is indicated not only by the style of architecture but by the considerable number of inscriptions, which form an almost continuous chain from the first century to the fourth. They belong to the Emperors Marcus Aurelius, Lucius Aurelius Verus, Commodus, Septimius Severus, Alexander Severus, &c.

These **Roman cities** became converted to the religion of Christ, and then **not** only were the sanctuaries of paganism transformed into Christian sanctuaries, but new churches were erected adapted to the new worship; houses, palaces, and tombs were built; even entire cities were founded. At length all these Christian cities were abandoned at the same time—probably at the epoch of the Mohammedan invasion—and since then they have not been touched. Except that earthquakes have thrown to the ground many of the walls and columns, they lack only beams and planks, or they would be perfect edifices, which soon might be made habitable again.

But how intensely interesting the exploration of the district becomes when we learn that underneath these towns of Roman date are the dwellings of the earlier inhabitants! For example, *Burak* is a city of the Hauran which has been identified with the episcopal city Constantia, founded, it is supposed, or at least embellished, by Constantine. But Rev. W. Wright tells us that while the houses seem to stand on a mound of black earth, they are in reality built on the foundations of houses of a more remote antiquity. In one place he descended to a depth of 16 or 18 feet, to see some pottery which had lately been discovered, and he found the walls at that depth formed of enormous undressed and unsquared stones, unlike the stones of the superstructure, which are small in size and have been better prepared for the walls. "Nor will it be doubted" (he says) "that beneath that raised mound are buried the remains of one of the 'three-score cities' that once existed in Bashan, and which still exist under changed circumstances, sometimes under different names."

At another place, called *Dra'a*, Dr S. Merrill desired to explore the underground caves or chambers which were known to exist, and the sheikh sent his son as a guide. They went through several chambers, galleries, and avenues, and then entered a small room, and followed a passage leading out of it that had been cut in the solid rock. Soon they were obliged to go on their hands and knees, and after proceeding about thirty yards the guide came upon a human skeleton, at which he was so shocked that he refused to go any farther, and the party were obliged to return. How the skeleton came there was a mystery : some wild beast may have dragged a body to the place, or a murder may have been committed, or some person may have been trying to explore the caverns and failed to find his way out. *Dra'a* ought to be a rich field for excavations, because at least three cities exist there, one beneath another. The present Arab buildings and heaps of filth are, for the most part, on the top of a Greek or Roman city, as is evident from the walls which are exposed in a multitude of places, and the masons' marks which appear on them. And the Roman town appears to rest on one still older, in which bevelled stones were used. But whether there are two or three cities above ground, there is certainly a large one beneath them, entirely excavated in the rock on which the upper cities stand.

The underground dwellings at this place had been visited some years before by Dr J. G. Wetzstein, and he also was prevented from making a thorough exploration ; for when his attendant's light went out he was so impressed with a sense of the danger they would be in if both lights went out together, that he thought it prudent to retreat. But he had seen a good deal. After passing a difficult passage he found himself in a broad street which had dwellings on both sides of it, and whose height and width left nothing to be desired. Farther along there were several cross streets, and soon after they came to a market-place, with numerous shops in the walls, exactly in the style of the shops that are seen in Syrian cities. After a while they turned into a side street, where a great hall attracted his attention, the roof formed of a single slab of jasper, and supported by four pillars. Dr Wetzstein speaks of this remarkable place as "old Edrei, the subterranean labyrinthine residence of King Og."

Herr Schumacher has also visited this underground city of *Dra'a* or *Ed Der'aah*, and describes it, giving plans, in his work, "Across the Jordan." He regards such cities as the work of the earliest inhabitants of Hauran, the so-called giants of Scripture. He was assured by the sheikh Naif, and by many others, that this underground city extends below the whole of *Ed Der'aah*.

Although the chambers and passages were ventilated, the question arises, why any people should choose to live in such gloomy seclusion instead of in the light of day? Mr Schumacher's conjecture is that they did ordinarily live in the daylight, and that these subterranean places were hollowed out in order to receive the population in time of danger. They were thus prepared to stand a siege, as long as their magazines were filled with food, their stables with cattle, and their cisterns with water. If, however, the enemy had found out how to cut off their supply of air, by covering up the air-holes, the besieged would have been compelled to surrender or perish. Another circumstance also might have proved disastrous—if armies of wasps found their way into the underground city the inhabitants would be driven out. Some writers think that this occurrence is actually spoken of in Exodus xxiii. 28—"And I will send the hornet before thee, which shall drive out the Hivite, the Canaanite, and the Hittite from before thee;" and Deut. vii. 20—"Moreover the Lord thy God will send the hornet among them, until they that are left, and hide themselves, perish from before thee"—*they that are left, and hide themselves!*

Herr Schumacher and Mr Laurence Oliphant find many names and traditions which lead them to regard the country of Western Hauran as probably the land of Uz. "There was a man in the land of Uz whose name was Job" (Job i.). The old village of *Sheikh Sa'ad* is a spot which from the most ancient times has been held sacred to the memory of Job (*Neby Ayyub*). We find there the ruins of the Monastery of Job (*Deir Ayyub*), much venerated by the ancient people of the Hauran. At the south-eastern extremity of the long, low hill upon which the village is built, and elevated about 40 feet above the surrounding plain, is the "Rock of Job," which stands now in a mosque. Here, so says the legend, Job sat when he was leprous, and received his friends. The rock is a monolith of basalt, 7 feet high and about 4 feet broad, and on its surface are some illegible letters. There may be no truth in the legend; but it serves to show how closely the name of Job is associated with this region.

About half a day's journey due east from Bethshan is a place called *Mahneh*, which several writers, on account of the similarity of name, have been inclined to identify with Mahanaim, where Jacob met the two companies of angels, and where David sojourned during Absalom's rebellion. A mound exists here, and Dr Tristram picked up some pieces of old pottery, scattered about, so that it might be worth while to excavate: but we must look elsewhere for Mahanaim.

Mahanaim must have been some little distance north of the Jabbok, because Jacob came to it before he crossed that stream. It must have been in or near the Jordan Valley, for Jacob, in his prayer at that place, says, "With my staff I passed over this Jordan," language which would not have been used if the Jordan were not within sight. The city was assigned to one of Solomon's commissariat officers (1 Kings iv. 14), from which we may infer that it represented a district. These conditions appear to point to *Khurbet Suleikhat*, a large ruined city at the mouth of

Wady Suleikhat, 9 miles north of the Jabbok. If we fix Mahanaim here we can understand why the name is in the dual form—the two Mahans or camps—for the ruins lie on both sides of the stream which here runs down the *Wady Suleikhat* into the Jordan. *Khurbet Suleikhat* is some 300 feet above the plain, and among the foot-hills, in such a way that it overlooks the valley, while the road running north and south along the valley passes nearly a mile to the west of it. A watchman from a tower could see to the north a considerable distance, also clear across the valley to the west, and down the valley to the south a long stretch, nearly or quite to the point where the Jabbok and the Jordan unite, at the foot of *Kurn Surtabeh.*

We can now understand the account of the messengers who bore the news of Absalom's death to David. The battle between Joab and Absalom took place a little to the south-east of Mahanaim. Josephus says that Joab " put his army in battle array over against the enemy in the great plain where he had a wood behind him " (Antiq. vii. 9, 8, and 10, 1-5). Absalom's men were routed, and fled through the forests and valleys, pursued by David's men. The battle was scattered over the face of all the country (2 Sam. xviii. 8), and probably extended to the foot-hills. The two messengers appear to start from some point on the hills, where Joab stood on vantage ground. " The Cushite," an Ethiopian slave of Joab's, attempted to go across over deep wadies and broken ground ; but Ahim-aaz, who knew the country better, struck down to the Jordan Valley, and ran by the way of the Plain (the *Kikkar*), where he had a level and smooth road all the rest of the way. Consequently, although he started second, he arrived first. David sat between the two gates at Mahanaim, and the watchman went up to the roof of the gate unto the wall, whence he descried the messengers approaching.

Succoth also was a city east of Jordan, for Jacob came to it before he crossed the Jordan from the east, and Gideon passed it after he had crossed the Jordan from the west (Judges vii. 4). From the account of Jacob's return it would seem to be at no great distance from Mahanaim. But notwithstanding that Jacob had crossed the Jabbok southward before he met Esau, and journeyed to Succoth after parting with Esau, there is reason for placing Succoth north of the Jabbok. Jacob recrossed the stream. The Jerusalem Talmud tells us that Succoth, one of the cities "in the valley," came to be called Darala; and just north of the Jabbok we find *Deir 'Alla*, one of the most conspicuous mounds or *tells* in the plain, 60 feet high, and covered with broken pottery of many colours and qualities. The site was mapped by Warren in 1868.

The word Succoth means "tents," and perhaps the place was named from the tents of the Arabs so constantly seen there. The region about the mouth of the Jabbok is fertile, with abundant grass and water, and is very much frequented now by the powerful desert tribes for the purpose of pasturing their flocks and herds. When Gideon, who crossed the Jordan near *Beisan*, had followed the Midianites down the valley to Succoth, it is said that "he went up by the way of them that dwell in tents," apparently some well-known route leading up the Jabbok Valley to the eastern deserts.

A fair interpretation of the circumstances leads to the conclusion that Penuel was not far east of Succoth. It was a fortified city, for it had a tower, which Gideon threatened to break down; and was regarded by Jeroboam as an outpost, useful in the defence of Shechem (1 Kings xii. 25). Dr Merrill finds that there is but one suitable site for it, and that is at the mounds called the "Hills of Gold," about 4 miles east of Jordan, in the valley of the Jabbok. The mounds are very striking objects; they are covered with ruins, and on the eastern side are the remains of an ancient castle. The work is not Moslem, Christian, or Roman ; the stones are unhewn blocks, and appear to date from a remote period.

A large district east and south-east of the Sea of Galilee was called Decapolis, or the region of the Ten Cities. The name occurs frequently in Josephus and other writers, and three times in the Gospels. Immediately after the conquest of Syria by the Romans (B.C. 65), ten cities appear to have been rebuilt, partially colonised, and endowed with peculiar privileges. One of the cities was Scythopolis, west of the Jordan ; the others included Gadara, Geraza, Philadelphia, Pella, &c., all on the east. The region, once so populous and prosperous, is now almost without inhabitants ; and the few families that do remain—in Scythopolis, Gadara, and Canatha—live amid the crumbling ruins of palaces, and in the cavernous recesses of old tombs.

Herr Schumacher has explored Abila of the Decapolis (now *Tell Abil*), and Gadara (at *Umm Keis*), and Pella (*Fahil*).

Pella—situated just opposite *Beisan*, on the other side of the Ghor—is the city to which the Christian believers fled when Titus advanced to besiege Jerusalem. Epiphanius says that " they removed because they had been forewarned by Christ himself of the approaching siege." Seventy years later (A.D. 135) when Hadrian rebuilt Jerusalem as a Roman city, and changed its name to Ælia, the Christians again left it and sought refuge in this elegant city of Pella in the Jordan valley. Dr Merrill is inclined to think that Christ himself had been in Pella (for we know that he visited Perea), and met with such favour and success as to make the city a fitting asylum for his followers. Herr Schumacher, after describing a rock-cut chamber of rectangular shape, having a ceiling cut in the shape of a cross vault, with two pillars on the southern and northern walls says, " It may be accepted as beyond doubt that we have here a cave, once inhabited by those Christian anchorites, who, in the beginning of the Christian era and during the Jewish wars, found a refuge at Pella. The flooring consisting of earth and remains of charcoal, as well as the plan of the whole, has no sepulchral character, but rather that of a habitation; the passages being used to secure air and afford a way of escape in case of persecution, for these small caves, if their door entrance was carefully shut, were hardly visible from below, and the passage still less. The entire northern slope is honey-combed with such caves."

The wonder is that Pella should ever have been forsaken, it is so favoured in position. Even after the long summer drought, the springs gushing out among the broken columns and ruins of former splendour are abundant enough to make fertile all the neighbouring land, which, situated on the upper level of the Ghor, and 250 feet below the sea, enjoys, perhaps, the finest climate, from an agricultural point of view, that can be found in Syria.

The capital of Perea was Gadara, a city mentioned in the Gospel narrative of the demoniac who had his dwelling among the tombs. The population of *Umm Keis* may be about two hundred souls, and the people cultivate tobacco, vegetables, and grain. Below the ground occupied by the present village, many caves and ancient burial places have been discovered. The ruins include a Roman theatre and what may be the remains of a castle.

Gilead.—The boundary of the tribe of Gad was some few miles north of the Jabbok, for the territory included Mahanaim; while on the south it extended to the Arnon. The region had belonged to the Ammonites; and it was long before they were driven out, for even after Saul was anointed King of Israel, Nahash the Ammonite besieged Jabesh Gilead and sought to lay a hard condition of surrender upon the Israelites there (1 Sam. xi.). This district

is the land of Gilead or " Mount Gilead " of the Bible.   It
is a good land for cattle, and would be prized by agricultural people in any part of the world.   " It is not to be
wondered at," says Dr Merrill, "that the two and a half
tribes were perfectly willing to stay on the east of Jordan.
Judea has no land to compare with it ; neither has Samaria,
except in very limited portions.   The surface of the country
is slightly rolling, but the fields are broad and comparatively free from stone.   Here common Arab trails broaden
out into fine roads.   Here are rich pasture lands and luxuriant fields of wheat and barley, and the ignorant Bedouin
who own the soil point with pride to the green acres that
are spread out beneath the sun."

Amman, called in the Bible Rabbath Ammon (Deut. iii.
11 ; 2 Sam. xi. 1, &c.), was the chief city of the children of
Ammon fifteen hundred years before Christ.   Here the
bedstead of Og, the king of Bashan, was taken by Joab,
David's general (2 Sam. xi. xii.), and Uriah the Hittite was
killed in one of the sorties.   Rabbath Ammon was rebuilt
by Ptolemy Philadelphus, king of Egypt, and its name
changed to Philadelphia.   Again it was destroyed by the
Saracens when they conquered Syria.   The stream of the
Jabbok ran right through Rabbath Ammon, and it was
called the " City of Waters."   It was after Joab had taken
the City of Waters that he sent to David and suggested
that he should come and capture the citadel himself, lest
all the glory should go to his servant.

Major Conder regards *Amman* as the most important
ruin surveyed in Palestine, as regards its antiquarian
interest, and the best specimen of a Roman town that he
visited, except the still more wonderful ruins of Gerasa,
which yield only to Baalbec and Palmyra among Syrian
capitals of the second century of our era.   The Roman
remains include two theatres, baths, a street of columns,
and remains of what was once a very great temple on the

highest part of the acropolis of the city. Several noble families must have lived in the town, as shown by the magnificent private tombs surrounding the city.

But the oldest remains visible at *Amman* are the dolmens, of which, with other rude stone monuments, there are some twenty in all. Next to these come the old rock-cut tombs, which Conder supposes to be of the early Hebrew period. But who knows whether there be not a buried city underneath *Amman?* The whole region south of *Amman,* and also north and west of it, abounds in ruins.

Moab.—The country south of Gilead was given to the tribe of Reuben. It was the land of the Moabites, and a land where Moabite kings continued to reign, notwithstanding the rights of Reuben. From this land came Ruth, to dwell at Bethlehem with Naomi, to marry Boaz, and be held in memory by-and-bye as the ancestress of David. Perhaps it was on account of Ruth that David found the king of Moab willing to give safe asylum to his aged parents, while he himself braved the dangers of the outlaw's life (1 Sam. xxii. 3). Yet the time came when David fought against the Moabites and conquered them, treating the captives with a severity which makes us suspect that there had been some act of perfidy or insult. It has been conjectured that the king of Moab betrayed the trust which David reposed in him, and either killed Jesse and his wife or surrendered them to Saul. We do not know.

The strong fortress of Moab was Kir-Haraseth, or Kir-Hareseth, or Kir-Heres (2 Kings iii. 25; Isaiah xvi. 7, 11); and it was on the walls of this city that King Mesha offered his son for a burnt-offering, and by the moral effect thus produced turned the tide of battle. We have reasonable ground for identifying Kir-Heres with the modern *Kerak,* near the south-eastern part of the Dead Sea. The allied armies marched round the southern end of the Dead Sea to reach it, instead of crossing the Jordan. "No chain of evidence," says Dr Tristram, "can be less open to cavil than that which identifies Kerak with Kir-Moab (Isaiah xv. 1) or Kir-Hareseth. It was the castle 'Kir,' as distinguished from the metropolis 'Ar' of the country, *i.e.*, Rabbath Moab, the modern *Rabba*." The Targum translates the name as "Kerakah." The Crusaders mistook it for Petra, and gave to its bishop that title, which the Greek Church has still retained, but the name in the vernacular has continued unchanged. No wonder, as we look down from the neighbouring heights upon it, that the combined armies of Israel, Judah, and Edom could not take it, and that "in Kir-Haraseth left they the stones thereof; howbeit the archers went about it and smote it," but to no purpose.

The position is so strong by nature that it would be seized upon as a fortress from the very earliest times. The platform on which the city is built is on a lofty brow, which pushes out like a peninsula and is only connected with other ground by a narrow neck. Two deep *wadies* flank it north and south, with steeply scarped or else rugged sides. There have been originally only two entrances to Kerak, and both of them through tunnels in the side of the cliff, emerging on the platform of the town.

Another town — reckoned to Reuben in an ancient fragment of poetry, but rebuilt by Gad (Num. xxi. 30, xxxii. 34,)—was Dibon. It is now identified with *Dhiban*, on the Roman road, about 3 miles north of the Arnon, a spot where there are extensive ruins. It is described by Dr Tristram as being quite as dreary and featureless a ruin as any other of the Moabite desolate heaps. "With its waterless plain," he says, "the prophecy is fulfilled—'Thou daughter that dost inhabit Dibon, come down from thy glory, and sit in thirst; for the spoiler of Moab shall come upon thee, and he shall destroy thy strongholds' (Jer. xlviii. 18). The place is full of cisterns, caverns, vaulted underground storehouses, and rude semicircular arches. All the hills about are limestone, and there is no trace of any basalt but what has been brought here by man. Still there are many basaltic blocks among the ruins, dressed to be used in masonry.

It was among these ruins that the famous Moabite Stone was found in the year 1868. It is a block of basalt measuring about 3½ feet by 2 feet, and has upon its face thirty-four lines of writing in the character known as Phœnician. As the language also is Phœnician—or probably Moabite, though closely related to Phœnician, and certainly closely related to Hebrew—there would have been no great difficulty in reading the inscription; but, unfortunately, when the Arabs found that the stone was valued by Europeans, they quarrelled about the possession of it and broke it up. About two-thirds of the fragments, however, were recovered and pieced together; besides which, a " squeeze " of the whole had been hurriedly taken before it was broken, and from this it was possible to fill in some of the gaps. The restored monument is now preserved in the Louvre at Paris, and a plaster cast is to be seen in the British Museum. The inscription shows that the monument was set up by Mesha, king of Moab (nearly nine hundred years before Christ), to record victories which he had gained and public works which he had accomplished. It would appear that after the allied armies retired from the siege of Kir-Haraseth, the fortune of war changed and went in Mesha's favour. The translation of the inscription is as follows :—

"I, Mesha, am the son of Chemosh-Gad, king of Moab, the Dibonite. My father reigned over Moab thirty years, and I reigned after my father. And I erected this stone to Chemosh at Korcha, a (stone of) salvation, for he saved me from all despoilers, and made me see my desire upon all my enemies, even upon Omri, king of Israel. Now they afflicted Moab many days, for Chemosh was angry with his land. His son succeeded him, and he also said, I will afflict Moab. In my days (Chemosh) said, (Let us go) and I will see my desire on him and his house, and I will destroy Israel with an everlasting destruction. Now Omri took the land of Medeba, and (the enemy) occupied it in (his days and in) the days of his son, forty years. And Chemosh (had mercy) on it in my days; and I fortified Baal-Meon, and made therein the tank, and I fortified Kiriathaim. For the men of Gad dwelt in the land of (Atar)oth from of old, and the king (of) Israel fortified for himself Ataroth, and I assaulted the wall and captured it, and killed all the warriors of the wall for the well-pleasing of Chemosh and Moab; and I removed from it all the spoil, and (offered) it before Chemosh in Kirjath; and I placed therein the men of Siran and the men of Mochrath. And Chemosh said to me, Go, take Nebo against Israel. (And I) went in the night, and I fought against it from the break of dawn till noon, and I took it, and slew in all seven thousand (men, but I did not kill) the women (and) maidens, for (I) devoted them to Ashtar-Chemosh, and I took from it the vessels of Yahveh, and offered them before Chemosh. And the king of Israel fortified Jahaz and occupied it, when he made war against me; and Chemosh drove him out before (me, and) I·took from Moab two hundred men, all its poor, and placed them in Jahaz, and took it to annex it to Dibon. I built Korcha, the wall of the forest, and the wall of the city, and I built the gates thereof, and I built the towers thereof, and I built the palace, and I made the prisons for the criminals within the walls. And there was no cistern in the wall at Korcha, and I said to all the people, Make for yourselves, every man, a cistern in his house. And I dug the ditch for Korcha by means of the (captive) men of Israel. I built Aroer, and I made the road across the Arnon. I built Beth-Bamoth, for it was destroyed ; I built Bezer, for it was cut (down) by the armed men of Dibon, for all Dibon was now loyal ; and I reigned from Bikran, which I added to my land, and I built (Beth-Gamul) and Beth Diblathaim and Beth-Baal-Meon, and I placed there the poor (people) of the land. And as to Horonaim, (the men of Edom) dwelt therein (from of old). And Chemosh said to me, Go down, make war against Horonaim, and take (it. And I assaulted it, and I took it, and) Chemosh (restored it) in my days. Wherefore I made . . . year . . . and I . . ."

In 1881 Major Conder, aided by Lieutenant Mantell, was sent out to begin the systematic survey of Eastern Palestine. The country at that time was very much disturbed ; but the party crossed the Jordan into Moab, and for two anxious months laboured at very high pressure. After measuring a base-line and connecting their triangulation with that west of the river, they worked over 500 square miles in detail. And even after attention was drawn to their presence they were able to extend their work over a considerable area, and they came back from the desert with their hands full of valuable results.

One of the most remarkable discoveries was the abundance of menhirs, dolmens, and stone-circles. They are numbered by hundreds, whereas in Judea and Samaria there are none, and in Galilee only half a dozen. Dr Merrill and Herr Schumacher found them abundant also in the Jaulan and the rest of the Hauran. According to Herr Schumacher, an examination of many specimens in Eastern Jaulan makes it apparent (1) that the dolmens are always built on circular terraces, which elevate them about 3 feet above the ground ; (2) that in most cases they are formed by six upright and two covering slabs ; (3) that the major axes of the dolmens all run east and west ; (4) that the western end of the dolmens is broader than the eastern ;

(5) that the western end is often distinguished by headings, one on each corner of the top slab ; and (6) that they vary in size from 7 to 13 feet in length. He finds it difficult to avoid the conclusion that these dolmens were built originally as burial places. The covered chamber, elevated above the ground, and shut in by slabs, was the first beginning of a sarcophagus ; and the body was laid facing the rising sun, with its head in the west. On the other hand Major Conder, who finds in Moab many rude stone monuments of a different kind, bids us remember that stones may be placed on end for more than one purpose. After examining seven hundred examples in Moab and Gilead, he has come to the conclusion that the sepulchral theory is often quite untenable, though we cannot deny that bodies were buried in such stone chambers sometimes. In many cases in Moab it was certain that no mound of earth had ever covered the stones ; there was nothing but hard rock to be found, and sometimes the structure was not large enough to cover even the body of a child. We must turn to local superstitions in order fully to understand the use of trilithons and dolmens. Wild as are the legends, they preserve, in Conder's opinion, what was once the religion of the dolmen-building tribes. After making measured drawings of about a hundred and fifty dolmens in Moab, it seemed to him that the purpose of the builders was to produce a flat table-like surface, which they perhaps used as an altar. True that the dolmens are often more numerous in a confined area than we should expect altars to be, but we must not forget the story of Balaam and Balak, in which seven altars are built on the same mountain top, and again seven more on a neighbouring mountain top. Then, as to the absence of such monuments in Judea and Samaria, Conder suggests that they may very probably have once existed, and may have been purposely destroyed. Israel was commanded to "smash" the *menhirs* of the

Canaanites, to "upset" their altars, and to destroy their images.   These commands Josiah, the zealous king of Judah, is recorded to have carried into practice.

Who built these structures?   They are very likely the surviving work of Canaanite tribes.   Herr Schumacher assigns those of the Hauran to the same period as the subterranean cities.

There is a curious archæological note in Deuteronomy, which speaks of the bedstead of Og, the king of Bashan, a bedstead 9 cubits long by 4 cubits wide.   The passage had very much exercised the ingenuity of commentators, and some of them supposed it to refer to a sarcophagus of basalt.   The Bible indeed speaks of a bedstead of iron ; but basalt is a material which resembles iron in appearance, and which is actually known by the name of iron among the Arabs, while a stone coffin might allowably be spoken of as a bed or bedstead.   But Conder says there is no basalt at Rabbath, and thinks it doubtful if Og was likely to be buried in a sarcophagus at all.   He is disposed to render the words as Og's *strong throne,* instead of "iron bedstead."   A memory of Irish dolmens suggested to him a possible connection between Og's throne and some rude stone monument which tradition might have indicated as a giant's seat, just as in Ireland dolmens are the "beds of Grain and Diarmed," and connected with legends of giants. It was, therefore, very striking to find a single enormous dolmen standing alone in a conspicuous position near Rabbath Ammon, and yet more striking that the top stone measured 13 feet (or very nearly 9 cubits of 16 inches) by 11 feet in extreme breadth.

If we look for a coffin or a bedstead rather than a dolmen, it is very striking to find that parallels exist both for bedsteads and coffins of the same gigantic dimensions.   Dr Erasmus Wilson, describing the coffins and mummies found at *Deir-el-Bahari,* says that, " the coffin of Queen Nefertari is gigantic in stature, measuring with its feathered crest 13 feet long. It is made of cloth-board and modelled into the shape of a statue, resembling, with arms crossed upon the chest, one of those architectural columns which are denominated Caryatides." Still more remarkable is the bedstead of the Babylonian god Bel, described by Mr George Smith in his account of the "Temple of Bel." After some description of the principal buildings, he says, "In these western chambers stood the couch of the god, and the throne of gold mentioned by Herodotus, besides other furniture of great value. The couch is stated to have been 9 cubits long and 4 cubits broad (15 feet by 6 feet 8 inches)." These are exactly the dimensions assigned to Og's bedstead.

Before leaving Moab it was Major Conder's privilege to stand where Moses stood, and view the landscape on all sides. There can be no doubt about the identification of Mount Nebo. It was ascertained by Canon Tristram; it has been confirmed by Conder, who finds the field of Zophim close by; and Sir Charles Warren discovered the ruins of the ancient city of Nebo at its foot. Moreover, it retains the name *Neba*, and from the summit you obtain the celebrated "Pisgah view" (Deut. xxxiv. 1-3). Naphtali, Gilead, Ephraim, and Manasseh, Judah, and the Negeb, or "dry land" south of Hebron, are all in sight, with the plains of Jericho "unto Zoar." But, according to Conder, the Mediterranean Sea is not visible from Nebo, being hidden throughout by the western watershed of Judea and Samaria. Dr Tristram says, in his "Land of Moab," "Carmel could be recognised, but we never were able to make out the sea to the north of it; and though it is certainly possible that it might be seen from this elevation, I could not satisfy myself that I saw more than the haze over the plain of Esdraelon." But even if the waters of the "great sea" in the Bay of Haifa could be seen distinctly from Mount Nebo, the fact would hardly be relevant, for Deut. xxxiv. points rather to the sea south of Joppa. It is sufficient, however, that from no other summit can you get so extensive a prospect as from Mount Nebo.

Conder's work was abruptly stopped. Even when the party went out in 1881 there was great excitement in the East. A Moslem Messiah was expected to appear in the year 1300 of the Hegira, and the war in Egypt was brewing. The British Government had served Conder with a notice that any expedition he might take out would be at his own risk, and they could not be responsible for the consequences. After fifteen months, during which the work was carried on at great risks, the Sultan heard that English captains were surveying the land, and sent orders for them to cease. In the same year Mr Rassam's researches in Mesopotamia were stopped. Finally, Conder and his party left Syria on a steamer crowded with refugees from the Alexandria massacres.

[*Authorities and Sources :*—"East of the Jordan." By Selah Merrill. London: Bentley & Son, 1881. "Across the Jordan." By Gottlieb Schumacher. Bentley & Son, 1886. "The Jaulan." By G. Schumacher, Bentley, 1888. "Abila," "Pella," and "Northern Ajlun." By G. Schumacher. London: Palestine Exploration Society, 1888, 1889. "Palestine." By Major Conder. London: George Philip & Son, 1889. "Heth and Moab." By Major Conder. Bentley & Son, 1883. "The Land of Moab." By Rev. Canon Tristram. London: John Murray, 1873. "Unexplored Syria." By Burton and Drake. London: Tinsley Brothers, 1872.]

CHAPTER III.

EVER since the days of David Jerusalem has been the chief city of Palestine, and although so small a city now that it would go conveniently into Hyde Park—and perhaps never much larger than at present—it has been the theatre of great events, and it claims an attentive study. Small as it was, it stood upon several hills, which were more or less easy to defend by fortifications, and offered some choice to the monarch desirous of building a palace, a tower, or a temple. The variety of local features, of hill and ravine and watercourse, finds frequent mention in the history, and is sometimes so much inter-twined with the events related, that it becomes necessary to look at the topography before we can hope to under-stand the narrative. For instance, when David wrested the city from the Jebusites :—

"David took the strong hold of Zion. . . . And David dwelt in the strong hold, and called it the City of David. And David built round about from Millo inward" (2 Sam. v. 7-9).

"So he took the Lower City by force, but the Citadel * held out still. . . . When David had cast the Jebusites out of the Citadel, he also rebuilt Jerusalem, and named it the City of David"—Josephus, Antiquities, vii. 3, 1-2, (Whiston's Translation).

Here we should like to know at least which part of

---

* *Greek* "Akra."

Jerusalem was called the City of David; because David built a house there, and most of the kings of Judah were buried there.

Again, in 1 Kings i., " Adonijah slew sheep and oxen and fatlings by the Stone of Zoheleth, which is beside En-Rogel," and sought to get himself proclaimed king. But when Nathan the prophet, and Bathsheba the mother of Solomon, had acquainted David with the proceeding, David gave orders to place Solomon upon the king's mule, and "bring him down to Gihon," and proclaim him as king. There the trumpet was blown, the people piped with pipes, and Adonijah and his guests heard the noise. Before we can fully realise these scenes we must know all the localities, and how they stood related to one another, and to the position of David's house.

The Old Testament history is full of such local references, and so are the Books of the Maccabees; and perhaps most of all, the chapters of Josephus which describe the siege of Jerusalem by Titus. Let us then try and make ourselves acquainted with the features of the ground, and learn to apply the names to the proper localities.

1. *The City as it is.*

Its position.—Jerusalem lies near the summit of the broad mountain ridge, or high, uneven table land which extends from the Plain of Esdraelon to the desert of the south. This tract is everywhere not less than from 20 to 25 miles in breadth, and has a surface rocky and uneven. Its height at Jerusalem is 2500 feet above the Mediterranean Sea; but it continues to rise towards the south, until, in the vicinity of Hebron, the elevation is nearly 3000 feet.

The city occupies the southern termination of a table-land which is cut off from the country round it on the

west, south, and east sides, by ravines more than usually
deep and precipitous.   These ravines leave the level of the
table-land, the one on the west and the other on the north-
east of the city, and fall rapidly until they form a junction
below its south-east corner.   The eastern one—the Valley
of the Kedron, commonly called the Valley of Jehoshaphat
—runs nearly straight from north to south.   But the

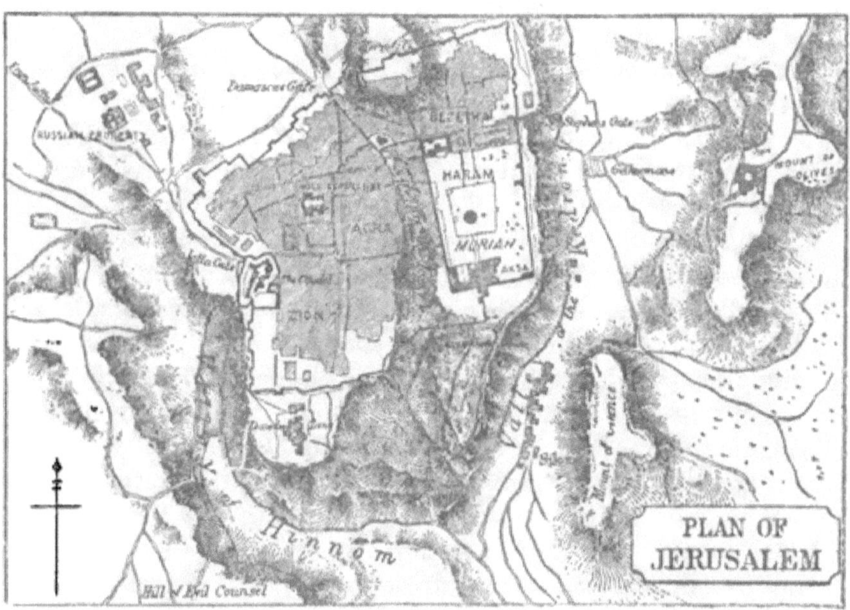

[By favour of the Palestine Exploration Fund.

western one—the Valley of Hinnom—runs south for a
time, and then takes a sudden bend to the east until it
meets the Valley of Jehoshaphat, after which the two rush
off as one to the Dead Sea.   How sudden is their descent
may be gathered from the fact that the level at the point
of junction—about a mile and a quarter from the starting-
point of each—is more than 600 feet below that of the upper
plateau from which they commenced their descent.   Thus

while on the north there is no material difference between the general level of the country outside the walls and that of the highest parts of the city, on the other three sides, so steep is the fall of the ravines, so trench-like their character, and so close do they keep to the promontory, at whose foot they run, as to leave on the beholder the impression of the ditch at the foot of a fortress, rather than of valleys formed by nature.

The promontory thus encircled is itself divided by a longitudinal ravine—called the Tyropœan Valley, running up it from south to north, rising gradually from the south like the external ones, till at last it arrives at the level of the upper plateau, dividing the central mass into two unequal portions. Of these two, that on the west—the Upper City of the Jews, the Mount Zion of modern tradition—is the higher and more massive ; that on the east—Mount Moriah—is at once considerably lower and smaller, so that, to a spectator from the south, the city appears to slope sharply towards the east. The central valley, at about half-way up its length, threw out a companion valley on its left or west side, which made its way up to the general level of the ground at the present Jaffa Gate.

One more valley must be noted. It was on the north of Moriah, and separated it from a hill on which, in the time of Josephus, stood a suburb or part of the city called Bezetha, or the New-town. Part of this depression is still preserved in the large reservoir with two arches, usually called the Pool of Bethesda, near the St Stephen's Gate.

All round the city are higher hills : on the east the Mount of Olives ; on the south the Hill of Evil Counsel, rising directly from the Vale of Hinnom ; on the west the ground rises gently to the borders of the great wady ; while on the north, a bend of the ridge connected with the Mount of Olives bounds the prospect at the distance of more than a mile. Towards the south-west the view is somewhat more open ; for here lies the Plain of Rephaim, commencing just at the southern brink of the Valley of Hinnom, and stretching off south-west, where it runs to the western sea.

This rough sketch of the *terrain* of Jerusalem will enable the reader to appreciate the two great advantages of its position. On the one hand the ravines which entrench it on the west, south, and east—out of which the rock slopes of the city rose almost like the walls of a fortress out of its ditches, must have rendered it impregnable on those quarters to the warfare of the old world. On the other hand its junction with the more level ground on its north and north-east sides afforded an opportunity of expansion, of which we know advantage was taken, and which gave it a remarkable superiority over other cities of Palestine, and especially of Judah, which, though secure on their hill-tops, were unable to expand beyond them.

The western side of the city is more than 100 feet higher than the eastern ; but the Mount of Olives overtops even the highest part of the city by more than 150 feet.

The Walls and Streets of the City.—Jerusalem is surrounded by walls some 40 to 50 feet high, imposing in appearance but far from strong. For the most part they were erected as they now stand by Sultan Suleiman, in the year 1542, and they appear to occupy the site of the walls of the middle ages, from the ruins of which they are mostly constructed. On the eastern side, along the brow of the Valley of Jehoshaphat, the section of the wall south of St Stephen's Gate is of far earlier date, and is constructed in part of massive bevelled stones. A great stone at the south-eastern corner is estimated to weigh more than one hundred tons ; and this block is one of a course of stones, 6 feet in thickness, which extends along the south wall for 600 feet, though not without gaps. The walls nearly resemble York and other ancient cities in England, having steps at intervals leading up to the battlemented breastwork ; and the circuit of them, according to Robinson and others, is something less than 2½ English miles. The form of the city is irregular, the walls having many projections and indentations ; but it is easy to make out four sides ; and these nearly face the cardinal points.

There are at present five open gates in the walls of Jerusalem—two on the south and one near the centre of each of the other sides. They all seem to occupy ancient sites, and are by name (1) the Jaffa Gate, or Hebron Gate, on the west, to which all the roads from the south and west converge. (2) The Damascus Gate, or Gate of the Column, on the north, from which runs the great north road, past the Tombs of the Kings, and over the ridge of Scopus, to Samaria and Damascus. (3) St Stephen's Gate, or Gate of my Lady Mary, or Gate of the Tribes, on the east, whence a road leads down to the bottom of the Kedron, and thence over Olivet to Bethany and Jericho. (4) The Dung Gate, or Gate of the Western Africans, on the south, and near the centre of the Tyropœan Valley. A path from it leads down to the village of Siloam. (5) Zion Gate, or the Gate of the Prophet David, on the summit of the ridge of the hill now called Zion. Besides these, there are two gates now walled up, one being the Gate of Herod, on the north side, about half-way between the Damascus Gate and the north-east angle of the city ; the other the Golden Gate, in the eastern wall of the Haram. The Arabs call this the Eternal Gate, and it is sometimes called the Gate of Repentance.

About one-sixth of the area of the city is occupied by the Haram or Sanctuary, on Mount Moriah, within which stands the great mosque, called the Dome of the Rock, and where also there is ample breathing space.

Jerusalem is not a fine city according to western ideas. It is badly built, of mean stone houses : and its streets and

lanes are narrow, dirty, and ill-paved. There are, however, some beautiful bits of architecture; there are the
grand walls of the temple area; and there is, above all,
the intense interest of its Scriptural associations.

Entering the city by the Jaffa Gate we find on our right
the citadel, with the so-called Tower of David. The street
right before us is now called the Street of David, and
descends eastward to the principal entrance to the Haram.
Another main street commences at the Damascus Gate and
traverses the city from north to south, passing near the
eastern end of the Church of the Holy Sepulchre, and
through the principal bazaar, and terminating a little east
ward of the Zion Gate. These two streets divide the city
into four quarters. The north-east is the Moslem quarter,
the north-west the Christian quarter, the south-west the
Armenian, and the south-east the Jewish. The Church of
the Holy Sepulchre is, of course, in the Christian quarter,
where also we have the Latin Convent, very conspicuous
from its lofty position near the north-west angle of the city.
In the Moslem quarter is the Serai or palace, and most of
the Consulates, and the beautiful little Church of St Anne.
The Armenian Convent, the largest building in the city,
occupies a noble site on the south-western hill. Near it, on
the north, is the English church. But by far the most remarkable and striking building in this quarter of the city is
the Citadel, whose massive towers loom heavily over all
around them. The Jewish quarter has no structure of note
with the exception of the new synagogues.

Jerusalem is not like Damascus, where the Moslem
religion and oriental customs are almost unmixed with
any foreign element, but is a city in which every form of
religion and every nationality of east and west are represented at one time. "So motley a crowd" (says Major
Conder) "as that which is presented daily in David Street
and in the market-place under David's Tower, is perhaps

to be found nowhere else. The chatter of the market people, the shouting of the camel drivers, the tinkling of bells, mingle with the long cry of the naked Santon, as he wanders, holding his tin pan for alms, and praising unceasingly "the Eternal God." The scene is most remarkable in the morning, before the glare of the sun, beating down on the stone city, has driven its inhabitants into the shadow. The foreground is composed of a tawny group of camels, lying down, donkeys bringing in vegetables or carrying out rubbish, and women in blue and red dresses slashed with yellow, their dark faces and long eyes (tinged with blue) shrouded in white veils, which are fringed perhaps with black or red. Soldiers in black and Softas in spotless robes are haggling about their change, or praying in public undisturbed by the din. Horsemen ride by in red boots with red saddles, and spears 15 feet long. The Greek Patriarch walks past on a visit, preceded by his mace-bearers and attended by his secretary. Up the narrow street comes the hearse of a famous Moslem, followed by a long procession of women, in white "izars," which envelop the whole figure, swelling out like balloons, and leaving only the black mask of the face-veil visible; their voices are raised in the high-pitched tremulous ululation which is alike their cry for the dead and their note of joy for the living. Next, perhaps, follows a regiment of sturdy infantry marching back to the Castle, with a colonel on a prancing grey—men who have shown their mettle since then, and fat, unwieldy officers, who have perhaps broken down under the strain of campaigning. Their bugles blow a monotonous tune, to which the drums keep time, and the men tread, not in step, but in good cadence to the music. If it be Easter the native crowd is mingled with the hosts of Armenian and Russian pilgrims, the first ruddy and stalwart, their women handsome and dark-eyed, the men fierce and dark; the Russians, yet stronger in build and more barbarian in air, distinguished from every other nationality by their unkempt beards, their long locks, their huge fur caps and boots. Not less distinct are the Spanish, Mughrabee, Russian, and German Jews, each marked by a peculiar and characteristic physiognomy."

Ten sects or religions are established in Jerusalem, and if their various sub-divisions are counted they amount to a total of twenty-four, more than half of which are Christian. The late Mr C. T. Tyrwhitt Drake gives the different races and creeds as follows :—

1. Abyssinians.
2. Armenians : (*a*) Orthodox, (*b*) Catholic.
3. Copts.
4. Greeks : (*a*) Orthodox, (*b*) Catholic.
5. Jews : (*a*) Ashkenazim, (*b*) Sephardim, (*c*) Karaite.
6. Latin or Roman Catholics.
7. Maronites.
8. Moslems : *Sunni*,—(*a*) Shafii, (*b*) Hanefi, (*c*) Hambeli, (*d*) Maleki. *Shiaï*,—Metawili, &c.
9. Protestants : (*a*) Church of England, (*b*) Lutheran.
10. Syrians : (*a*) Jacobite, (*b*) Catholic.

All these sects have their churches, synagogues, monasteries, hospices, which take up no inconsiderable portion of the square half mile of space within the city walls. Yet the population of Jerusalem was estimated at 20,000 in 1878, and there has been further influx since. But many of the new comers build dwellings outside the walls, and there is now quite a large suburb on the north-west.

The Haram esh Sherif, or Noble Sanctuary, on Mount Moriah, is a large, open space, of peculiar sanctity in the eyes of all true Moslems. Its surface is studded with cypress and olive, and its sides are surrounded in part by the finest mural masonry in the world. At the southern end is the Mosque El Aksa, and a pile of buildings formerly used by the Knights Templars; nearly in the centre is a raised platform paved with marble, and rising from this is the well-known Mosque, Kubbet es-Sakhrah, with its beautifully proportioned dome. Within this sacred enclosure stood the temple of. the Jews; but all traces of it have long since disappeared, and its exact position was a fiercely contested question before the time of the recent explorations.

The Haram is a quadrangle of about 35 acres in area. The angles at the south-west and north-east corners are right angles, and the south-east angle is 92° 30′. The true bearing of the east wall is 352° 30′ (general direction). The length of the south wall is 922 feet on the level of the interior. The west wall is 1601 feet long; the east wall, 1530 feet. The northern boundary for 350 feet is formed by a scarp of rock 30 feet high, projecting at the north-west of the Haram.

The modern gateways giving entrance into the interior are eleven in number: three on the north and eight on the west. Of the ancient gateways there were two on the south, now called the Double and Triple Gates; while east of the latter is the mediæval entrance, known as the Single Gate, beneath which Colonel Warren discovered a passage. On the east wall is the Golden Gate, now closed; and two small posterns in the modern masonry are found south of this portal. On the west wall the Prophet's Gateway (sometimes called Barclay's Gate) is recognised as the southern of the two Parbar (or Suburban) Gates, mentioned in the Talmud; while the Northern Suburban Gate appears to have been converted into a tank, and lies immediately west of the Dome of the Rock. (This is Tank No. 30, Ordnance Survey.)

The raised platform in the middle of the Haram enclosure has an area of about 5 acres, and is an irregular quadrangle. The Kubbet es-Sakhrah, or Dome of the

Rock, on this platform, covers the sacred rock, which rises 5 feet above the floor of the building, the crest being at the level 2440 feet above the Mediterranean. The Dome of the Chain is immediately to the east of the Kubbet es-Sakhrah.

The Jami'a el-Aksa, or "distant mosque " (that is, distant from Mecca), is on the south, reaching to the outer wall. The whole enclosure of the Haram is called by Moslem writers Masjid el Aksa, "praying-place of the Aksa," from this mosque.

Entering by the gate of the Cotton Bazaar we stand within the temple courts. Before us are the steps which lead up to the platform where shoes must be removed ; for while the outer court, like the old court of the Gentiles, is a promenade, the paved marble platform is a sacred enclosure, not to be trodden except barefoot.

Over the outer arcade of the Dome of the Rock runs the great Cufic inscription, giving the date of the erection of the building in 688 A.D. "The Dome of the Rock " (says Conder) "belongs to that obscure period of Saracenic art when the Arabs had not as yet created an architectural style of their own, and when they were in the habit of employing Byzantine architects to build their mosques."

From the bright sunlight we pass suddenly into the deep gloom of the interior, lit with the "dim religious light " of the glorious purple windows. The gorgeous colouring, the painted wood-work, the fine marble, the costly mosaics, the great dome, flourished all over with arabesques and inscriptions, and gilded to the very top—all this splendour gleams out here and there from the darkness.

And in honour of what is this beautiful chapel built? A low canopy of rich silk covers the dusty limestone ledge round which the " Dome of the Rock " has risen. According to Arab tradition this Rock of Paradise is the source of the rivers of Paradise and the Foundation-stone of the world. From this rock Mohammed ascended to heaven (here is the impression made by the hand of the angel Gabriel, who held the rock down to prevent it from following the prophet), and this Rock is the Place of Prayer of all the Prophets.

Even more mysterious than the Sacred Rock is the Sacred Well below it. Descending a flight of steps at the south-east corner of the rock we enter a cave, in the rocky floor of which is a circular slab of marble, which returns a hollow sound when struck, but which is never uplifted. The Arabs appear to regard it as the mouth of Hell, for they call it the Well of Souls, and have a dread of the consequences if any evil spirit should escape. It is a tradition that in the Temple the ark of the covenant used to stand over this cave, and that it was afterwards concealed in the cave, or below it, by Jeremiah, and still lies hidden beneath the sacred rock.

The ground of the Haram enclosure is honeycombed with tanks, into some of which the water finds its way by unknown channels. One of the tanks is called the Great Sea, and would hold 2,000,000 gallons of water; another would hold 1,400,000, and all the tanks together 10,000,000 of gallons at the least. This would be more than a year's supply for the city in its best days, a valuable resource in times of siege.

Solomon's Stables.—Under the Haram area, at the south-eastern part, are the vaults known as Solomon's Stables— thirteen rows of vaults of a variety of spans. They were used as stables by the Crusaders, and the holes in the piers by which the horses were fastened may still be seen. The name of Solomon's Stables is supposed to have been given by the Crusaders, who may, however, have been guided by some earlier tradition. The vaults are in part ancient and in part a reconstruction, probably about the time of Justinian (sixth century A.D.).

The Jews' Wailing Place.—Outside the Haram, on the west, and not very far from the south-west corner, is the Wailing Place of the Jews. From the Jaffa Gate we may reach it by going down David Street and through the fruit bazaar, and then turning through a by-lane. The Wailing Place is a narrow court, in which the temple rampart happens to be free and exposed in the Jews' quarter. Every Friday the court is crowded with Jews who come to read and pray, and bemoan the condition of their temple, their holy city, and their scattered people. The scene is striking from the great size and strength of the mighty stones, which rise without door or window up to the domes and cypresses above, suggesting how utterly the original worshippers are cast out by men of alien race and faith. Here we may see venerable men reading the Book of the Law, women in their long white robes kissing the ancient masonry, and praying through the crevices of the stones, Russian Jews, Spanish Jews, German Jews, men, women, and children, with gray locks, or blue-black hair, or russet beard, and dressed variously, according to their country— strange and unique is the spectacle! "It reminds one forcibly" (says Conder) "of the unchanged character of the Jews. After nineteen centuries of wandering and exile they are still the same as ever, still bound by the iron chain of Talmudic law, a people whose slavery to custom outruns even that of the Chinese to etiquette, and whose veneration for the past appears to preclude the possibility of progress or improvement in the present."

Pools and Fountains of Jerusalem.—Jerusalem is at present chiefly supplied with water by its cisterns. Every house of any size has one or more of them, into which the winter rains are conducted by little pipes and ducts from the roofs and courtyards. These private cisterns are generally vaulted chambers with only a small opening at the top, surrounded by stonework, and furnished with a curb and wheel. Many of them are ancient.

But besides these covered cisterns in the houses and courts, there are many large open reservoirs in and around the city.   In the upper part of the Valley of Hinnom, west of the city, is the *Birket el Mamilla*, often called the Upper Pool of Gihon.   Lower down in the same valley, and not far from the south-western angle of the city wall, is the *Birket es Sultan*, frequently called the Lower Pool. Because these pools are clearly related to one another as upper and lower, it has been usual to assume that they are upper and lower pools of Gihon, which seem to be referred to in 2 Chron. xxxii. 30, and elsewhere.   But although the Sultan's Pool has been called Gihon from the fourteenth century downwards, it is known to have been constructed by the Germans only two centuries before, and the word Gihon means a spring-head.   From the Sultan's Pool we may ride down the deep valley, on the south bank of which are the traditional Aceldama and the tombs of many Christian pilgrims, till we come to *Bir Eyub* (Joab's Well), where the Valley of Hinnom unites with the Valley of Kedron.   The Crusaders, who were never too well informed, identified Joab's Well with the Biblical En Rogel. From this place we ride northward to the junction of the Kedron wi· he Tyropœan, and there, in a verdant spot, we find the Pool of Siloam, with dry stone walls and a little muddy water.   With the village of Siloam on our right, we ride up the Kedron Valley some 300 yards, and arrive at the Fountain of the Mother of Stairs, also called the Virgin's Fountain.   Descending by a flight of sixteen steps we reach a chamber, its sides built of old stones and its roof formed of a pointed arch.   Then going down fourteen steps more into a roughly hewn grotto, we reach the water.   *Mejr ed Deir* states that the water of this fountain was a great test for women accused of adultery; the innocent drank harmlessly, but the guilty no sooner tasted than they died !   When the Virgin Mary was accused, she submitted to the ordeal, and thus established her innocence. Hence the spring was long known as the Fountain of Accused Women. Dr Robinson imagined that this was the true Bethesda, because the water is considered to possess healing virtue, and every day crowds of men and women, afflicted with rheumatism and other maladies, descend the steps and wait for the moving of the waters. The flow is intermittent—due, it is supposed, to a natural syphon—and the waters rise suddenly, immersing the folks, fully clothed, nearly up to the neck.

The water wells up in the cave, and when it has attained a height of 4 feet 7 inches runs away through a passage near the back, into a small tunnel, and goes to supply the Pool of Siloam.

About 100 yards north-east of St Stephen's Gate is the Pool of My Lady Mary, outside the walls.

Within the city, on your left as you enter by St Stephen's Gate, is the *Birket Israil*, Pool of Israel, the traditional Pool of Bethesda (but only so since the twelfth century). It is now a receptacle for ashes and rubbish of all kinds ; but it has at some time been used for water, for Warren found the bottom lined with concrete 16 inches thick.

Sometimes the Virgin's Fountain is spoken of as the only spring of living water at Jerusalem, but it is possible, as suggested by Warren, that another existed at the *Hammam esh-Shefa*, or Bath of Healing, in the Tyropœan. The entrance to the fountain is by a narrow opening in the roof of a house behind the bath.

We need only mention further the Pool of Hezekiah, a large reservoir which lies in the centre of a group of buildings, in the angle made by the north side of David Street and the west side of Christian Street. It is stated that a subterranean conduit from the *Birket el Mamilla* passes underneath the city wall near the Jaffa Gate, and supplies both the Pool of Hezekiah and the cisterns of the citadel.

In ancient times water was brought into the city by two aqueducts, the "low level" and the "high level," but the course of the former can alone be traced within the walls of the city. It crosses the valley of Hinnom a little above the *Birket es Sultan,* and winding round the southern slope of the modern Zion, enters the city near the Jewish alms-houses; it then passes along the eastern side of the same hill, and runs over the causeway and Wilson's Arch to the Sanctuary. The numerous Saracenic fountains in the lower part of the city appear to have been supplied by pipes branching off from the main, but the pipes are now destroyed, and the fountains themselves are used as receptacles for the refuse of the town. This aqueduct derived its supply from the Pools of Solomon (near Bethlehem), from *Ain Etan,* and a reservoir in *Wady Arûb,* and still carries water as far as Bethlehem; its total length is over 14 miles, not far short of the length of the aqueduct which Josephus tells us was made by Pontius Pilate.

The Pools of Solomon near the head of *Wady Urtas* are three in number; they receive the surface drainage of the ground above them and the water of a fine spring known as the Sealed Fountain. The pools have been made by building solid dams of masonry across the valley, and are so arranged that the water from each of the upper ones can be run off into the one immediately below it. The lower pool is constructed in a peculiar manner, which appears to indicate that it was sometimes used as an amphitheatre for naval displays; there are several tiers of seats with steps leading down to them, and the lower portion of the pool, which is much deeper than the upper, could be filled with water by a conduit from one of the other reservoirs.

The "high level aqueduct," called by the Arabs that of the Unbelievers, is one of the most remarkable works in Palestine. The water was collected in a rock-hewn tunnel 4 miles long, beneath the bed of *Wady Byar,* a valley on the road to Hebron, and thence carried by an aqueduct above the head of the upper Pool of Solomon, where it tapped the waters of the Sealed Fountain. From this point it wound along the hills above the valley of Urtas to the vicinity of Bethlehem, where it crossed the watershed, and then passed over the valley at Rachel's Tomb by an inverted stone syphon, which was first brought to notice by Mr Macneill, who made an examination of the water supply for the Syria Improvement Committee. The tubular portion is formed by large perforated blocks of stone set in a mass of rubble masonry; the tube is 15 inches in diameter, and the joints, which appear to have been ground, are put together with an extremely hard cement. The last trace of this aqueduct is seen on the Plain of Rephaim, at which point its elevation is sufficient to deliver water at the Jaffa Gate, and so supply the upper portion of the city; but the point at which it entered has never been discovered, unless it is connected in some way with an aqueduct which was found between the Russian convent and the north-west corner of the city wall.

The present supply of water is almost entirely dependent on the collection of the winter rainfall, which is much less than has generally been supposed, as, by a strange mistake, the rain-gauge was formerly read four times higher than it should have been. According to Dr Chaplin's observations, the average rainfall during the years 1860-64 was 19·86 inches, the maximum being 22·975 inches, and minimum 15·0 inches.

In addition to Bir Eyûb, which has been described above, the inhabitants draw water from the Fountain of the Virgin and the Hammam esh-Shefa.

[*Authorities and Sources:*—Smith's "Dictionary of the Bible." "Survey Memoirs," Jerusalem volume. "The Recovery of Jerusalem." Sir Charles Warren.

"Palestine." Major Conder. "Modern Jerusalem." C. F. Tyrwhitt Drake. "Walks about Jerusalem." W. H. Bartlett. "Quarterly Statements of P. E. Fund."]

2. *The Sieges of Jerusalem, and the Fortunes of its Walls.*

" In considering the annals of the city of Jerusalem," says Mr W. Aldis Wright, " nothing strikes one so forcibly as the number and severity of the sieges which it underwent. We catch our earliest glimpse of it in the brief notice of the first chapter of Judges, which describes how 'the children of Judah smote it with the edge of the sword, and set the city on fire;' and almost the latest mention of it in the New Testament is contained in the solemn warnings in which Christ foretold how Jerusalem should be compassed with armies, and the abomination of desolation be seen standing in the Holy Place. In the fifteen centuries which elapsed between these two points, the city was besieged no fewer than seventeen times; twice it was razed to the ground, and on two other occasions its walls were levelled. In this respect it stands without a parallel in any city ancient or modern."

The first siege appears to have taken place soon after the death of Joshua. The men of Judah and Simeon "fought against it and took it, and smote it with the edge of the sword, and set the city on fire " (Judges i. 8). Josephus adds that the siege lasted some time, and that the part of the city captured at last was "the lower," but that the part above them * was so difficult, by reason of its walls and from the nature of the place, that they relinquished their attempt upon it. As long as the strongest part of the city remained in the hands of the Jebusites they practically had possession of the whole. The Benjamites followed the men of Judah to Jerusalem, but

* ἡ καθύπερθεν **αὐταῖς**.

they could not drive out the Jebusites (Judges i. 21). A Jebusite city it remained until the days of David.

Jerusalem was taken by David, *circa* 1044 B.C. He took the castle of Zion, which is the City of David, and dwelt in the castle (2 Sam. v. 6; 1 Chron. xi. 4). Then David built round about, from Millo and inward, and Joab repaired the rest of the city.

As long as Solomon lived the visits of foreign powers to Jerusalem were those of courtesy and amity; but with his death this was changed. Rehoboam had only been on the throne four years when Shishak, king of Egypt, invaded Judah, and advanced against the capital. Rehoboam opened the gates to him, and Shishak did not depart without plundering the temple and the palace. B.C. 886.

In the reign of Jehoram, the son of Jehoshaphat, the Philistines and Arabians attacked Jerusalem, broke into the palace, spoiled it of all its treasures, sacked the royal harem, and killed or carried off the king's wives and all his sons but one. This was the fourth siege. B.C. 881.

Amaziah, king of Judah, victorious over the Edomites, was foolish enough to challenge Jehoash, king of Israel. The battle took place at Bethshemesh of Judah, 12 miles west of Jerusalem. Amaziah was routed, and the victorious Jehoash, after the gates of Jerusalem had been thrown open to him, broke down 400 cubits length of wall, from the Corner Gate to the Gate of Ephraim. (This must have been at the north-west part of the city walls, the favourite point of attack in after times.) B.C. 857.

King Uzziah, after some campaigns against foreign princes, devoted himself to the care of Jerusalem. He rebuilt the wall broken down by Jehoash, and fortified it with towers. In Uzziah's reign the city suffered from an earthquake; a serious breach was made in the Temple, and below the city a large fragment was detached from one of the hills and rolled down the slope, overwhelming the king's paradise or park. B.C. 770.

The hill above En Rogel was called Ophel, and might be otherwise described as the slope south of the Temple. The royal palaces were there, and it was protected by a strong wall. We have no record of the first erection of this wall ; but Jotham, the son of Uzziah, built much upon it, and also built the upper gateway to the Temple (2 Chron. xxvii. 3). According to Josephus, he also repaired the city walls wherever they were dilapidated, and strengthened them by very large and strong towers. B.C. 740.

Before the death of Jotham the clouds of the Syrian invasion began to gather, and they broke on the head of Ahaz, his successor. Rezin, king of Syria, and Pekah, king of Israel, joined their armies and invested Jerusalem (2 Kings xvi. 5). In a battle which took place outside the walls Ahaz was defeated. This induced him to send to Assyria and obtain help from Tiglath Pileser, whose vassal he became, and whose sun-worship he adopted. B.C. 730.

And now approached the greatest crisis that had yet occurred in the history of the city. Hezekiah reformed the worship and declined to be a dependent on Assyria. Sennacherib had succeeded Tiglath Pileser, and the dreaded Assyrian army approached. Hezekiah stopped the springs round Jerusalem, repaired the walls of the city, breaking down houses to get the material—even raised the wall in some places up to the towers ; and built a second wall at some exposed part, and strengthened Millo (2 Kings xx. 20; 2 Chron. xxxii. 3-5, 30; Isaiah xxii. 10). On this occasion it would appear that the city escaped, but at the cost of the treasures of the palace and the temple. B.C. 700.

In the middle of the long reign of Manasseh Jerusalem was taken by Assur-bani-pal, the grandson of Sennacherib. B.C. 650.

But Manasseh, in the latter part of his reign, sought to repair and strengthen the city. He built a fresh wall, extending "from the west side of Gihon-in-the-valley to the Fish Gate ;" and he also continued the works which had been begun at Ophel, and raised the structure to a very great height. B.C. 640.

During the reign of Jehoiakim Jerusalem was visited by Nebuchadnezzar, with the Babylonian army lately victorious over the Egyptians at Carchemish, and it is thought that there must have been a siege, but we have no account of it. Jehoiakim was succeeded by his son Jehoiachin, and hardly had his short reign begun before the terrible army of Babylon reappeared before the city, again commanded by Nebuchadnezzar (2 Kings xxiv). Jehoiachin surrendered, and the city was pillaged. Jehoiachin being carried off to Babylon, his uncle Zedekiah was made king ; but he was imprudent enough to seek the help of Pharaoh Hophra of Egypt, and upon this Nebuchadnezzar marched to Jerusalem again and began a regular siege. The walls and houses were battered by rams, and missiles were discharged into the town. After some delays a breach was made in the north wall, and the city suffered all the horrors of assault and sack. Zedekiah had stolen out of the city on the south side, but was pursued and overtaken. The Babylonians burnt the Temple, the palace, and other public buildings, and threw down the city walls. B.C. 577.

When Nehemiah obtained leave to return and rebuild the city of his fathers he found heaps of disordered rubbish everywhere on the ground. By his amazing zeal and energy he stirred up the people to work ; and in due time all the gates and walls were set up, on the old foundations. B.C. 457.

There is no need for us to pursue the history in detail. Further stormy periods succeed. B.C.

    Ptolemy, son of Lagus takes Jerusalem,   305.

    Antiochus the Great takes the city,   219.

	B.C.
Antiochus Epiphanes takes the city without siege,	170.
Antiochus Eupator takes the city,	163.
Jonathan builds a new wall,	143.
Simon takes the Akra citadel,	139.
Antiochus Sidetes besieges Jerusalem,	134.
Aretas, the Arab, besieges the city,	65.
Pompey takes the city,	63.
Antipater rebuilds the walls,	58.
Herod and Sosius take Jerusalem,	37.

	A.D.
Agrippa builds the third wall,	43.
Cestius Gallus attacks Jerusalem,	66.
Titus takes Jerusalem (fifteenth siege) and utterly destroys it,	70.
Bar Cocheba revolts,	132.
Bar Cocheba is expelled,	135.
Rufus ploughs the temple site,	135.
Hadrian founds Ælia Capitolina,	136.
The Jews revolt and are excluded from the city,	339.
Eudoxia rebuilds the walls,	450.
Chosroes II. takes Jerusalem,	614.
Omar the Caliph takes the city,	637.
Caliph Moez takes possession of the city,	969.
Turkomans expel Egyptians from the city,	1094.
The Egyptians retake Jerusalem,	1098.
Crusaders take Jerusalem (nineteenth siege),	1099.
Walls of Jerusalem repaired,	1178.
Saladin takes Jerusalem (twentieth siege),	1187.
Saladin repairs the walls of the city,	1192.
Melek el Muazzam dismantles the walls,	1192.
Frederic II. rebuilds the walls,	1229.
Daud, Emir of Kerak, destroys the walls,	1239.
Christians obtain Jerusalem by treaty,	1243.
Soliman the Magnificent builds walls,	1542.

A.D.

Muhammed Aly takes Jerusalem (no siege),   1832.
The Fellahin seize Jerusalem,   1834.
Syria and Jerusalem restored to Turkey,   1840.

In reflecting upon such a history as this, two things become very clear; the first is that the details of the events would be much better understood if we had an accurate map before us; the second is that the events themselves—the successive destructions and rebuildings—must have changed the city considerably from what it was. Even in the city of London the floors of Roman dwellings are found 15 or 18 feet below the present surface of the streets. In Jerusalem, we need not be surprised to learn, the depth of *debris* is much greater, and since it has accumulated chiefly in the valleys, and very nearly obliterated some of them, it has, of course, obscured the topography. An accurate map of modern Jerusalem is in our hands, but it does not show us what the ancient city was like. Therefore it is not sufficient to have this modern map before us when we read the ancient history. We read in the history that Zedekiah fled (from his palace) through the gate between two walls and by the way of the king's gardens; but in modern Jerusalem there is no king's palace or garden and no gate between two walls. The history describes how Nehemiah rebuilt the wall, from the Sheep Gate to the Tower of Meah, and thence to the Fish Gate, and the Old Gate, &c., but in modern Jerusalem we find no such places and names. We are still worse off when we read in Josephus about Titus encamping within the third wall, and then making a breach in the middle wall and encamping in the middle city, and still having a wall between him and the Jews in the Upper City: for the Jerusalem of to-day shows only one wall besides the rampart of the temple. Naturally there has been much conjecture concerning the ancient

P

city, and the best authorities have differed from one another in their ideas. It was with the hope of settling the disputed questions as well as with the object of uncovering antiquities, that the Palestine Exploration Society began the work of excavation.

It has often been said that there is not a single topographical question connected with ancient Jerusalem which is not the subject of controversy. This is, however, rather overstating the case, for there are points concerning which all authorities are in accord. First, as regards the natural features of the site, it is agreed that the Mount of Olives is the chain of hills east of the Temple Hill, and that the valley beneath it on the west is the Brook Kedron. It is agreed that the Temple stood on the spur immediately west of the Kedron, and that the southern tongue of this spur was called Ophel. It is also agreed that the flat valley west of this spur is that to which Josephus applies the name Tyropœan, although there was a diversity of opinion as to the exact course of the valley, which has now been set at rest by the collection of the rock-levels within the city. It is also agreed by all authorities that the high south-western hill (to which the name Zion has been applied since the fourth century) is that which Josephus calls the hill of the Upper City, or Upper Market Place.

The site of the Pool of Siloam is also undisputed, and the rock Zoheleth was discovered by M. Clermont Ganneau at the present village of *Silwan.* As regards the walls of the ancient city, all authorities, except Fergusson, agree in placing the Royal Towers (of Herod) in the vicinity of the present citadel, and all suppose the scarp in the Protestant cemetery to be the old south-west angle of the city. The Tyropœan Bridge—or stairway and arch—is accepted by all writers since Robinson as leading to the royal cloisters of Herod's temple, and all plans of Herod's temple start with the assumption that the south-west angle of its courts coincided with the present south-west angle of the Haram. All plans also agree in accepting the east wall of the Haram as an ancient rampart of the city. We have thus various data to begin with which must be considered as certain, because writers who differ on all other points agree on these.*

The "other points" upon which writers have differed may be stated as follows :—

1. What was the extent of the city on the north before the destruction of A.D. 70?

2. What was the line of the second wall, which bounded the city on the north, in those early times before there was any third wall, or any need of one?

3. What was the line of the south wall in Nehemiah's time, and again in the time of the siege by Titus?

4. Which is the true Mount Zion or City of David?

5. On what spot did the Temple itself stand within the Haram enclosure; and what were the limits of its courts, first in Solomon's day, and secondly, after they were enlarged by Herod?

6. Does the Church of the Holy Sepulchre stand upon the true site of Calvary?

7. What is the probable site of the royal sepulchres where David and so many other kings lie buried?

[*Authorities and Sources :*—Smith's "Dictionary of the Bible." "Survey Memoirs," Jerusalem volume.]

3. *Excavations at Jerusalem.*

In the beginning of 1867 Lieutenant Warren, R.E. (now Colonel Sir Charles Warren), began his work of excavation in Jerusalem, assisted by several corporals of sappers, and employing native Arabs as labourers. Scores of shafts

---

* "Survey Memoirs."

SPRING STONE OF ROBINSON'S ARCH.   (*By favour of the Palestine Exploration Fund.*)

were sunk through the accumulated rubbish, and were always carried down to the natural rock. In cases where the miners came upon artificial structures—arches, aqueducts, cisterns, or other works of man—they were carefully explored and measured, and plans of them made to scale. It was considered important to examine the underground masonry of the Temple rampart ; but as the walls are regarded as sacred, and it was desirable not to offend the susceptibilities of the inhabitants, this was accomplished by sinking shafts at a distance from the wall and driving lateral galleries. Sometimes when an unsympathising Turkish official came to inspect the works, a twist was given to the rope as he descended, and so, having lost his bearings, he could not be sure that he gazed upon the foundations of the Temple when they were really shown to him. The work was continued until the year 1870, and the results are recorded in the Jerusalem volume of the Memoirs. Let us now glance at some of the more striking discoveries on all the four sides of the Haram.

In the Tyropœan Valley.—On the west side of the Haram, about 39 feet from the south-western angle, a great stone is seen projecting from the wall. Dr Robinson, the American traveller, believed it to be the spring-stone of an arch—perhaps the first arch of a bridge going to the Upper City—but others took a different view, and the question could only be settled by excavation. The span of the arch, as deduced from the curve of the spring-stone, should be about 42 feet. At that distance from the wall Warren discovered the pier of the arch, resting on the rock at a depth of 42 feet. It is 12 feet 2 inches in thickness, 52 feet 6 inches in length (the spring-stone above ground is 50 feet) and is constructed of long drafted stones, similar to those in the wall, one of them being over 13 feet in length and weighing ten tons. Three courses of stones were in place on the eastern side and two on the western.

To the west of the pier is a rock-hewn channel, close to
the pier, with a perpendicular scarp below the pier of 4

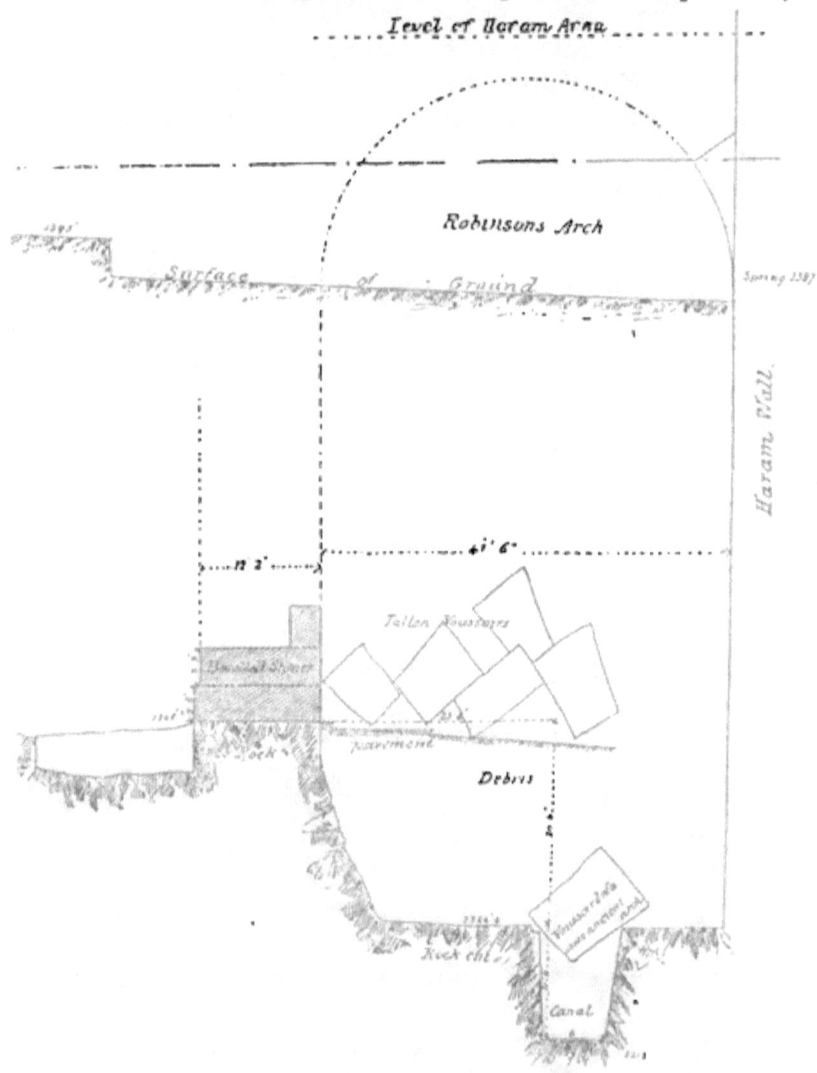

ROBINSON'S ARCH (SECTION.)   (*By favour of the Palestine Exploration Fund.*)

feet; and on the east side of the pier the rock is scarped
down nearly perpendicularly for a depth of about 18 feet.

But nearly on a level with the base of the pier, on the east side, a pavement extends from the pier to the Haram wall ; and on this pavement rest the fallen voussoirs of the arch. Below the pavement is a mass of *debris*, and in the bottom of the space is an aqueduct cut in the rock nearly 12 feet deep, arched over, but with the roof crushed in at one place by the voussoirs of a more ancient arch.

Following the aqueduct to the south we presently come to a pool or cistern, 16 feet in diameter ; and beyond this the channel turns the corner of the Haram and ends to-day in a drain. Following the aqueduct to the north it brings us to another pool, and presently to a third, this third one being partly underneath the wall of the Haram. The channel was evidently intended to supply the city with pure water, for after the *debris* had accumulated, shafts were made from the pavement before spoken of, to allow of buckets being let down.

The chief explorers, Warren and Conder, whose matured opinion is given in the Jerusalem volume of the Memoirs, find "no grounds for supposing that the roadway over Robinson's Arch led up to the Upper City, either by steps or by a bridge ; it was probably one of the suburban entrances spoken of by Josephus. There may have been other arches in continuation of Robinson's Arch, but there is no indication of this existing on the ground."

Proceeding from Robinson's Arch up the valley, we come to the Gate of the Chain, a chief entrance to the Haram. The street running westward from it is the Street of the Chain, and would bring us, with one little elbow, into David Street, whence we go straight to the Jaffa Gate. But in front of the Gate of the Chain it is found that the Street of the Chain passes over a fine arch (now called Wilson's Arch) 42 feet in span, like Robinson's Arch lower down. From an old book, called " La Citez de Jherusalem," we learn that the street coming south from the Damascus

Gate to the Dung Gate used to pass under this arch in the Middle Ages. The road passing over the arch is about 80 feet above the rock. But the rock under the western pier is 10 feet higher than under the Noble Sanctuary, and the lowest point in the valley is about 16 feet west of the Sanctuary wall. Westward of the pier the Street of the Chain rests upon a Causeway, made up of a complication of structures difficult to describe. There is a long passage or tunnel running along under the street, which for convenience is called the " Secret Passage." North of this run two parallel rows of vaults, which are broken up by more recent work, apparently Saracenic. But when the vaults were made they interfered at one place with a very ancient chamber of drafted stones, the " Ancient Hall," which has all the appearance of being one of the oldest buildings in Jerusalem. A shaft was sunk in the floor of the chamber to a depth of 11 feet 6 inches, through rough masonry as hard as a wall, but without finding rock. With regard to the Secret Passage, an Arabic writer, Mejr ed Din, says that the Street of David is " so named from a subterranean gallery which David caused to be made from the Gate of the Chain to the Citadel called the Mihrab of David. It still exists, and parts of it are occasionally discovered. It is solidly vaulted." It would, however, be unsafe to accept the Arab writer's opinion as to the date and use of the passage.

As touching the original contours of the ground, it appears from the excavations in the Tyropœan that two valleys descend, one from the Damascus Gate, the other from near the Jaffa Gate, and that they were originally very deep, giving the lower part of the north-western hill a rounded and gibbous form. The accumulation of rubbish at Wilson's Arch is 80 feet, at Robinson's Arch it is still more, and the true bed of the valley passes under the Haram and comes out on the south side at a distance of

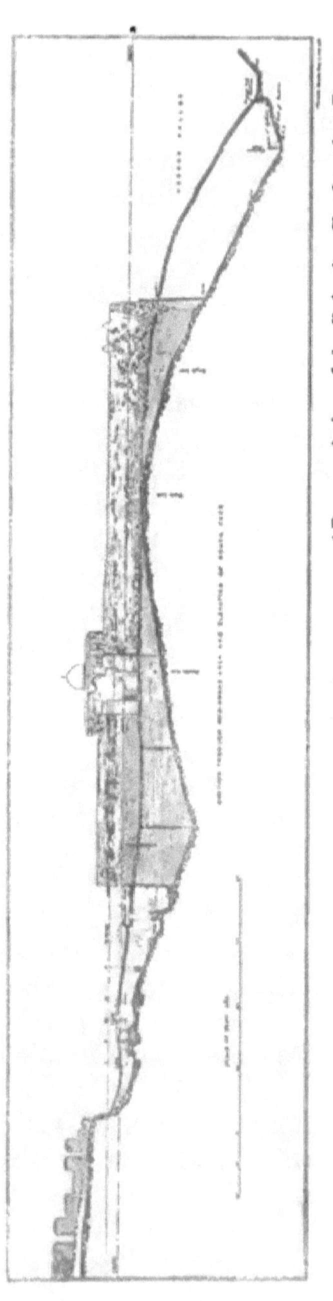

90 feet from the south-west angle. There is a steep scarp from the Upper City down to the present Tyropœan, and thence the rock shelves down to the ancient valley bed.

On the Ophel Hill.—Ophel is the southern slope of Mount Moriah; and as we stand on the slope, looking northward, we face the south wall of the Noble Sanctuary. Right in the middle of it is the Triple Gate, from which the surface of the ground shelves down 22 feet to the south-east angle, while westward it maintains its level. Yet really, in that western part (hidden from us just now by the wall of the city) the true bed of the Tyropœan runs out, and the depth of soil or rubbish is 85 feet. At the Triple Gate itself the rock is found about 2 feet below the sill; but at the south-east angle again we should have to sink a shaft 80 feet deep to find it. Thus the original surface of Ophel is all covered up, and its true contour disguised. Buried in the rubbish Warren has found the Wall of Ophel, abutting on the wall of the Sanctuary at the south-east angle. It is about 12 feet wide at the top and 15 feet at the bottom ; it runs southward for 76 feet, and then makes a bend to the west, in which direction it extends for 700 feet, and there ends abruptly. At the bend it is strengthened by a projecting tower, and below the bend there are several towers, one standing out very prominently. (*See* Plan of Haram Area, p. 212.)

The whole space of ground within this wall, wherever the spade was put in, proved to be rich in antiquities of various dates. One of the most interesting discoveries was that of a cavern with fullers' vats, close to the traditional spot where St James was thrown over the Temple wall and despatched by a fuller's baton.

At the South-Eastern Angle.—At this corner the wall stands about 70 feet high above the ground. At a height of 22 feet we observe the great stone which is estimated to weigh more than one hundred tons ;

and the courses below that have the appearance of being
ancient work. But we still have to go 78 or 80 feet beneath

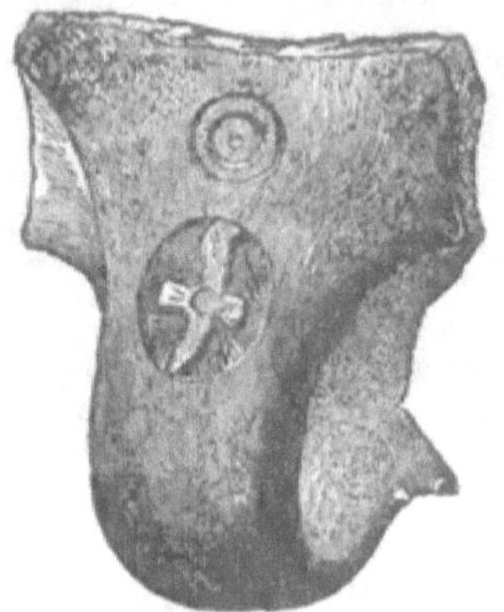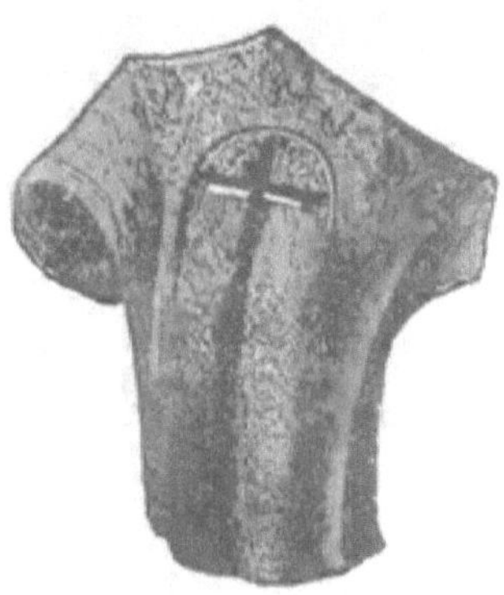

JAR HANDLES FROM SOUTH-EAST ANGLE.
(*By favour of the Palestine Exploration Fund.*)

the surface to find the foundations of the wall. It appears
that the lowest or foundation course is partially sunk in the

VASE FOUND AT S.-E. ANGLE.
(*By favour of the Palestine
Exploration Fund.*)

rock at the angle. When the
builders of the Temple came to
work here, they found upon the
rock an accumulation of 8 or 10
feet of fat mould, abounding in
potsherds. This they cut through
in order to lay their foundation
stones on the solid rock. In the
red earth were found fragments of
pottery and fat-lamps, which probably are of the earliest type of
lamp used in Jerusalem. Resting
on the red earth was a layer of
broken pottery, and in this was
found a rusty nail, some charred
wood, and several jar handles.
Some of these last had well-defined figures impressed on

them, resembling in some degree a bird, but believed to represent a winged sun or disc, possibly the emblem of the Sun god. On each handle, above and below the wings, are some Phœnician letters, corresponding in one case to LMLK ZPH, and in the other to LK SHT. At 3 feet east of the angle a hole was discovered scooped out of the rock, and in it was found a little earthen jar, standing upright as though it had been purposely placed there.

More interesting still, Warren discovered on some of the

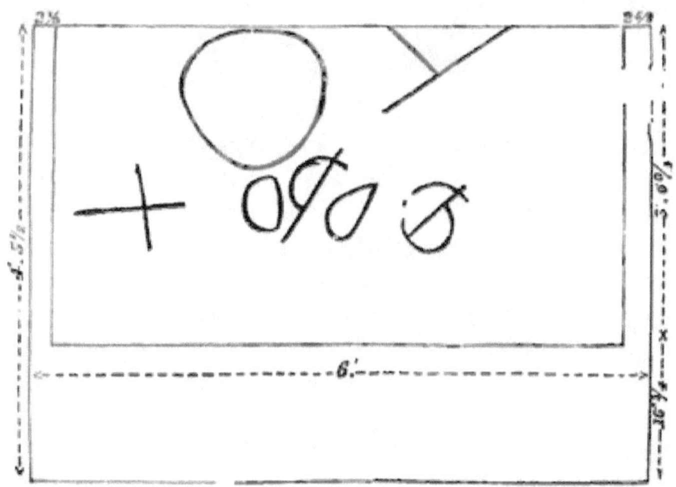

MASONS' MARKS, S.-E. ANGLE. (*By favour of the Palestine Exploration Fund.*)

lower stones near the south-east angle a number of marks in red paint, with two or three characters also inscribed with the chisel. The late Emanuel Deutsch declared them to be partly letters, partly numerals, and partly special masons' marks, exactly corresponding to some which he found on the substructures of the harbour of Sidon, and the very oldest ruins in the city of Tyre. As we know from the Bible that Solomon employed Phœnician masons to build the Temple, this discovery was thought at first to prove the Solomonic age of this part of the wall. But further reflection warns us that it is not of itself sufficient; the old alphabet might be but little changed in the days when Herod rebuilt the Temple, and the forms of masons' marks might be the same with Phœnicians and with Romans. As, however, they appear to be quarry signs, they seem to imply that the stones were shaped at the quarry, and not upon the ground, and thus support the Scripture statement that the Temple was erected without sound of axe or hammer. The same may be said of the marginal drafts or bevels, which on some stones are carried all round, on some round three sides, or only two, and exhibit no pattern or design when we look at the wall as a whole. The quarry whence the stones appear to have been brought is called the Cotton Cavern ; its entrance is outside the walls, east of Damascus Gate, and it extends under the north-eastern part of the city for more than a quarter of a mile. The cavern was not unknown in the time of the Sultans, but it was afterwards lost sight of, until in the year 1852, a dog scratching away the earth and stones, again uncovered the mouth of it. In this quarry we go over ground covered with chips, we see some blocks of stone in the rough, and others cut, and some only partially severed from the rock. We see also the places where lamps rested to give light to the workers. But in the fat mould at the angle of the wall we do not find any stone chippings.

In the Kedron Valley there is an accumulation of nearly 100 feet of loose stone chippings and other *debris*, lying against the wall of the Sanctuary, covering all the western side of the valley, and resting at its eastern part upon the slope of Olivet. The true bed of the Kedron is 40 feet west of its present surface bed. On the west side of the true bed was found a masonry wall, 3 feet thick ; and at intervals, as the rock rises other walls are encountered, built apparently for supporting terraces.

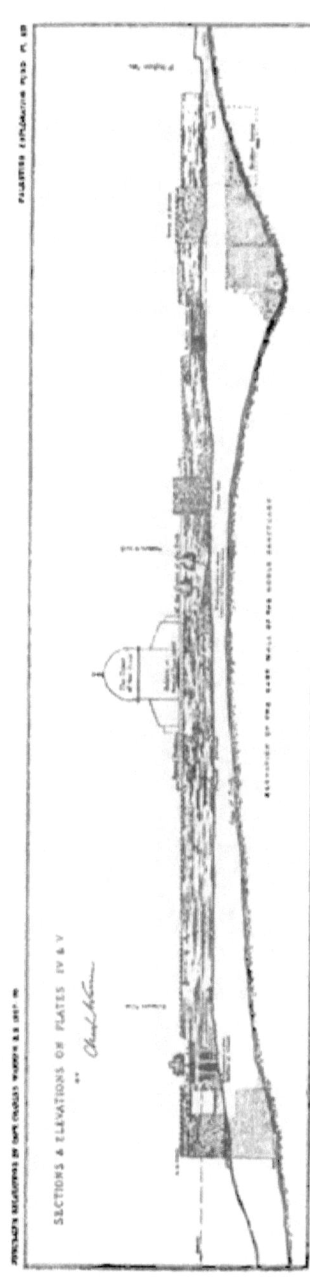

From the south-east angle the foundation of the wall rises, to about the middle of the eastern side, and then falls again, down to the Golden Gate and beyond. The construction of the Golden Gate is still a vexed question; it is possibly a reconstruction of comparatively late date, but it stands on the ancient foundations of a gateway, which in some measure correspond with those of the Triple Gate. North of the Golden Gate the rock still falls, and the depth of rubbish in the depression is in the deepest part 125 feet. Yet the wall is built up from the bottom, and is carried across the depression to the higher rock surface north of it. It extends beyond the north-east angle of the Haram without showing any break at that point ; and this seems to favour the idea that a break may be found more to the south, where the Haram terminated before Herod enlarged its area. In fact the masonry north of the Golden Gate is of a rougher sort than that south of it. But it is impossible to examine the buried portion of the east wall at all points, because a Mohammedan cemetery covers the ground, and excavation among the graves is forbidden. It was only by sinking shafts at a distance from the wall, and employing a method of laborious tunnelling, that the depth of the foundations could be ascertained. Warren's work hereabout has been pronounced by Sir Charles Wilson to be without a parallel in the history of excavation. "In one shaft alone no less than 600 feet run of shaft and gallery was excavated."

If we might only explore freely within this cemetery Warren is confident that we should come upon those huge stones—20 cubits long and 6 cubits thick—which Solomon laid down on this side when he built the temple (Josephus, Ant. xx. 9, 7). One would suppose that the present north-east angle, added by Herod, was of much later date than the south-eastern ; yet here again " Phœnician " masons' marks are found. Masons' marks, however, may have a tendency to remain the same through many ages. It is a curious fact that the red paint with which they were put on has "run" in one instance, while still wet, and the trickling is *upwards* as the stone stands in the wall. This shows that the marking was done before the stone was placed, and very likely at the quarry.

North of the Haram enclosure.—The excavations just referred to were sufficient to show that a deep valley once existed to the north of the Temple, as described by Josephus, in "Antiquities" xiv. 4, 2 and "Wars" i. 7, 3, where he states that Pompey found it a difficult business to fill it up. This valley commences to the north of the city wall, passes down west of the Church of St Anne, and runs into the Kedron, past the Sanctuary wall, at a distance of 145 feet south of the north-east angle. The great reservoir, called the *Birket Israil*, which extends along the northern side of the Sanctuary for 360 feet, lies across this valley. It is 126 feet wide and 80 feet deep. The west wall of the reservoir is rock, and the east wall is partly rock and partly masonry; while the south wall of the pool is at the same time the north wall of the Sanctuary.

The excavations on all sides of the Sanctuary, and the examination of the cisterns within the enclosure, show that Mount Moriah was originally somewhat pear-shaped in contour, the rock shelving off on all sides from the summit, which is now under the Dome of the Rock. At the north-western corner, however, the rock was high, and there was a narrow neck which joined this hill to Bezetha and made it a sort of peninsula in form. This neck has been artificially cut through.

The Tunnels from the Virgin's Fountain.—From the Virgin's Fountain, about 320 yards south of the Triple Gate, and on the eastern side of Ophel, a tunnel has been excavated through the hill to the Pool of Siloam. The distance between these two places is not much more than 300 yards, but the tunnel winds about and its length is 1708 feet (or 569 yards). Robinson and others had been through it, and found it difficult to traverse, for it is necessary to go part of the way crawling on hands and feet. Colonel Warren, accompanied by Serjeant Birtles and a fellah, patiently explored it, taking compass bearings at every turn, and giving us at last an accurate plan of it. It was no easy work crawling in three or four inches of water, recording observations with pencil and paper, and carrying candles at the same time. Nor was the business unattended with danger, for the flow of water being intermittent, and an unexpected flow occurring while they were in the tunnel, it proved very difficult to keep their mouths above water.

An inscription within this tunnel escaped the notice of all explorers until lately, and was not detected even by Warren.

The present Pool of Siloam measures about 55 feet

north and south by 18 feet east and west, and is about
20 feet deep.   At the north end an archway, 5 feet wide,
appears, leading to a small vault, 12 feet long, in which is a
descent from the level of the top of the pool to the level of

PLAN OF THE SILOAM TUNNEL.
(*By favour of the Palestine Exploration Fund.*)

the channel supplying it.   In the year 1880 one of the
pupils of Herr Conrad Schick, the architect of the Church
Missionary Society, while climbing down fell into the
water, and on rising to the surface noticed the appearance

of letters on the wall of the rock. The rock had been smoothed so as to form a tablet about 27 inches square, which contains six lines of writing on its lower portion. The inscription is about 5 yards from the mouth of the channel, and is on the right hand of an explorer entering from the Siloam end. It could hardly be read at first, because a deposit of lime had formed over it. Dr Guthe removed this by washing the tablet with a weak solution of hydrochloric acid. Major Conder, with the aid of Lieutenant Mantell, expended much labour and patience in taking a "squeeze," sitting for three or four hours cramped up in the water in order to obtain a perfect copy, and repeating the experience in order to verify every letter. Conder's squeezes were the basis of the earliest correct representation published in Europe. Professor Sayce, who had already visited the tunnel and made a provisional translation of the text, was now enabled to improve it; and the following is the translation :—

" 1. (Behold the) excavation ! Now this is the history of the excavation. While the excavators were still lifting up

" 2. The pick, each towards his neighbour, and while there were yet three cubits to (excavate, there was heard) the voice of one man

" 3. Calling to his neighbour, for there was an *excess* (?) in the rock on the right hand (and on the left ?). And after that on the day

" 4. Of excavating the excavators had struck pick against pick, one against another,

" 5. The waters flowed from the spring to the pool for a distance of 1200 cubits. And (part)

" 6. Of a cubit was the height of the rock over the head of the excavators." *

The meeting of the two parties of excavators near the

---

* This is Dr Sayce's improved translation, in " Records of the Past," Second Series, vol. ii. The inscription has since been cut out and stolen.

middle of the tunnel accords with Warren's discovery of two false cuttings, one on either side, at a distance of 900 feet from the Siloam end.

The inscription is in ancient characters, very much resembling those on the Moabite Stone, but possessing certain peculiarities. It is probably the oldest bit of Hebrew writing on stone that we possess, and opens out a new chapter in the history of the alphabet. It gives the first monumental evidence of the condition of civilisation among the Hebrews in the days of their kings; and altogether it is the most important discovery of the kind since the finding of the Moabite Stone.

Major Conder says that the general impression resulting from an examination of the conduit is that it was the work of a people whose knowledge of engineering was rudimentary. It is well known that in mining it is very difficult to induce the excavator to keep in a truly straight line, the tendency being to diverge very rapidly to one side. It is possible that this is the real reason of the crooked run of the canal; but another reason may have been the comparative hardness of the strata met in mining at a uniform level through a hill, with beds having a considerable dip. It will, however, be observed, that, after passing the shaft, the direction of the tunnel changes to a line more truly directed on the Virgin's Fountain. The excavators from the Siloam end became aware, probably by the impossibility of seeing a light at the head of the mine, when standing at the mouth of the tunnel, that they were not going straight, and the only means they had of correcting the error consisted in making a shaft up to the surface to see where they had got to. After ascertaining this they went straight for about 140 feet, and then diverged gradually to the left; but their general direction, nevertheless, agrees roughly with that of the rock contour, which may be due to following a particular seam of rock.

SHAFTS DISCOVERED AT THE VIRGIN'S FOUNTAIN. (By favour of the Palestine Exploration Fund.)

It is recognised by Colonel Warren that the tunnel running southward to the Pool of Siloam was not the first tunnel excavated in connection with the Virgin's Fountain. A channel had previously been made from the Virgin's Fountain due west, for a distance of 67 feet, into the heart of the hill, and there communicated by a shaft and corridors with the surface. When the longer tunnel came to be made the engineers wisely availed themselves of the channel already existing, and began their new excavation at a distance of 50 feet from the Virgin's Fount. The priority of the channel running due west to the shaft appears to be undoubted; and it is clear that whatever mistakes of direction might be made by unscientific engineers when they had got some distance into the hill, they never would *begin* by working due west from the Virgin's Fount when their object was to make a channel south-south-west to Siloam Pool.

At the bottom of the shaft, which is 67 feet due west, Warren found the rock scooped out into a basin 3 feet deep, for the water to lie in, and at the top of the shaft an iron ring to which the rope of the bucket could be tied. The shaft was 40 feet in height, and then the space began to open out westward into a great cavern, there being a sloping ascent at an angle of 45°, covered with loose stones of about a foot cube. Warren says it was ticklish work ascending, for the stones all seemed longing to be off, and one starting would have sent the mass rolling, himself with it, on top of the serjeant, all to form a mash at the bottom of the shaft. After ascending about 30 feet they got on to a landing. The cave now opened out to south-west and north-west. Following it in the latter direction they arrived at a passage 40 feet long, at the far end of which was a rough wall. Creeping through a hole in this they ascended a steep staircase for 50 feet, passed another wall, and found themselves in a vaulted chamber. The exit at last was on the Hill of Ophel, a few feet from the ridge, and almost certainly, some writers maintain, within the ancient walls. The object of the cuttings was to get a supply of water from within ; and perhaps the piles of loose stones which were found in the long passage were intended to be thrown down the shaft if an enemy should attempt to ascend it. In the passage were found three glass lamps of curious construction, placed at intervals as if to light the way; and in the vaulted chamber a little pile of charcoal as if for cooking, one of these lamps, a cooking dish glazed inside, for heating food, and a jar for water. Evidently the place had been used as a refuge.

A similar arrangement for closing the entrance to a spring, and using a secret passage from the hill above, has lately been discovered at *El Jib* (ancient Gibeon),* and only a few years ago at *'Amman* (Rabbath Ammon). In connection with the latter, Conder quotes Polybius to the effect that when Antiochus the Great besieged the forces of Ptolemy Philopater, at *Amman*, in 218 B.C., the garrison held out until a prisoner revealed a secret communication with a water supply outside the walls.

Difficulties of the Work.—It is impossible to read the detailed accounts of Warren's work at Jerusalem without feeling an admiration for the courage and patience of the explorers, and without being sometimes amused at the ludicrous predicaments into which they occasionally got. They have been jammed in aqueducts, wedged in chasms, and walled up behind falling heaps of *debris*. They have had to go down ladders too short for reascending, to squeeze down apertures that have taken the skin off the shoulders, and have been half drowned in cisterns at the bottom. In the Tyropœan the soil is so soaked with sewage that it poisons the flesh wherever it touches a scratch. In the Kedron Valley the soil is so loose that it rushes into the

* " Quarterly Statement," Jan. 1890.

galleries, almost flowing like a fluid, and drives the men out. In the Siloam tunnel they more than once ran the risk of being drowned. In the Ophel shaft a loose stone, weighing eight cwt., threatened momentarily to fall upon their heads. Once when the Arab labourers had gone down a shaft, where the ancient bed of the Tyropœan runs out, 90 feet from the south-west angle, they had descended 79 feet when they came upon a stone slab. They began breaking it up with a hammer, when presently the pieces fell in, the hammer disappeared, and the men, in terror lest they should fall into unknown depths, rushed to the surface, sought out the serjeant, and assured him that they had found the bottomless pit! The awful depth proved to be just 6 feet more to the solid rock!

Warren had often to dig in people's gardens, or to mine under their houses, or sink shafts near to their sacred places, and it required much tact to deal with the prejudices of the Mohammedans, and to satisfy all claims for compensation. In the neighbourhood of Jerusalem a piece of garden ground may belong to one man, be rented by another, while a dozen people claim an interest in the crops that grow upon it. Sometimes Warren's labourers have been dragged before the judges and threatened with imprisonment, or told that they shall be sent to do forced labour on the Jaffa Road. When Warren was working at the Virgin's Fountain there was much commotion among the people of Siloam. Work was to be resumed in the morning; but one cantankerous sheikh, taking it into his head that Englishmen had no business out of their own country, effectually stayed proceedings by sending a bevy of damsels to the Fount to wash. On one occasion a Turkish officer of Engineers, dressed in full uniform, approached, in no friendly spirit, to examine one of the shafts. If he had chosen to give an adverse report the work would have been stopped. He knew that Warren was in command, but he marched magnificently past him without deigning to notice him, and was going straight for the head of the shaft. But Warren passed on rapidly before him, threw over the ladder which some lady visitors had been using, blew out the light, and descended by a rope. The Turk, hearing a crash, and seeing Warren disappear in the darkness, was afraid that something terrible had occurred, which he did not wish to be responsible for, and lost no time in turning his steps away. But, after all, when we consider that the Sanctuary at Jerusalem is as sacred to the Mohammedans as the precincts of Westminster Abbey to ourselves, it is marvellous how much Sir Charles Warren succeeded in effecting, and with how little friction he did it.

[*Authorities and Sources :*—" Quarterly Statements of P. E. Fund." " Recovery of Jerusalem." Sir C. Warren. "Tent-Work in Palestine." Major Conder.]

5. *Jerusalem as it was.*

The Hills and Valleys.—Sir Charles Warren was the first to point out the necessity of ascertaining the depth of the rock below the present surface, in as many places as possible, and of referring all the measurements to one fixed datum, the level of the sea. In the study of the ancient topography the original appearance of the ground is the first consideration, for although a certain amount of soil may always have existed, still the ancient surface must have conformed far more closely to that of the rock than does the present.

To this work very great attention has been given, first by Warren himself, in his exploration of numerous tanks and sinking of scores of shafts ; next by Herr Schick, who, in his professional capacity of architect, has measured the position when sinking foundations for houses in every quarter of Jerusalem. Contours had also been given in the Ordnance Survey conducted by Sir C. Wilson in 1864. At length Conder was able to take all the data and send home a plan of rock levels for the entire city. From this he also prepared a reduced shaded sketch of the original rock site of the town. The sketch is here reproduced, and by the help of it the reader will find it comparatively easy to understand Josephus's description, as well as the reconstruction of the ancient city which will be attempted in this section.

Josephus says—" The city of Jerusalem was fortified with three walls, on such parts as were not encompassed with unpassable valleys, for in such places it had but one wall. The city was built upon two hills, which are opposite to one another, and have a valley to divide them asunder, at which valley the corresponding rows of houses on both hills end. Of these hills that which contains the Upper City is much higher and in length more direct. Accordingly it was called the Citadel (φρούριον) by King David, but it is by us called the Upper Market Place. But the other hill, which was called Akra, and sustains the Lower City, is curved on both sides (ἀμφίκυρτος).* Over against this was a third hill, but naturally lower than Akra, and parted formerly from the other by a broad valley. However, in those times when the Maccabees reigned, they filled up that valley with earth, and had a mind to join the city to the temple. They then took off part of the height of Akra, and reduced it to be of less elevation than it was before, that the temple might be superior to it. Now the Tyropœan Valley, as it was called, and was that which we told you before distinguished the hill of the Upper City from that of the Lower, extended as far as Siloam." (Wars, v. 4, 1.)

* Might mean **arched, or** gibbous, **or** humped.   Conder **understands** it " rising to a peak." Q. S.   Oct. 1873.

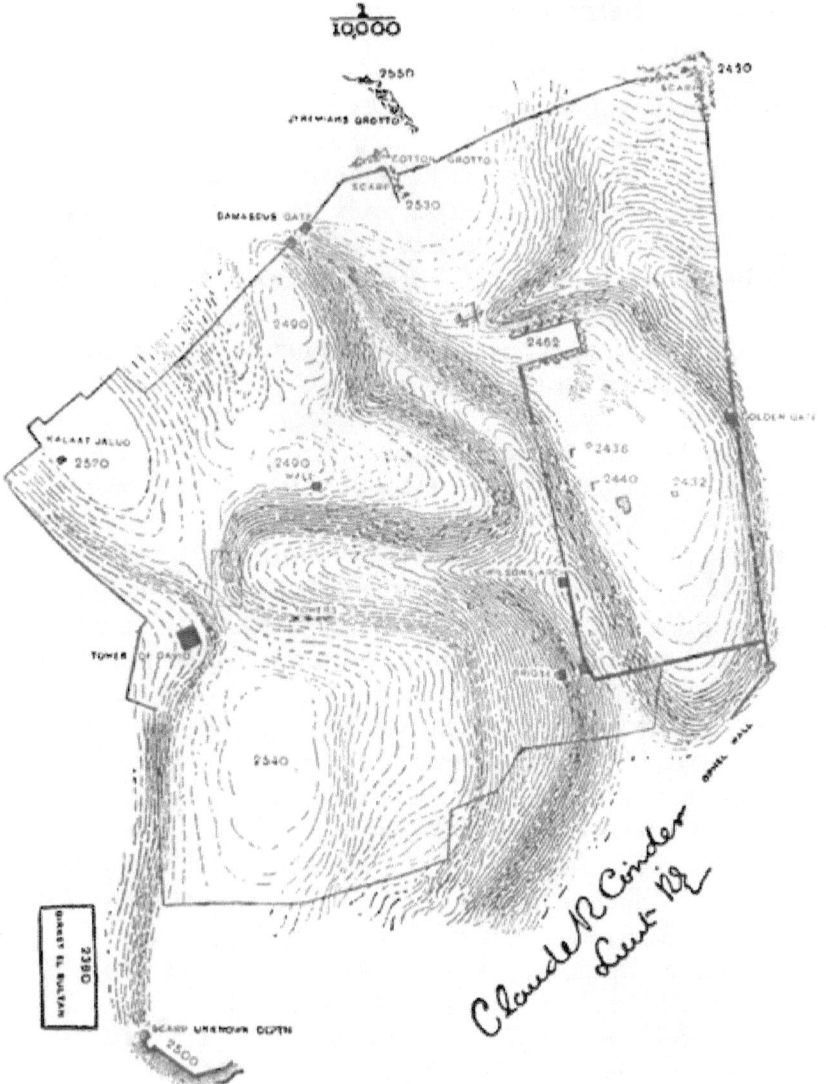

ROCK SITE OF JERUSALEM. (*By favour of the Palestine Exploration Fund.*)

In the next section Josephus tells us that as the city grew more populous it crept beyond its old limits, "and those parts of it that stood northward of the temple and joined that hill to the city, made it considerably larger, and occasioned that hill, which is in number the fourth, and is called *Bezetha* (or New City), to be inhabited also. It lies over against the Tower of Antonia, but is divided from it by a deep valley, which was dug on purpose, and that in order to hinder the foundations of the Tower of Antonia from joining to this hill."

When we read these descriptions in the light of our plan, things become tolerably plain. The south-western hill was the Upper City—a large flat-topped hill surrounded with deep valleys, and having a level of about 2550 to 2500 feet above the sea. The eastern hill is known to be the Temple Hill, which is number three in Josephus's description. Bezetha (number four) is distinctly described as the hill north of the Temple Hill, and only divided from it at one point by an artificial cutting. The explorers have found this cutting, carried through a narrow neck of high ground, at the north-western corner of the Haram. Thus there is no room to question that "the second hill, which was called Akra and sustained the Lower City" is the hill projecting down from the north-west like a promontory, gibbous in its form. The Upper City was divided from Akra "by a broad valley," now partly filled up, which was called the Tyropœan Valley, and beginning near the Jaffa Gate, "extended as far as Siloam Fountain." The summit of Akra is not more than 2480 feet above sea level—considerably lower than the Upper City—and looks lower than it is, because the whole site of Jerusalem is tilted up from the west like an inclined plane, and because the valleys about the Upper City are deeper. Josephus says the Akra hill used to be higher, and sustained the Macedonian fortress called the Akra, which dominated the

Temple. Being so near and so high, it enabled the garrison to look down into the Temple courts. They used also to run out and molest the Jews who were passing from the Upper City into the Temple by the western gate (Joseph. Ant. xii. 9, 3; 1 Macc. i. 36; and Warren in "Transactions of the Society of Biblical Archæology," vii. 314).

The Macedonian fortress was a thorn in the side of Jerusalem until Simon Maccabæus captured it and demolished it. At the same time he cut down the top of the hill itself; and perhaps it was with the material so obtained that he filled up the valley between Akra and the Temple. By the filling up of this valley, which it is convenient to call the Asmonean Valley, the two hills were joined together; and it would not be surprising if the terms "Akra" and "Lower City" soon after began to have an extended meaning, and to embrace all the buildings on both the hills which were now united into one.

Having now a definite conception of the original lie of the ground, and knowing the four hills of Jerusalem by name and location, we can proceed to plant a few of the ancient buildings in their proper places.

The Temple of Solomon.—We have already seen reason for placing the Temple over the very summit of Moriah; but we must now make our reasons quite conclusive, and also show the limits of the Temple courts.

In the first place the summit of the mountain is the natural position for the Temple, rather than any position on the slope. The rock called the Sakhrah and the Foundation-stone of the World has been sacred from time immemorial. It seems to be referred to in Isaiah xxviii. 16—"Behold, I lay in Zion for a foundation a stone, a tried stone, a precious corner (stone), of sure foundation." Ezekiel also, with Josephus and the Talmud, all agree in placing the temple on the summit of the mountain (Ezek. xliii. 12).

As remarked by Dr Chaplin,* the question whether the "stone of foundation" was a portion of the solid rock or a movable stone is one of considerable interest in connection with the topography of the Temple. If the former, it will be easy to fix with all but absolute certainty its position, and from it as a starting-point, to lay down the sites of the temple, altar, and courts with no more uncertainty than the uncertain value of the cubit renders inevitable. The use of the word *Eben* would imply that it was a movable stone, but its (supposed) history, as given by the Rabbis, quite removes it from the category of ordinary stones, and represents it as the centre or nucleus from which the world was founded. The *Toldoth Yesu* represents it as a movable stone, and states that King David, when digging the foundation of the temple, found it "over the mouth of the abyss" with THE NAME engraved upon it, and that he brought it up and placed it in the Holy of Holies. "On the whole" (says Dr Chaplin) "it is difficult to come to any other conclusion than that the stone which the Rabbis write about was a portion of rock projecting three finger-breadths upwards from the floor of the Holy of Holies, covering a cavity which was regarded as the mouth of the abyss, reverenced as the centre and foundation of the world, and having the ineffable name of God inscribed upon it."

The statements made in the Talmud and repeated over and over again with great accuracy by Rabbinic writers, supply us with the following precise information : (1) The stone of foundation (in other words, the solid rock) was the highest point within the Holy of Holies, projecting slightly above the floor, and from it the rock sloped downwards on all sides. (2) A "solid and closed foundation," 6 cubits high, was made all round the house in order to raise the floor to (within three finger-breadths of) its summit. On the eastern side this solid foundation was covered by steps

* "Quarterly Statement," January 1876.

leading down to the court, 22 cubits below the summit on that side. We must agree with Dr Chaplin that the summit of the Sakhrah under the great Dome of the Rock is the only spot in the whole enclosure which answers to these data.

The Holy House, with its courts, was not in the centre of the enclosure, but had a position north-west of the centre. The altar court was at a lower level than the Holy House; and lower still, by successive descents, were the court of Israel, the court of the women, and the court of the Gentiles. The courts being in terraces one above another, and the Holy House at the summit, the temple was a far more conspicuous object than is the Dome of the Rock at the present day.

The Talmud describes the Temple area as 500 cubits square. The prophet Ezekiel says " it had a wall round about, the length five hundred and the breadth five hundred, to make a separation between that which was holy and that which was common " (xlii. 20). Then we are told by Maimonides, the learned Jewish writer, that " the men who built the second temple, when they built it in the days of Ezra, they built it like Solomon's, and in some things according to the explanation in Ezekiel."

Taking then the centre of the Sakhrah as the centre of the Holy of Holies, and allowing ourselves to be guided by the Talmud measurements, which are given with great exactitude, we shall not be far wrong if we draw the boundaries as follows :—On the north, the northern limit of the present platform, the line of which if continued eastward would cut the east wall of the Haram a little north of the Golden Gate. The platform is raised 12 feet above the present general surface of the Haram enclosure. One day when the rain had loosened a stone near the north-eastern corner of the platform and revealed the existence of vaults, Warren went down and took

measurements; and it appears that the northern end of
the platform consists of rock which has been scarped away
perpendicularly. On the south the boundary would come
to within a few feet of the entrance of El Aksa mosque,
and would fall short of the south wall of the Haram by
300 feet. On the east and west the boundaries would fall
a little way within the present walls of the Haram. We
may reasonably conclude that the present east and west
walls of the Haram either represent walls of the Temple
enclosure, or else were built a little without them, as
retaining walls for gradually accumulating *debris*.

When the Temple of Solomon was destroyed, with all
the buildings that surrounded it, the *debris* would be piled
up in the courts. Probably it would never be thought
worth while to remove it all from the lower courts, but
rather to cover it over and lay a neat pavement on the
surface. Spaces and corners where the rubbish was less
gathered would be filled in or built up to complete the
levelling ; and as the rubbish increased, both within and
without the walls, after successive sieges, the walls
themselves were further built up, to keep them of sufficient
height. It never was intended in the first instance, to
build walls up from the foundation and make them 150
feet high. By successive changes, the result of calamities
as much as the fruit of improvement, the terraced mountain
grew to be an elevated plateau, such as the Haram
enclosure is at the present day. Josephus says that when
Herod rebuilt the Temple he extended the area of the
courts and made it twice as large as it was before. With
that, however, we need not concern ourselves while we are
seeking to restore the city of Old Testament times.

Solomon's **Palace** we find reasons for placing south of
Solomon's **Temple**, on the slope of the terraced mountain,
with its south-eastern angle coinciding with the present
south-eastern corner of the Haram. Those deep-buried

stones with the Phœnician masons' marks upon them may be the very foundation stones of the palace. The palace was a great work, and occupied thirteen years in building. It was necessary to build up at this corner, but as soon as a level was reached that permitted the work to be carried through from east to west, the six-feet course was laid as the true base for the more splendid super-structure. This six-feet course extends for 600 feet westward from the south-east angle, and gives us the limit in that direction. Northward we are limited by the courts of the temple to 300 feet. This, then, is where Sir Charles Warren places Solomon's palace, and these are the dimensions he assigns to it. Mr James Fergusson had already been led, from architectural reasons, to consider it an oblong of 550 feet by 300. The level of the six-feet course is 60 feet below the summit of the mountain. A patient examination of the wall led Warren to the con-clusion that all below this great course is old work, and that the walls of the Haram generally correspond to the description of Josephus, in whose day the great wall of Solomon still existed.

The Temple and the palace being thus located, there is left, beyond the west end of the palace, a plot of ground, 300 feet square, not enclosed at the time we are speaking of, although at the present day it forms the south-western corner of the Sanctuary and has the mosque El Aksa covering it. But the great depression of the Tyropœan Valley falls just there, and it would not be raised and enclosed until a late day. Warren says, in the "Recovery of Jerusalem" : "Our researches show that the portion of the wall to the west of the Double Gate is of a different construction to, and more recent than that to the east. This is a matter of very great importance, and, combined with other results, appears to show the impossibility of the Temple having existed at the south-west angle, as restored by Mr Fergusson and others. The only solution of the question I can see, is by supposing the portion to the east of the Double Gate to have formed the south wall of Solomon's palace, and that to the west to have been added by Herod when he enlarged the courts of the Temple."

Before this addition was made the south wall was but 600 feet in length. The Triple Gate stood in the middle of it, and as we have seen, it is exactly on the ridge of the hill. The sill is 38 feet below the present level of the Sanctuary, and from the gate three avenues ascend gently to the Sanctuary floor. May they not represent " the way by which Solomon went up to the House of the Lord " ?

The Wall of Ophel, as already described, has been discovered by Warren, and abuts against the south-eastern angle of what we are now prepared to regard as Solomon's palace.

The Tower of Antonia.—Josephus tells us that the tower which Herod built and named in honour of Antony stood on a rock 50 cubits high, at the north-west corner of the Temple. The rock was separated from Bezetha by a cutting made on purpose, yet the tower was so near to Bezetha that it adjoined the New City. At the same time it was so near to the Temple that the south-eastern turret overlooked the Temple courts, while passages from the tower led to the west and north cloisters. This description is precise enough. As Conder says, there is just such a rock fortress in the north-west part of the Haram. It is a great scarp, with vertical faces on the south and north, standing up 40 feet above the interior court, and separated from the north-eastern hill of Jerusalem by a ditch 50 yards broad, in which are now the Twin Pools— the Bethesda of St. Jerome. This block of rock is " the top of the hill " spoken of by Josephus, and occupies a length of 100 yards along the course of the north wall of the Haram. No other such scarp exists in or near the enclosure of the High Sanctuary. Can we then hesitate to place Antonia here?

Herod, after all, only repaired and strengthened this tower, for it had been built by Hyrcanus and passed under the name of Baris before being renamed Antonia, and even Hyrcanus was not the first at this work (page 265).

[*Authorities and Sources:*—" Quarterly Statements of P. E. Fund." "The Recovery of Jerusalem." Sir C. Warren. "The Works of Josephus."]

5. *The Walls and Gates of the City.*

"Even stone walls," says Mr Lewin, "cannot fail to awaken some degree of interest, when it is remembered that upon the result of the inquiry depends the question, Where was Calvary? and where the Holy Sepulchre?" If we desire to understand Old Testament events as well as those of the Gospels we shall take some interest in the question of the correct line of the walls. The walls were perambulated by Nehemiah's two companies on the Thanksgiving Day; certain of the gates are mentioned by name in connection with events of the history; and our reading of the narrative will gain in vividness if we can follow the events like those acquainted with the ground.

The First Wall, or Wall of the Upper City.—Josephus says there were three walls; but as the third or most northerly was not built until A.D. 43, we will leave it out of account for the present. We shall endeavour to fix the lines of the walls and the positions of the gates as they were in Nehemiah's time, and then we shall have those of still earlier date, for Nehemiah only repaired walls and gates which had been thrown down, and did not build afresh.

Beginning at the remarkable neck of land near the present Jaffa Gate a wall ran eastward along the northern brow of the hill, and in the line of the Causeway, and

ended at the west cloister of the Temple. This was the
north wall of the Upper City. That city had a wall all
round it ; and on the west, south, and east the wall simply
followed the brow of the hill. From the Jaffa Gate it ran
southward (facing westward) along the brink of the Valley
of Hinnom, by Bethso (the Hebrew term for Dung place)
to the Gate of the Essenes. At the south-west corner of
the hill an escarpment of the rock was noticed by Robinson ;
was further traced by Mr Maudslay, who in 1872 found
there a tower, reached by rock-cut steps ; and is clearly
marked in Conder's plan. From this corner the wall faced
the south for a while, and then, according to Josephus, made
a bend above Siloam ; and this must have been, as Mr
Lewin points out, a bend up the Tyropœan Valley, along
the edge of the High Town (to the Causeway), and then
back again along the edge of the Low Town on Ophel
(until it joined the Wall of Ophel discovered by Warren).
The wall from Siloam, we learn from Josephus, bending
there, faced to the east at Solomon's Pool, and holding on
as far as the place called Ophla, joined the eastern cloister
of the Temple.* The eastern cloister of the Temple—*i. .*,
the south-eastern angle of the enclosure—was, in Josephus's
day, coincident with the south-east angle of Solomon's
palace of earlier time ; and the city wall which joined it
was the Wall of Ophel itself.

According to this description Solomon's Pool was in the
Tyropœan Valley, between the two walls of the High
Town and the Low Town. Probably at a very early
period many houses were built in this valley, and it became
an intramural suburb. In view of war it would be deemed
necessary to protect it ; and for its defence the most
obvious plan would be to build a dam or a wall athwart
the valley. Such a work would greatly strengthen the
city itself, by preventing all access up the valley, especially

* "Wars" v. 4. 2.

if the mound or wall was aided by a castle at the Ophel end of it. We shall see reason to believe that the dam and the castle were built and were called Millo and the House of Millo. The suburb thus became immured in the city, but continued to be called the Suburb; and we read that the west wall of the Temple enclosure had two gates leading to the Suburb (Josephus, "Antiquities" xv. 11, 5; 1 Chron. xxvi. 16, the gate Shallecheth).

The course of the first wall as thus described by Josephus does not appear to differ much from its course in Nehemiah's time; and in all essentials it seems to be the wall of David's day, preserved upon the old foundations. Josephus indeed states as much in the following passage :—"Now of these three walls, the old one was hard to be taken, both by reason of the valleys and of that hill on which it was built, and which was above them. But besides that great advantage as to the place where they were situated, it was also built very strong ; because David and Solomon and the following kings were very zealous about this work."

The Second Wall.—The description of the second wall, given by Josephus, is short, and may be quoted entire, " It took its beginning from that gate which they called Gennath, which belonged to the first wall; it only encompassed the northern quarter of the city, and reached as far as the tower Antonia."

The necessity for this wall arose as follows. Through the increase of the population a suburb had sprung up, not only in the upper reach of the Tyropœan Valley, but on the hill beyond it. On the spur of this hill, which projected toward the Temple, stood the Akra fortress, but north-west of the fortress the ground was high and open, and unprotected by any deep valley. To protect this suburb it was necessary to carry a wall across the saddleback, sweeping round from the corner of the High Town to the

north-west corner of the eastern hill; and this was probably done as early as David's day.

There is not now much difficulty in finding approxi-
mately the position of the gate Gennath, the starting point
of this wall. We observe on Conder's plan of the rock
site that a narrow ridge runs north and south, immediately
east of the Tower of David, and separates as a shed the
broad head of the Tyropœan from the western valley. The
Tyropœan deepens very suddenly, and any wall carried
across it would of necessity be commanded by the ridge
to the west of it. The only sensible course for the builders
was to carry the wall along the ridge itself, on ground
commanding all without it. Exactly along this ridge, at
its western side, a wall was discovered in the year 1885,
during the rebuilding of the Greek Bazaar. At a depth
15 feet below the present street Dr Merrill found two
layers of stone, and at some points three, still in position ; and the stones were of the same size and character
as the largest of the stones in the Tower of David opposite.
Broken Roman pottery was found in these excavations,
and a stone ball, such as the Romans used in warfare.
The discovery of these foundations enables us to lay down
the second wall for a distance of 40 or 50 yards, with accuracy.* Thus we know where the wall began, and where
it ended. Its intermediate course can only be ascertained
by arguments of probability, and by mapping every bit of
ancient wall uncovered in connection with building operations and the making of drains. Upon the true course of
this wall depends the answer to the question whether the
site of the Church of the Holy Sepulchre was without the
the city or within. We are contented here to adopt the
line of wall arrived at by Herr Conrad Schick, who has
studied the question on the ground, who is acquainted with
every bit of ancient wall that has come to light, and has a

* "Quarterly Statement," Jan. 1886.

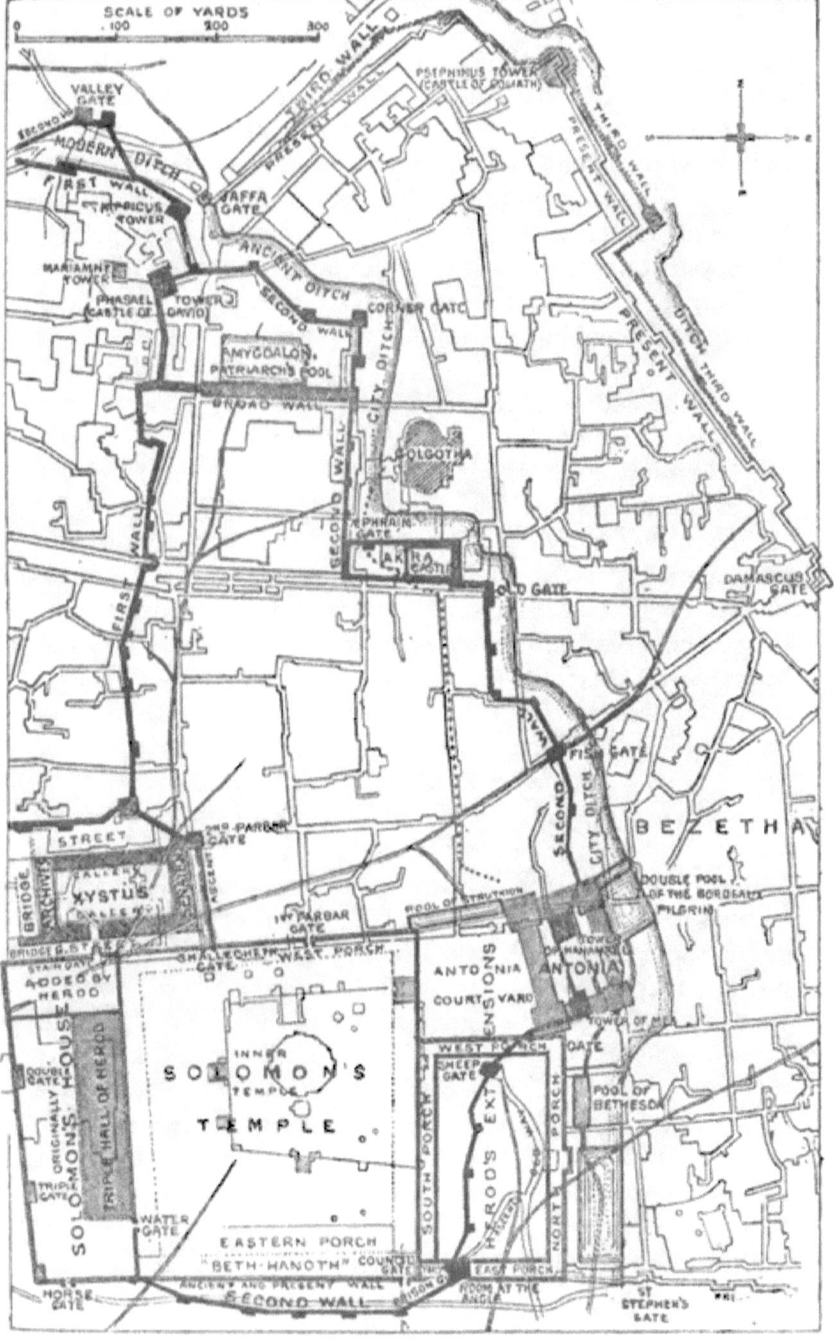

SCHICK'S LINE OF SECOND WALL.

reason for every twist and turn and every gate and tower here represented. It will be seen by his plan that he does not stop at the Tower of Antonia, but continues his line of wall so as to defend the northern and eastern sides of the Temple. This is required by Nehemiah's descriptions. But when Herod enlarged the Temple courts, if not before, these portions of the wall would be interfered with—the northern portion would be removed, the eastern portion had perhaps become buried—and so Josephus is silent about them.

With the course of the walls thus definitely marked out, it becomes possible to follow the descriptions in the Book of Nehemiah, and to identify the towers and gates and places there mentioned.

Nehemiah's Night Ride to Survey the Ruins.—Jerusalem had been destroyed by Nebuchadnezzar's general, and although the Chaldeans entered by a breach on the north side, they afterwards burnt the palace and every great house, and brake down the walls of Jerusalem round about (2 Kings xxv. 4). Nehemiah returned from the captivity to rebuild the city of his fathers, and prudently decided to make first a quiet survey of the extent of the destruction.

In chapter ii. 13, we read, "I went out by night by the Valley Gate, even towards the dragon's well, and to the Dung Gate." This Valley Gate was at or near the Gennath Gate, at the head of the Tyropœan Valley, and at the same time close to the Valley of Hinnom. It could not be far from the present Jaffa Gate. The Dung Gate—Josephus's "Bethso"—comes between the Jaffa Gate and the south-west corner of the city; a position also required by chap. iii. 13. "Then I went on to the Fountain Gate and to the King's Pool." The Fountain Gate would be a convenient exit from the city to a path leading down to Siloam Pool; The King's Pool (*el-Berekath*) was probably Solomon's Pool, mentioned by Josephus as being by the

east face of the old wall.   In after times it would be called
in Scripture the King's Pool, because it was appropriated
and used by Solomon's successors, just as Solomon's Palace
is called the king's house in Neh. iii. 25.   This pool would
be within the protected suburb.   Nehemiah continues,
" But there was no place for the beast that was under me
to pass."   Why? Because here we have two walls in a
narrow space, and the destruction of both of them had
filled the valley with *debris*.   "Then I went up by the
brook (*nachal*, the Kedron) and viewed the wall : and I
turned back and entered by the Valley Gate, and so
returned."

The Rebuilding of the Walls and Gates.—Nehemiah decides
that the walls can be and shall be rebuilt ; and he parcels
out the work among forty-six of the principal people, who
each have their retainers.   The work is sacred, and is ap-
propriately begun by the high priest, who naturally selects
a spot near the Temple—the Sheep Gate of the city wall,
which would seem to have been about mid-way between
the north-eastern and north-western corners of the temple
area of that time.   The description of the repairs takes us
westward, or to the left, and carries us all round the city
to the same point again.   "Then Eliashib the high priest
rose up with his brethren the priests, and they builded the
Sheep Gate ; they sanctified it, and set up the doors of it ;
even unto the tower of Hammeah * they sanctified it, unto
the tower of Hananel."   These two towers, we may suppose, with Mr Lewin and Herr Schick, already occupied
the site of the future Antonia.   In fact they were parts of
the Baris or Castle where Nehemiah himself intends to
reside (Neh. ii. 8, where the Hebrew word is the
Birah).

---

* In the Authorised Version it is Meah, in the Revised Version Hammeah.
It might be translated Tower of the Hundred.

After these towers of the Baris the various gates and places come before us in the following order :—

The Fish Gate, placed in Herr Schick's plan where the first main line of street ran out into the country.

The Old Gate, where the next main line of street ran out. It is where these two roads cross one another that we get, at a later period, the Damascus Gate set up. Streets running direct towards a city wall seem to demand a gate in that wall to complete their usefulness.

Next we have the Throne of the Governor-beyond-the-River. This, like the preceding, is some structure occurring in the course of the wall. In chap. ii. 7, 9, the phrase "beyond the river" seems to mean westward of the Jordan, where the district was governed by a viceroy of the king of Assyria. The viceroy lived or had lived in Jerusalem,[*] and his castle appears to have come into the line of the second wall, in the part which is south-east of the Church of the Holy Sepulchre, and perhaps exactly at the re-entering angle.

The Broad Wall, which is named next, was not necessarily broad in itself. Open spaces, such as we should name Squares, were in Jerusalem called Broads. There was one such broad space south of the Temple water gate, on Ophel, in which the people sometimes assembled (Neh. viii. 1 ; Ezra x. 9). There seems to have been another near one of the city gates, where Hezekiah addressed the people, alarmed at the approach of Sennacherib (2 Chron. xxxii. 6). Sennacherib would approach the city on the north-west, and the people were very likely gathered by the Valley Gate discussing the matter, in an open space afterwards utilised by the construction of the "Pool of Hezekiah." The "Broad" wall might be so called from running along one side of this broad space. It perhaps started from the second wall at the point which Nehemiah's

* Ezra iv. 16, 20 ; v. 3, 6 ; vi. 6, 8, 13 ; viii. 36.

description has now reached, and extended southward to the wall of the high town, and so constituted an inner line of defence. Nothing is said of repairing it : perhaps it had not been thrown down ; or, as an inner wall, Nehemiah neglects it for the present, as he does also the north wall of the Upper City. At any rate the description carries us beyond it. At the north-west angle of the second wall there was a Corner Gate (2 Kings xiv. 13 ; 2 Chron. xxv. 23), which is called also the Gate that Looketh. A gate here would command a view of the city walls as far as the Fish Gate on the one hand and the Valley Gate on the other. But this gate also is passed over in the present description.

We have next the Tower of the Furnaces, probably west of the " Pool of Hezekiah." The word may mean hearths furnaces, ovens, or altars ; but we cannot say to what it related.

And then we come to the Valley Gate, which we have already seen must have been near the present Jaffa Gate, and probably was exactly where the present David Street passes the end of the wall discovered, by the Greek Bazaar, in 1885. Unless a gate existed there, the street would lose half its use. Yet there is Herr Schick's alternative, that the name was given to a gate south-west of the Citadel, and opening on to the Valley of Hinnom.

In verse 13, from the Valley Gate it is " 1000 cubits on the wall to the Dung Gate." This forbids any identification with the present dung gate, in the Tyropœan, and fixes within a little the position of *Bethso.*

In verse 15, Shallun, who repairs the Fountain Gate, repairs also " the wall of the Pool of Shelah by the king's garden." Allow that Shelah is Siloam, yet this need not be a wall running down to Siloam—if we were to take that line we should go wrong all the rest of the way—it is

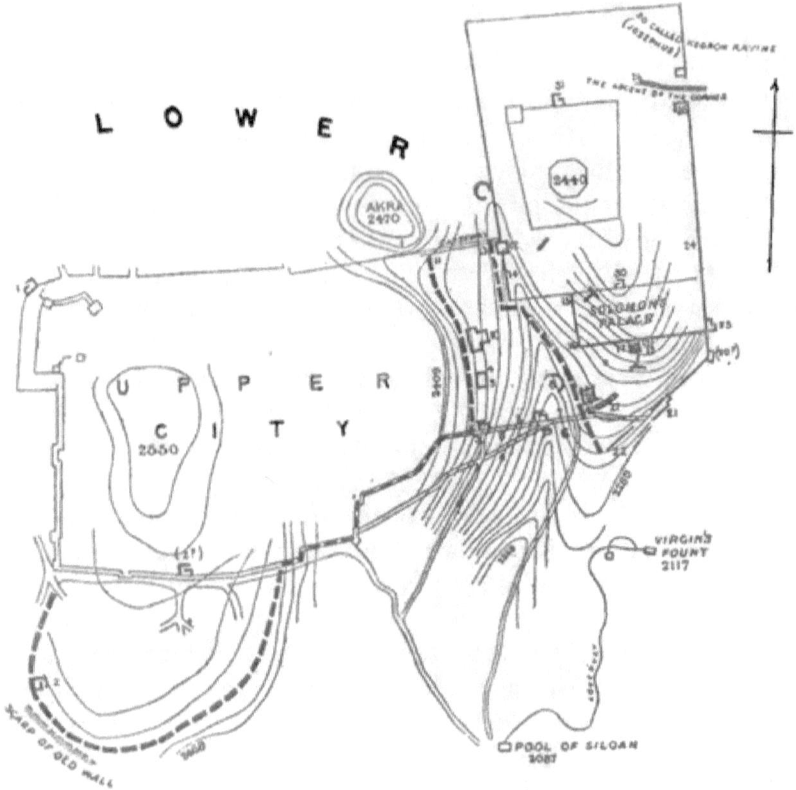

NEHEMIAH'S SOUTH WALL, ACCORDING TO GEORGE ST CLAIR.

*** The contour lines represent successive steps of ten feet. The height at the Triple Gate
is 2379 feet.

REFERENCE.

Suggested line of wall ▬▬▬

1 Valley gate.
2 Dung gate.
3 Fountain gate.
4 King's pool.
5 Wall of Pool of Shelah.
6 King's Gardens.
7 Stairs of the City of David.
8 Sepulchres of David.
9 The Pool that was made.
10 House of the mighty.
11 Turning of the wall.
12 The Armoury.
13 Turning of the wall.
14 House of Eliashib.
15 Turning of the wall.
16 The Corner

17 Turning of the wall.
18 Tower at King's house.
   (Tower that standeth out.)
19 Water gate.
20 Tower that lieth out.
21 Great Tower that lieth out.
22 Wall of Ophel.
23 Horse gate.
24 Houses of priests.
25 Gate Miphkad.
26 Ascent of the corner.
27 Going up of the wall.
28 House of David.
29 Gate between two walls.
30 Gate of the Guard (2 Kings. xi. 19).
31 Gate of the Guard (Neh. xii. 39).

the transverse wall in the same valley above. Through a gate in this wall the Pool of Siloam would be conveniently reached from the Suburb; and this would be the "Gate between two walls," through which Zedekiah fled away (2 Kings, xxv. 4; Jer. xxxix. 4; lii. 7). The wall was by the king's garden (*le* = by or near). Shallun pursues his work along the transverse wall eastward "unto (*ad*) the Stairs (*maaloth*) that go down from the City of David." So the City of David includes Ophel, and the Stairs descend the Ophel slope westward into the bed of the Tyropœan.

Verse 16, "After him repaired Nehemiah, the son of Azbuk, unto the place over against (*neged* = in front of) the sepulchres of David." The wall of the Pool of Shelah was an offshoot from the wall of the High Town, so the writer returns and continues his description of the wall of the High Town. Nehemiah, the son of Azbuk, takes up the repairs at the Fountain Gate and works northward. He comes over against the royal sepulchres, which are therefore on the Ophel side of the Tyropœan, a little north of the Stairs. The entrance would have to be low down in the valley bed to be outside the wall which protects Ophel on the west; but there is no reason why it should not be low down. The only doubt we need have is whether the spot marked in the plan is quite far enough north. In either case the excavations for royal tombs were so extensive as at length to approach the south wall of the Temple, perhaps even to touch the wall (at a point now under the mosque El Eksa). This is complained of by the prophet Ezekiel as a desecration. "The house of Israel shall no more defile my holy name, neither they, nor their kings, by their whoredom, and by the carcases of their kings in their death; in their setting of their threshold by my threshold, and their door-post beside my door-post, and there was but the wall between me and them" (Ezek. xliii. 7, 8).

Nehemiah, the son of Azbuk, continues working northward "unto the pool that was made" (*berekah*, probably the "king's pool" of ii. 14, and the "reservoir between two walls" of Isaiah xxii.). He goes on "unto the house of the mighty men." If this is the house of the king's bodyguard, the men of war mentioned in 2 Kings xxv. 4, we shall find that they are conveniently placed about midway between the armoury and the king's house.

In the remaining short space on the west side of the Tyropœan we have no less than four bands of workers, indicating that the destruction had been very great, as indeed Nehemiah found it to be when there was no possibility of his beast getting along ; and the next indication of locality is in

Verse 19, " the turning " of the wall, "over against the ascent to the armoury." The armoury, therefore, was in or near the north-eastern angle of the suburb.

Verse 20. We are now carried from "the turning " of the wall by the armoury, southward, " unto the door of the house of Eliashib, the high priest ; " and we are not surprised to find his house here, for we are close alongside the Temple courts. The workers come *unto* the door of Eliashib's house, which thus seems to project westward, so as to be quite near to the line of wall ; but they only come *over against* the less important houses which follow.

Verse 24. The sixth worker down this side comes to "the turning " of the wall and "unto the corner." The turning is not the same as the corner ; the Hebrew language uses different words for a re-entering and a salient angle. Each of the two turnings at the causeway (vv. 19, 20) is called a *miqtzoa* (= a re-entering angle) ; but now, in v. 24, they come to a *miqtzoa* and to a *pinneh* (= a projecting angle). It is to be observed that we should not have such angles at this part but for the vacant square which Warren's examination of the masonry compelled him to leave—the wall for 300 feet each way from the south-west corner of the Haram being more recent than the rest.

The first salient angle is passed over because the worker who begins north of it continues his labours till he comes south of it, and so its mention is not necessary in defining the work done. (In like manner, in vv. 6-8, the Gate of Ephraim is passed by without mention, although, according to xii. 38, 39, it existed between the Broad Wall and the Old Gate; and the Corner Gate, which we know existed, is passed over by Nehemiah.)

Verse 25. The mention now of another re-entering angle might perplex us, only that the same verse speaks of a "tower standing out from the king's upper house," and this may easily afford the angle.

Verse 26. We are now fairly on the Hill of Ophel, and accordingly the workers who have been set to labour here are "the Nethinim dwelling in Ophel." There is also mention in v. 31 of a house of the Nethinim near the northern end of the east wall—still outside the Temple precincts.*

As soon as the Nethinim of Ophel get far enough south to look beyond the projecting tower and see the Triple Gate, they are stated to be over against the Water Gate. Lewin says that "the Water Gate proper was that of the inner Temple, to the south of the altar, and led down to the great southern gate of the outer Temple, which was probably also called the Water Gate." The Nethinim find themselves at the same time looking eastward, or their wall facing toward the sun-rising. They are also over against the tower that standeth out. This is not the tower mentioned in the previous verse as projecting from the king's house, but may perhaps be the one at the bend of the Ophel wall, discovered by Warren.

Verse 27. Where the Nethinim cease their work it is taken up by the Tekoites, who presently come " over

* The Nethinim were but servants of the Levites.

against the great tower that standeth out," namely, the large tower which Warren found.   This identification struck Warren himself, and he mentions it in the " Recovery of Jerusalem," p. 295. It now wanted but a little extension of the work to complete the junction with the Wall of Ophel, at the point where Warren found that wall to end abruptly, and the narrative tells us that the Tekoites effected the junction.

Verse 28. The Ophel Wall being in good repair, is no more referred to ; but the next thing mentioned is the Horse Gate. As Warren could not find any gate in the Ophel Wall, the Horse Gate must have been north of it ; and here it would be at a point convenient for entrance to Solomon's Stables, which would be under the palace, and perhaps under the present vaults known as Solomon's Stables.   There is a depth of about 100 feet of unexplored rubbish between the floor of Solomon's Stables and the rock at the south-eastern angle.   The true stables may lie buried in this rubbish.

" Above the Horse Gate repaired the priests, every one over against his own house."   These houses of priests are in a position exactly corresponding with the house of Eliashib and others on the west side.   The expression "over against," implies that the city wall which is being repaired stands removed from the priests' houses, which border the Temple courts, and it would be eastward of the present Haram wall.   Herr Schick draws it so.

Verse 29. An East Gate is referred to (*Mizrach*), not to be confounded with the Gate Harsith, the so-called East Gate of Jeremiah xix. 2 in the Authorised Version.   It may be the Shushan Gate, which, according to the Talmud, stood over against the east front of the Temple.

When we come over against the Golden Gate—which Nehemiah calls the Gate Miphkad—we are just where Warren's tunnelling work was arrested by a massive masonry barrier—probably a part of the ancient city wall —50 feet east of the Haram wall. The wall was built of large quarry-dressed stones, and was so thick that a hole made into it for 5 feet 6 inches did not go right through. A few feet north of the Golden Gate the wall began bending north-west, as though following the contour of the hill ; and Warren was also led to suspect that the wall is a high one, extending upward through the *debris* to near the surface, since immediately above it, in the road, there are some large roughly-bevelled stones lying in the same line.*

In Nehemiah's description we are now immediately at "the ascent of the corner" (*pinneh*, a projecting angle). There is no corner now visible at the surface immediately north of the Golden Gate, and no ascent from a depth. But we have seen already that the northern cloister of the Temple would strike the east wall of the Haram a little north of the Golden Gate, and consequently here would be the *corner* of the Temple courts. We have also seen that the rock now shelves down to the north, for the valley from Herod's Gate came out here, and at 300 feet north of Golden Gate the rubbish is 125 feet in depth, so that from this low ground there would be an *ascent* in turning west. The wall itself would go up, ascending toward the ridge of the hill. There is no more likely spot for the elbow of the wall than that marked by the little building called the Throne of Solomon. The great depth of the valley here gave fearful height to the corner tower ; and eastern imagination would be not unlikely to suggest that only Solomon or the demons could have built it.

Having reached "the ascent of the corner," one more band of workers brings us to the Sheep Gate, where the description began.

The Route of the Processionists.—Chapter xii. affords striking confirmation of the foregoing positions. At the

* "Recovery of Jerusalem," pp. 155-9.

dedication of the walls two companies start from the Valley
Gate and go opposite ways to meet in the Temple.　Presumably the Valley Gate was chosen to afford journeys of
about equal length ; and this is another indication that the
wall did not go down to Siloam.　The party going south
pass the Dung Gate, and reach the Fountain Gate.　And
now which way will they go ?　The wall has been repaired
right ahead of them, and also the wall turning north, and
they will have to choose between two routes.　The Revised
Version says they went " by (*ad*) the Fountain Gate and
straight before them," and ascended *by* the Stairs of the
City of David at the going up of the wall (not *by* this time,
nor really " at," but " *in* "—*ba-maaleth le-chomah, i.e., in* the
stairway of the wall *by* the Stairs of David—a different
stairway from the Stairs of the City of David, which
descended into the valley bed).

Their way up these stairs and beyond carried them "above
the house of David, even unto the Water Gate."　The
house of David here is close by the king's garden of iii. 15 ;
and its position on the slope of the hill suggests a reason
for calling Solomon's palace the king's upper house (or
high house, iii. 25).　Some say "the house of David"
means David's tomb ; but if that be so, it only confirms
the position which I am led to assign to the tomb.　Observe
also that the position required for the Water Gate here is
again that of the present Triple Gate, the same as in iii. 26.

It deserves particular attention that the processionists
pass quickly from the Stairs of David to the Water Gate,
whereas in the rebuilding, these two places are very wide
apart, because the bend of the wall is followed.　In iii. 15,
we have the Sepulchres, the Pool, the House of the Mighty,
four more bands of workers, the turning of the wall, the
armoury, the house of Eliashib, the turning, the corner, and
the outstanding tower—all between the point over against
the Stairs of David and the Water Gate ; but none of these

things come in the route of the processionists. This is
easy to understand if the wall makes a bay up the
Tyropœan, for then the short cut in the text corresponds
with the short cut in the plan; but it can hardly be made
intelligible on any plan which omits this bay and carries
the wall down to Siloam.

A superficial objection may be raised that the detour up
the valley and *vià* the causeway, avoided by the processionists, would be avoided by Nehemiah in repairing the
walls, for why should he do more than repair the short
transverse wall, when his object was speed? My reply
would be that his object was strength and safety as well as
speed. The transverse wall was no sufficient protection by
itself, there being an easy approach up the valley, but it
was valuable as an addition to the inner walls. Besides,
Nehemiah had workers enough to be engaged at all these
parts at once, so that the completion of the work was not
at all delayed by repairing the two north-and-south walls
of the bend simultaneously with the cross wall, and indeed
with the walls all round the city.

The second company, with whom was Nehemiah, started
from the Gate of the Valley simultaneously with the first;
and the earliest note of their progress is that they pass the
Tower of the Furnaces and reach the Broad Wall. We
now, of course, meet with the places in the reverse order to
that in which we made their acquaintance, in following the
builders from east to west. The order then was—

Sheep-Gate.
Tower of the Meah.
Tower of Hananel.
Fish Gate.
Old Gate.
Broad Wall.
Tower of the Furnaces.

Passing these now, in reverse order, we find the Gate of Ephraim noticed, between the Broad Wall and the Old Gate. I incline to place the Gate of Ephraim at the junction of several streets near the north-east corner of the Muristan, and I will give two reasons. (1) Taking the wall as drawn by Schick, a principal street of the city going west abuts upon the wall at that point and requires a gate. (2) A Corner Gate existed, apparently at the north-western angle of the second wall, west of the Broad Wall ; the distance between the Corner Gate and the Gate of Ephraim was 400 cubits (2 Kings xiv. 13 ; 2 Chron. xxv. 23) ; and the place now proposed for the Gate of Ephraim corresponds to that distance. It may be that the tower of this gate was the throne of the governor, the viceroy of the Assyrian king.

Nehemiah's company having at length reached the Sheep Gate entered the Temple courts and stood still in the Gate of the Guard.

Thus the two companies stood on the north and south sides of the altar, and rendered thanksgiving to God, for that an unbroken wall once more protected Jerusalem.

The line of wall being established, with the positions of David's house, the gate between two walls, &c., we are confirmed in our conclusion that the City of David was the eastern hill and included Ophel. We see whereabouts the royal supulchres are likely to be found by future excavation. We gain something immediately by being able to follow step by step the work of Nehemiah. And this is not all, for we obtain fresh light upon the history of the house of David at various points.

[*Authorities and Sources :*—The author himself is responsible for the views of Jerusalem topography set forth in this volume. The reader who wishes to consult other writers may find the following references useful :—

"Jerusalem, a Sketch." By Thomas Lewin. "Siege of Jerusalem." Thomas Lewin. "Antient Jerusalem." Joseph Francis Thrupp. "The Recovery of Jerusalem." Sir Charles Warren. Trans. Soc. Bib. Archæol., vol. vii. ("Site of the Temple." By Sir C. Warren). "The Holy City." Rev. George Williams. "The Holy Sepulchre and the Temple." James Fergusson, F.R.S. "Murray's Handbook of Syria and Palestine." (Dr. Porter). "Quarterly Statements of the P.E. Fund" (numerous papers).]

6. *Incidents of the History better realised.*

The Taking of Jerusalem by David:—The king and his men went to Jerusalem against the Jebusites, who felt so secure in their stronghold that they mocked David by putting the lame and the blind upon the walls as defenders. Nevertheless, "David took the stronghold of Zion; the same is the City of David . . . and David dwelt in the stronghold and called it the City of David" (2 Sam. v.). The stronghold here spoken of is not that which is now called the tower of David, near the Jaffa Gate, nor is the Zion here spoken of the south-western hill. The parallel statement in Josephus is that David "took the Lower City by force, but the Akra held out still." Joab, however, scaled the fortress, the Jebusites were cast out of the Akra, and then David rebuilt Jerusalem, renamed it the City of David, and dwelt there (Antiq. vii. 3. 1 & 2). It is not the High Town which is here spoken of but the Akra; and in the place where Josephus gives a general description of the city he tells us that Akra was the hill of the Lower City, while the Upper City was called by King David the *Phrourion*, that is, the *hill-fort* or *watch-post*.

It would seem that in those early days the south-western hill was not yet inhabited, or at any rate was not yet enclosed by a wall, although a garrisoned watch-tower stood upon it. The highest hills are not always deemed the best positions for a citadel or castle. It was not so at Athens, and it is not so in Edinburgh. The Jebusite population of Jerusalem was mostly clustered on the eastern hill. In 1879 Sir Charles Warren said : "The strongest point, to my mind, in favour of Ophel having been the ancient site of the Jebusite city is the fact of the one spring of water being found there. I have carefully noted the manner in which the Kaffirs have located themselves close to water in their various strongholds, and I think that unless there were very urgent reasons, the Jebusites would have located themselves near what is now called the Virgin's Fountain."

But while the eastern hill was Zion,* the Akra was the stronghold of its owners and defenders, their castle occupying an advantageous promontory defended by valleys and ditches. A castle or fort so situated, could not, however, stand a siege, unless it possessed a secret supply of water ; and Warren has spoken of the Virgin's Fountain as the only spring. But there is some mystery about the *Hammam esh Shefa,* and many, including Warren himself, are inclined to believe it may be connected with a spring. The water is stated to be clear and free from the impurities of rain water, and the supply is never exhausted. The position of this "well" is in the Tyropœan Valley, in a line between Akra and the Dome of the Rock. The entrance to the fountain is by a narrow opening, but the shaft soon expands to about 12 feet square. At the bottom is an excavated chamber on one side, and a passage on the other. The passage expands into a vault, beyond which the channel becomes crooked and irregular. It appears that an ancient conduit enters the vault at the extremity of the horizontal passage, but its direction and

* Zion is only called Moriah as the hill of vision (2 Chron. iii. 1).

source are unknown. May not some conduit have enabled the besieged garrison of the Akra fort to draw water from this source?

A few years ago the Rev. F W. Birch, arguing on the supposition that it was the city on Ophel which Joab captured for David, suggested that he found his way into it by the secret tunnels and shafts from the Virgin's Fountain. That Ophel might be captured by surprise in that way seems likely; only it was not Ophel that Joab had to capture, but Akra. The Lower City had all been taken, except that the Akra held out still. If its garrison obtained water from the *Hammam esh Shefa*, may not Joab have effected an entrance from *that* spring? He did not have to *get up to* a "*gutter*," nor yet to a "water course," but to "reach them by the aqueduct" (*B'Tzinnor*).

David's flight and exile; the Spies.—David at first dwelt in the stronghold (the Akra fort), but we afterwards find references to a house which he had and which was on the Ophel slope. We have had evidence of this in the Book of Nehemiah, and we find confirmation in such passages as 1 Kings viii. 1-6, where the ark is *brought up* out of the City of David into the temple (and 2 Sam. xxiv. 18; 1 Kings ix. 24). When David decided to flee from Jerusalem because of the rebellion of Absalom, he would go down the stairs of the City of David, pass out by the Gate between two walls, and go through his own garden grounds; and then, as we are told, he passed over the Kedron, ascended Olivet, and went down to Jericho and over the Jordan.

But he left friends behind him at his house, and it was arranged that two sons of the priests should act as spies and bring him news (2 Sam. xvii.). They waited outside the city, at En Rogel, and a wench went and told them. En Rogel is now identified with the Virgin's Fountain; and it would not be a bad place for the spies to hide in, seeing that its passages were dark, and communicated both with the hill and the valley. The maid servant, descending the staircases from above, might take a pitcher or a bucket to draw water, and so escape suspicion ; the spies below, on receiving the message, could hie away over the mountain to the Jericho road and Jordan.

The evidence that the Virgin's Fountain is En Rogel will increase upon us as we proceed ; but one reason may be stated here. En Rogel is etymologically the Spring of the Fuller, and was so called, no doubt, because fullers washed clothes at the place ; but it may also be made to mean the Spring of the Steps, because fullers trode the clothes with their feet, and hence got their name (from *Regel*, the *foot*, and metaphorically a *step*). The Virgin's Fountain is now called by the Arabs, *Ain Umm ed Deraj*, " Fountain of the Mother of Steps," a designation commonly supposed to refer to the two flights of steps which lead down to it, but which may be derived by tradition from " En Rogel." The steps were not always there. The explorers of Jerusalem say, " The pool seems originally to have been visible in the face of a cliff, and the vault and steps are modern. Possibly the original exit of the water was down the Kedron Valley."

Adonijah's Banquet at the Stone of Zoheleth.—After Absalom's death David returned to Jerusalem. But by-and-bye he grew old and infirm, and then there were speculations and plots about the succession to the throne. Adonijah thought to gain favour by assuming royal state and showing princely generosity. He set up chariots and horsemen, and fifty men to run before him ; and he slew sheep and oxen and fatlings by the stone of Zoheleth, which is beside En Rogel. Abiathar the priest was at the banquet, and Joab the veteran general ; all was going merrily, and the guests shouted, " God save King Adonijah !" (1 Kings i.) But news of these proceedings was carried to

David at his house on Ophel. Bathsheba came in and told him what was occurring, and reminded him of his oath that Solomon her son should sit upon the throne. While the queen was yet speaking, Nathan the prophet was announced, who confirmed the story, and inquired anxiously who was to reign. Then David called for Zadok and Nathan, the priests, and Benaiah, the soldier, chief of the king's body-guard, to go with them as the representative of force, and indeed to take his men, and said, "Cause Solomon my son to ride upon mine own mule, and bring him down to Gihon (*i.e.*, Siloam Pool), anoint him there, and blow the trumpet, and say, God save King Solomon. Then ye shall come up after him, and he shall come and sit upon my throne ; for he shall be king in my stead." This was done, and all the people said, "God save King Solomon !"

We shall realize these events better when we look at the position of Zoheleth, the discovery of which was one of the happy results of M. Clermont Ganneau's investigations in 1870. Nearly in the centre of the line along which stretches the village of Siloam there exists a rocky plateau surrounded by Arab buildings, which mask its true form and extent : the western face, cut perpendicularly, slightly overhangs the valley. Steps rudely cut in the rock enable one to climb it, not without difficulty, and so to penetrate directly from the valley to the midst of the village. By this road, troublesome, and even dangerous, pass habitually the women of Siloam, who come to fill their vessels at the so-called Virgin's Fountain. Now this passage and this ledge of rock in which it is cut are called by the fellahin, " Ez Zehweile," which means " a slippery place," or perhaps "the serpent stone." This was M. Ganneau's discovery, and he knew at once the bearings of it, in helping to fix En Rogel at the Virgin's Fountain, and the king's garden somewhere in its neighbourhood. Perhaps the discovery would have been made earlier, only that the village of Siloam, owing to the turbulence of its inhabitants, is almost unvisited by Europeans.

Adonijah's feast, then, was being held at the foot of this cliff, about 70 yards across the valley from En Rogel. Solomon's party could not be seen because the rising ground of Ophel came between. But when the anointing had taken place at the Pool of Siloam, and the party were going back up the Tyropœan toward David's house, the people piped their music and shouted their joy till the earth rang again. The attention of Joab was attracted by the sound of the trumpet, and he enquired, "Wherefore is this noise of the city being in an uproar?" The truth was learned, and then Adonijah's guests were afraid, and rose up and went every man his way.

Solomon's Change of Residence.—Solomon would at first live in the house of his father David, which was near the stairs which went down to the valley bed. "And Solomon made affinity with Pharaoh, king of Egypt, and took Pharaoh's daughter and brought her into the City of David until he had made an end of building his own house," &c. (1 Kings iii. 1). "And Solomon was building his own house thirteen years." "He made also a house for Pharaoh's daughter" (close to his own house) (1 Kings vii. 1. 8). "And Solomon brought up the daughter of Pharaoh out of the City of David unto the house that he had built for her: for he said, My wife shall not dwell in the house of David, king of Israel, because the places are holy, whereunto the ark of the Lord hath come" (2 Chron. viii. 11). This incidental mention that he brought her up accords well with the relative positions of the two palaces —David's lower down the slope of Ophel, the new one higher up. The same remark applies to bringing up the ark from David's house to the Temple.

The Building of Millo.—David having taken the stronghold of Zion improved his new capital by building " round about, from Millo and inward " (2 Sam. v. 9). What Millo was, or where it was located, has been one of the great puzzles of Jerusalem topography. It seems, however, to have been the great dam athwart the Tyropœan Valley. It is possible that even the Jebusites had hit upon the device and had constructed a dam in some rude fashion, and named it by a word of their own language, which afterwards clung to it. Sir G. Grove, in the " Dictionary of the Bible," conjectures that it was the Jebusites who first built Millo, because it is difficult to assign a meaning to the word in Hebrew, while the Canaanites of Shechem also had a Millo (Judges ix. 6, 20), and because David seems to find it existing and not to build it. The statement that David built from Millo and *inward* suits very well the identification of Millo with the great dam which was the outer defence of the Tyropœan, and to a great extent of Zion itself. It is not unlikely either that the House of Millo was a castle on the Ophel Hill, close to the eastern end of the dam, and that this was adopted by David as a residence. He may also have strengthened both the castle and the dam.

But it was Solomon who so strengthened this work as to deserve the credit of having constructed it. It was one of the great works for the accomplishment of which he made a levy upon all parts of the kingdom (1 Kings ix. 15). The nature of the work is indicated in 1 Kings xi. 27— " Solomon built Millo (and so) closed up the fissure (or cleft) of the city of David his father : " either the two expressions relate to the same work, or the two works are closely associated together. Accordingly, before the work can be begun, Pharaoh's daughter must vacate the house of Millo. She came up " out of the City of David unto her house which Solomon had built for her : then did he build Millo " (1 Kings ix. 24). The Israelites employed upon the work were the children of Joseph, and their superintendent was Jeroboam, an Ephraimite, probably already acquainted with the similar work at Shechem (1 Kings xi. 28). It is stated in the Septuagint that Jeroboam completed the fortifications at Millo, and was long afterwards known as the man who had "enclosed the City of David." The work was so well done that Jerusalem was never again attacked from this side, although previously this side was found the most vulnerable, both by David and by the children of Simeon and Judah in earlier time.

If we are to find a Hebrew etymology for the name Millo, it seems to be a noun formed in the usual way by prefixing the letter M to the Aramæan verb *l'va*, equivalent to the Hebrew *lavah*,* having the meaning to wind or twist, and used to describe stairways as well as serpents and garlands. A dam across the Tyropœan would require the construction of two stairways at least, one from the bed of the Tyropœan to the top of the dam on the Ophel side, and one from the High Town down to the dam on the west.

The Death of Athaliah.—This incident affords indications of locality in beautiful agreement with Nehemiah. When this queen-mother heard that her son, the king, had been killed by Jehu, she snatched at the sovereignty for herself, and her policy was to slay all the seed royal. But one little child escaped, carried off by its nurse, and they were secreted in the Temple by Jehoiada, the high priest. In the seventh year Jehoiada assembled the chiefs of the people in the Temple, produced the little child Joash, stood him upon the platform (or by the pillar) appropriated to the kings, and said, This is the rightful heir! The chiefs shouted their joy, when Athaliah heard the noise and rushed into the Temple to learn the cause. That she should hear so readily and find such easy access to the Temple, accords

* The resemblances are better seen in the Hebrew.

well with the supposition that she was living in Solomon's palace, close adjoining the Temple, as Warren places it. When Athaliah saw the state of things, she cried—"Treason, treason!" But she found no friends there. The priest said, "Have her forth—slay her not in the house of the Lord! So they made way for her; and she went to the entry of the Horse Gate to the king's house; and they slew her there" (2 Chron. xviii. 15; 2 Kings xii. 16). It is implied in this narrative that the Horse Gate was not only by the king's house, but that it was also the nearest point which could be considered fairly beyond the sacred precincts; and this is in full agreement with the position which we have assigned it.

In the context of the passages just quoted we find that Joash is carried "by the way of the Gate of the Guard into the king's house." This gate must, of course, have been on that side of the palace adjoining the Temple courts; it was probably due north of the Water Gate (*i.e.*, the Triple Gate), and it thus again accords with Neh. iii. 25, where the tower standing out from Solomon's house is said to be "by the court of the guard." The court of the guard may very well have extended from the Water Gate without to the Gate of the Guard on the Temple side of the palace. From Neh. xii. 39, it appears that there was a corresponding Gate of the Guard at the corresponding point on the north side of the altar.

The Assassination of Joash. When Joash grew to man's estate he made changes which displeased his people; and the short statement is that his slaves slew him on his bed, "at the House of Millo, that goeth down to Silla" (2 Kings xii. 20, combined with 2 Chron. xxiv. 25). This has been generally regarded as obscure, and some have supposed Silla to be the same as M'sillah, a stairway at the west gate of the Temple, north of Wilson's Arch (1 Chron. xxvi. 16). But it is more naturally the stairway at Millo itself. Joash was living at Beth Millo, David's house, and when he heard of the conspiracy he designed to flee down the stairs and through the Gate between two walls ; but being a sick man he was being carried on a litter, as Lewin remarks, and while going down Silla,—not while going down *to* Silla, for there is no preposition here in the Hebrew text—the assassins killed him.

The Wall destroyed by Jehoash, king of Israel, when he came against Amaziah of Judah, extended from the Gate of Ephraim unto the Corner Gate, 400 cubits (2 Kings xiv. 13 ; 2 Chron. xxv. 23). We can now, by aid of Herr Schick's plan of the second wall, and our previous study of Nehemiah, see exactly this piece of wall, south of the Church of the Holy Sepulchre, and running east and west.

The Towers built by Uzziah were intended to strengthen the city just in this part where it had been found to be vulnerable. He "built towers in Jerusalem at the Corner Gate, at the Valley Gate, and at the turning of the wall, and fortified them" (2 Chron. xxvi. 9). The "turning" here spoken of is a re-entering angle, and not improbably that one south-east of the Church of the Sepulchre, where we find the "Throne of the Governor" in later time.

In the days of Ahaz, the grandson of Uzziah, Jerusalem was threatened by the allied forces of Rezin, king of Syria and Pekah, king of Israel. Ahaz and his people were greatly perturbed, and needed a message of advice and encouragement. The word of the Lord came to Isaiah, in the Temple, saying, "Go forth now and meet Ahaz, at the end of the conduit of the upper pool, in the highway of the Fuller's Field" (Isaiah vii. 3). The upper pool here spoken of is believed to be the Virgin's Fountain, where we find one end of a conduit which connects it with the lower pool at Siloam. But if this is what is meant, why is the spot not described shortly and plainly as En-Rogel, by which name it was already known? (1 Kings i. 9).

Surely it is not the pool itself which is meant but the end of a conduit, or channel, or passage belonging to it—the end of a passage, yet not a termination in any pool. That is to say, it refers to the top of the shaft and stairway on the Ophel Hill, which had been lost so long until re-discovered by Warren. This entrance was of course known to Isaiah, and known to the king, being close by the king's gardens. Ahaz would reach it by going out through the Gate between two walls, and was probably accustomed to walk there frequently. The place spoken of is not really stated to be "*in* the highway of the Fuller's Field :" in the Hebrew text the word *in* is not found, and the passage might be rendered—"The end of the channel of the upper pool, the staircase of the Fuller's Field." This is an exact description of the top of the shaft on the Ophel Hill.

Here, then, we have another interesting note of locality: it appears that the Fuller's Field was on Ophel, and Warren's shaft was in it. We cannot but recall the statement of Josephus that St James was martyred by being thrown over the outer wall of the Temple enclosure, and that "a fuller took the club with which he pressed the clothes, and brought it down on the head of the Just one." It is reasonable to infer that fullers were at work not far from the spot where St James fell. On the slope of the Ophel Hill Sir Charles Warren discovered a cavern which was apparently used by the fullers, for it contained vats or troughs cut in the rock. In the earth above the cave is a drain, which is of course more modern ; and yet here were found glass and pottery, supposed to be early Christian.

In the days of Hezekiah, the son of Ahaz, the stairway shaft in the Fuller's Field is spoken of again, and in a way that quite confirms our previous conclusions. Sennacherib, while besieging Lachish, sent his Tartan and his Rab-shakeh with a strong force against Jerusalem, as an easy prey.   The Assyrian officers pitched their camp at the north-west of the city, on the high ground, which was ever after known as the " Camp of the Assyrians."   But, seeing the strength of the city, they made no assault upon it; they sought a conference with Hezekiah to induce him to surrender.   Learning where his palace was, that is, David's house, on the slope of Ophel, they came and " stood at the passage of the upper pool, which is at the staircase of the Fuller's Field " (2 Kings. xviii. 17).   There they called to the king, and when Hezekiah, consulting his dignity, deputed his Prime Minister, his Secretary, and his Recorder to represent him, these officers spoke from the top of the wall.   The circumstances may seem to require that the wall should extend a little more southward than the wall found by Warren, but they seem to be good evidence that the Ophel shaft was outside the wall, and that the king's house was within shouting distance of the shaft, or at any rate that the Assyrian generals thought so.

Jerusalem was not taken at this time ; but in expectation of a siege, Hezekiah had made great defensive preparations. For one thing he gathered many labourers and choked up all the fountains outside the city and stopped the flow of the brook (2 Chron. xxxii. 3).   He stopped the upper spring of the waters of Gihon and brought them straight down on the west side of the City of David (2 Chron. xxxii. 30). He gathered together the waters of the lower pool ; he made a reservoir between the two walls for the water of the old pool ; he made a pool and a conduit and brought water into the city (Isaiah xxii. 9, 11 ; 2 Kings xx. 20). It is probable that most of these statements relate to the same piece of work, and that work the making of Siloam Pool and the tunnel to bring water to it from the Virgin's Fountain.   There had been an "old pool" of Siloam, which is clearly traceable south-east of the present one, and this was the "lower pool of Gihon ;" while the Virgin's Fount was the "upper pool" or the "upper spring of the waters of Gihon." The water had previously flowed from the one to the other, by an open channel down the Tyropœan Valley—a channel which has been struck at some points —and this was "the brook that flowed through the midst of the land." The lower pool and the waters of Siloah were referred to by Isaiah in the previous reign (that is, he speaks of the waters of Siloah that go softly, viii. 6, and he implies a lower pool by speaking of the upper pool). It is reasonably argued by Dr Chaplin* that Siloah and Gihon were identical, and that the terms applied not only to the spring or pool but to the canal that joined them. We may assent to this if we keep in mind that the open canal existed before the rock-cut tunnel. The only difficulty we have is in thinking of the new Siloam as a reservoir between the two walls, and in understanding the use of making the tunnel if Siloam was to be outside the city. Some writers, therefore, suppose that the first wall of the city actually bent round Siloam on the southward side.

Hezekiah, besides these hydraulic works, built up all the wall that was broken down, and raised it up to the towers ; and the other wall without (which it is just possible was south of Siloam Pool, only, even in that case, there is a great dam across the fissure to the north of it) ; and being so solicitous about this part of the city, he "strengthened Millo, the city of David" (2 Chron. xxxii. 5).

In the days of King Josiah we have mention of the prophetess Huldah, and it is stated that she lived in Jerusalem, in the *Mishneh* (or Second Quarter). The word means second in order or in dignity, and in the case of brothers the younger. It appears to designate that part of the city which lay in the Asmonean Valley, a part inferior to Zion in dignity, and younger as an inhabited district,

* "Quarterly Statement," April, 1890.

because originally a suburb outside the walls which encircled the hills.

The Capture of Jerusalem and Flight of Zedekiah.—Not to multiply incidents, let us come now to the last king of Judah—Zedekiah. In his day Nebuchadnezzer came up against the city, and pitched his camp, as all had done before him, against the northern quarter. The event to be expected in such a case is described in Zeph. i. 10. There is first a noise from the Fish Gate at the head of the Asmonean Valley. Of consequence there is next a howling from the Second Quarter of Jerusalem, for the forcing of the Fish Gate has brought the invaders into the northern "suburb." Next, the alarm having spread, there is a crashing from the hills on either side. Howl ye inhabitants of Macktesh—the "Hollow," the southern Suburb, where dwelt the men of Tyre which brought in fish and all manner of ware (Neh. xiii. 15), and after whom the Valley was probably named—howl ye, for all the merchant people are undone, all they that were laden with silver are cut off.

Nebuchadnezzar's generals effected an entrance at the middle gate of the north wall; and Zedekiah, as soon as he knew of it, fled away by night with his bodyguard. Whether living in Solomon's house or David's, his way would be down the Stairs of the City of David into the bed of the Tyropœan; and then we are distinctly told that he fled by the way of the Gate between the two walls, which was by the king's garden (2 Kings xxv. 4; Jer. xxxix. 4; lii. 7). His plan was to take the route which David had taken when he fled from Absalom. Josephus says "that he fled out of the city through the fortified ditch" ("Antiq." x. 8, 2)—a statement which quite supports our idea that the deep hollow "Suburb" was defended by a transverse wall or dam.

. *Jeremiah's Prophecy.*—In order to encourage the people

during the captivity, Jeremiah predicts that Jerusalem shall be again inhabited and its borders extended. The measuring line is to go forth over against it upon the hill Gareb (probably the later Bezetha, north-west of the Temple) and shall compass about to Goath (this seems to be a sweep round the north-western, western, and south-western parts of the city); and the whole valley of the dead bodies and of the ashes (*i.e.*, Topheth, the broad junction of the present Hinnom and Tyropœan Valleys), and all the fields (eastward) unto the Brook Kedron (and then northward), unto the corner of the Horse Gate toward the east shall be holy unto the Lord (Jer. xxxi. 28). This reference again confirms the position we have assigned to the Horse Gate.

Zechariah also describes Jerusalem in its length and breadth. It is to be lifted up and inhabited from Benjamin's Gate (the east gate of the temple in Ezekiel's plan, Ezek. xlviii. 32), unto the place of the first gate (the first gate of the city, a gate near the north-east corner—as the Hebrew language reads from right to left, so goes the numbering here), unto the Corner Gate. This is from east to west; the north and south extremes named by Zechariah are the Tower of Hananel (same position as Antonia) and the king's wine-presses (which we may guess to be southward of the king's garden).

The Locality of the King's Garden is an important point in Jerusalem topography. M. Clermont Ganneau inclines to place it on the eastern side of Ophel; but his reason seems to be insufficient. The great eastern valley of Jerusalem so commonly called the Kedron, is divided by the fellahin of Siloam into three parts, and the middle part—extending from the south-east angle of the Haram to the junction of valleys a little north of Joab's well—they call *Wady Fer'aun*, or "Pharaoh's Valley." M. Ganneau believes that this signifies, in their minds, simply the *Valley of the King,* and is equivalent to the King's Garden.* M. Ganneau might claim in his favour the statement of Josephus that Adonijah's feast, "by En Rogel," took place near the fountain that was in the king's paradise (or park).† But the paradise or park was something different from the garden, and Josephus does not use the word paradise to describe the king's gardens in which Uzziah was buried, but the word *kepois*.‡ It is worth notice also that if the Virgin's Fountain was in the king's park, it' was almost certainly outside the city. Again, the fact that the royal park included within it the spring of water makes it probable that the shaft in connection with it was on the royal property also, for the kings would hardly allow the free use of a spring which they deemed their own. And then, if the shaft was on the royal grounds (although that part was still traditionally called the Fuller's Field) it would be natural that Isaiah should find king Ahaz walking there.

Amos prophesied in the days of Uzziah, "two years before the earthquake" (Amos i. 1). This earthquake, although not noticed in the history, was of a terrible character, and the people fled before it (Zech. xiv. 5). As Josephus tells the story, it was just as Uzziah was entering the Temple that the building suddenly started asunder; the light flashed through,. and at the same moment the leprosy rushed into the king's face. The hills around felt the shock, and a memorial of the crash was long preserved in a large fragment, or landslip, which, rolling down from the western hill, was brought to rest at the base of the eastern hill, and there obstructed not only the roads but the paradises of the kings. Josephus says that this occurred at the place called Eroge, and Dean Stanley is confident that he means En Rogel ;§ but here again it is

* "Quarterly Statement," Jan.—March, 1870.
† Antiq., vii. 14, 4.   ‡ Antiq., ix. 10. 4.
§ "Sinai and Palestine," chap. iii.

necessary to notice that it is the king's paradises which are spoken of and not the king's gardens.

It is quite clear that the king's gardens were near the Gate between two walls, as mentioned in the account of Zedekiah's flight ; and it seems certain that the Gate between two walls was in the Tyropœan.

7. *Sieges of Jerusalem understood by the topography.*— The capture of Jerusalem by David, the investment of it by Sennacherib, and the overthrow of it by Nebuchadnezzar have already been described. Time would fail me to go into detail concerning all the sieges that followed ; and probably a brief treatment of two or three will be sufficient for the reader. We desire to show how much clearer the history becomes in the light of modern survey and investigation ; and for this purpose a few examples are enough.

Jerusalem on three sides was protected by deep ravines, and an enemy, looking up, saw the brow of every hill surmounted by high walls. At first he might imagine the Tyropœan Valley was accessible from the south, since the dam or transverse wall was lower in position than the walls which it joined together ; but no doubt the dam or wall was strongly built. Even if he could get within it, there was the Causeway in front and walls on either side, and he would only be in what Josephus calls a fortified ditch. The assailants of Jerusalem—who doubtless knew their business—always chose to assault it from the high ground north and north-west. The king's palace, therefore, on Ophel, was about the last place which an enemy could reach, and not until he had broken through two or three walls.

When Pompey advanced against Jerusalem (B.C. 64), the population was divided. The party of Hyrcanus opened the gates to him ; but the party of Aristobulus retired to the Temple, breaking down the bridge which communicated with the city. This may have been an arch

on the site of the present Wilson's Arch.   Pompey, having
sent a garrison into the city itself, laid siege to the Temple,
purposing to assault it from the north.   He "filled up the
ditch on the north side of the Temple."   That would be
the artificial cutting at the north-west corner.   He filled up
the valley also, Josephus tells us (Wars, i. 7, 3), "and
indeed it was a hard thing to fill up that valley, by reason
of its immense depth, especially as the Jews used all the
means possible to repel them from their superior station."
This is the valley which Warren found, crossing the present
Haram area, falling away from the north side of the platform to a depth of 200 feet, and passing out into the
Kedron north of the Golden Gate.   Probably it was only
partially filled up at this time.   Pompey then erected
towers upon the bank which he had made, and brought
engines to bear; but it was not until the third month of
the siege that he made himself master of the Temple.

In B.C. 37, Herod, like all preceding generals, pitched his
camp on the north side (Josephus, Wars, i. 17, 9).   The
Jews in this warfare made mines—perhaps in the ground
banked up by Pompey—and surprised the Romans by
sudden sorties from below.   But the first wall was captured
in forty days—(Antiq. xiv. 16, 2.   This was of course the
wall which we know as the second)—and the Lower City
being thus taken, the Jews retired into the Upper City
and into the Temple.   The Upper City was taken by
storm after fifteen days more.   But here the destruction
ceased.   Herod was going to reign in Jerusalem, and did
not wish to do more damage than was inevitable in the
capture of the city.   He sought to save the Temple, and
only some of the cloisters about it got burnt down.

Afterwards, to ingratiate himself with the Jews, Herod
rebuilt the Temple, and enlarged the precincts of it.   It
would seem that Solomon's palace had been destroyed by
Nebuchadnezzar's generals and never rebuilt.   Herod's

own palace was in the High Town. The area formerly occupied by Solomon's palace was now taken into the Temple precincts, the south-west corner was raised up from its low level and added also ; and along this southern front was built a royal cloister, 100 feet high. To make an approach to this cloister from the west, Robinson's Arch was erected, and if there was no viaduct from the western hill there must have been a staircase to ascend from the valley. On the north side also the Temple precincts were enlarged, by taking in the ground which Pompey had raised to a higher level. The Baris or castle in which Nehemiah had lived was reconstructed and strengthened, renamed Antonia, and connected with the Temple.

In another quarter Herod strengthened the city very much. The reader will have noticed that while it was a usual thing with assailants to attack the north wall, and take the Lower City as a preliminary to assaulting the Upper City, yet there was one spot where the Upper City might be approached at once from the outside. This was by the Valley Gate, and was owing to the fact that the second wall started from the Gennath Gate to go north-ward, whereas the wall of the Upper City was prolonged westward. Herod determined to strengthen this part of the city all the more because his own palace was in this part ; so he built three strong towers, which he named Hippicus, Phasaelus, and Mariamne. Hippicus was at the outer angle ; the base of it remains, and is the foundation of the north-west tower of the present citadel, which measures 45 feet square. Phasaelus remains, and is the one conspicuous object on the right hand as the traveller enters the Jaffa Gate. It is 70 feet by 56 feet, and is solid to the height of 60 feet ; the stones are bevelled, like those round the Haram, and do not appear ever to have been disturbed. The site of Mariamne is less certain, but it probably corresponded with the third tower which we see marked in almost every plan of the so-called Castle of David.

The Jerusalem of Herod's day was the Jerusalem which Jesus Christ would be familiar with.

In the year 43 A.D., Agrippa built a third wall, to enclose the suburban dwellings which had sprung up on the north. This third wall began at the tower Hippicus, went northward, and had a tower called Psephinus at its north-west angle, then passed eastward "over against" the monuments of Helena, queen of Adiabene (the so-called "Tombs of the Kings," half a mile out, on the great north road), then passed by the caverns of the kings, bent southward at the tower of the north-eastern corner, and finally joined the old wall at the valley "called the Valley of Kedron" (Josephus, Wars, v. 4, 2). "The city could no way have been taken if that wall had been finished in the manner it was begun." But Agrippa "left off building it when he had only laid the foundation, out of the fear he was in of Claudius Cæsar." The wall was 10 cubits wide, and was afterwards raised as high as 20 cubits, above which it had battlements and turrets. In the course of the third wall, according to Josephus, there were ninety towers, as compared with sixty in the first; and the whole compass of the city was 33 furlongs. He also says that the ninety towers were 200 cubits apart; but this would make the third wall alone more than 5 miles in length, and so we judge that some mistake has crept into the text. Therefore we shall venture to take the present north wall of the city as representing Agrippa's wall, notwithstanding that the entire circumference would then be less than 33 furlongs. There seems to be no sufficient evidence for going beyond the present wall. It is a wall which begins at the tower Hippicus, by the Jaffa Gate. The position of the great corner tower Psephinus seems to be indicated by the ruined castle called *Kalat Jalud* (Giant's Castle), just within the present north-west angle. The Damascus Gate is "over against" the so-called Tombs of the Kings, for a spectator standing at the Tombs would look down directly upon that gate. The "royal caverns" we may identify with the Cotton Cavern, the quarry whence the kings of Judah obtained the stone for the great buildings of the city. The entrance to them is in the face of the scarped rock, about 300 feet east of the Damascus Gate, and the city wall runs right across the entrance. At the north-east corner of the present wall we find the tower which Josephus assigns to that point—"the most colossal ruins after those at the north-west corner." A trench cut in the rock at the foot of the eastern wall is deflected here, passes round the corner, and goes west ; it does not go any further north as we might expect it to do if the wall ever extended further north. And then the wall from the north-east corner is brought southward and joins the Haram wall, the junction not being at the north-east angle of the Haram, but much nearer to the Golden Gate, at the deep valley which Pompey began to fill up. We have to bear in mind that this third wall had been built before the siege of Jerusalem by Titus, in A.D. 70.

Titus began by investing the city on the north and the west. The place he selected for his attempt on the outer wall was just west of the Pool of Hezekiah, because there the wall of the High Town was not covered by the second wall, and he thought to capture the third wall and then at once assault the first.

When Titus had taken the outer wall he encamped in the north-west part of the city between the second and third walls ; and at the same time extended his line from the "Camp of the Assyrians" to the Kedron Valley. His attempt to storm the High Town at the uncovered portion of the wall failed because of the strength of Herod's towers. He then made an attempt on the Temple platform from the north, but failed because the valley there was deep and the Temple was strongly fortified. He had hoped, when he took the Wall of Agrippa, to be able to assault Antonia from the north, without taking the second wall; but it now appeared to him that that castle might best be assaulted on the west. These considerations induced him to attack the second wall. After some effort, a breach was made, and the Romans entered the middle city. They were once driven out by the Jews, and kept out for a time; but by-and-bye they gained entrance again, and then, made wise by experience, they demolished the second wall, or the northern part of it, and so were able to keep their ground.

Antonia was now assaulted on its western side; but the business was difficult, and the struggle was long. The mounds which the Romans cast up were undermined by the Jews and destroyed. The mines, however, weakened the outer wall of the castle, and that fell also. The Romans were filled with hope; but the Jews had foreseen the event, and had run up another wall behind. The courage of the Romans was damped by the sight of this second wall. But a few days after, they scaled it by a night surprise, and at the same time forced their way into Antonia through the mine under the wall. The Jews, in a panic, rushed away into the Temple, where they were able to defend themselves as in a fortress. But fighting now took place daily, until at length the northern cloisters of the Temple were burnt down, the inner Temple was assaulted, and eventually the whole fabric was reduced to ashes.

The Jews were now crowded in the Upper City, and confined to that. Titus held a parley with them across the bridge above the Xystus—that is, at Wilson's Arch—offering them terms. But they declined his conditions, and so the siege had to go on. The Ophel quarter was now plundered and burnt; and then a grand effort was made against the Upper City. Mounds were thrown up, and the assault was delivered simultaneously from several points—on the west, by Herod's palace, on the north-west part of the town a little east of the tower Phasaelus, and on the north-east at the Xystus, which extended from Wilson's Arch southward. The strong city at last fell, and its walls and buildings were razed to the ground.

We know that it rose again from its ashes, and has had an eventful history since; but it is not our purpose to follow its fortunes farther.

In seeking to understand the descriptions given by Josephus, writers have been much puzzled by his mention of a ravine "called the Kedron ravine." It could not well be the Kedron Valley itself, or it would hardly be spoken of in this way ; besides which, we are told that the eastern portion of Agrippa's wall joined the old wall at the ravine called Kedron. This would be too indefinite a note of place if the wall and the ravine ran parallel with one another. Moreover, the north-east angle of the Temple cloisters was built over the said ravine, and the depth was frightful (Wars, vi. 3, 2). The depth was frightful at the angle, rather than at the eastern side. There could be no right understanding of the references, until Sir Charles Warren's labours showed that a deep valley crosses the Haram north of the Golden Gate, and contains within it the Birket Israil. It was only a "so-called ravine" to Josephus, because the western portion had been filled up by Pompey, and the eastern mouth was cut across by the Wall of Agrippa. Warren's discovery of this ravine, and demonstration of its depth, is a glorious instance of the value of excavation work in questions of Jerusalem topography.

[*Authorities and Sources :*—The Works of Josephus. "Siege of Jerusalem." Thomas Lewin. "Jerusalem, a Sketch." Thomas Lewin.]

CHAPTER IV.

1. *Christ in the Provinces.*

IN New Testament times Palestine was a Roman province, and its divisions were no longer tribal. East of Jordan were the districts of Perea Batanæa, Trachonitis, Auranitis, Paneas, and Gaulonitis. In this chapter, however, we have to do chiefly with Western Palestine. On this side the central position was held by Samaria, with Galilee north of it, Judea south, and in the extreme south Idumea.

The Samaritans were not pure Hebrews in blood, and not purely Jewish in their worship. When the ten tribes of Israel had been crushed, and their principal families carried into captivity, the Assyrian conquerors brought men from Cuthah, Sepharvaim, and other places in the far east, and set them down in Samaria. Of various nationalities themselves, these people intermarried with the poorer Jews who had been left behind, and so their descendants were of mixed blood. Naturally also, there was at first some admixture of religious beliefs and practices, and some confusion of dialects (2 Kings, xvii.).

But eventually the various elements of the population coalesced, and the Samaritans settled down as a people, speaking a language allied to that of the Jews, and accepting the Books of Moses as their guide. But they rejected all the later books excepting Joshua, and claimed that Mount

Gerizim was the place where it had always been intended that the Temple of Jehovah should be built. In the days of Ezra and Nehemiah the co-operation of the Samaritans in rebuilding Jerusalem and the Temple had been refused, and at no later period would the Jews consent to have friendly dealings with the Samaritans.

Nehemiah had seen the evils resulting from mixed marriages, and the contaminating influence of foreign merchants in Jerusalem. In later days, when Greek literature and Greek manners were spreading over Syria, the more zealous of the Jews contended earnestly against the corrupting innovations. The day when the Seventy Elders translated the Law into Greek for king Ptolemy was pronounced accursed—a day of evil, as when Israel made for itself a golden calf. The patriotic struggle of the Maccabees was all intended to get rid of foreign influence, and keep God's chosen people separate. The Pharisees were a party who by their very name claimed to be "separated," and made it their object to resist the slightest departure from the requirements of the Jewish Law. Their ideas and tenets came to be generally accepted by the Jews of Judea ; and hence in the days of Christ Jerusalem was a centre of exclusiveness, bigotry, and ceremonialism.

The Jews of Galilee, cut off from their brethren of the south by the interposition of Samaria, could seldom visit the Temple at Jerusalem ; they saw little of the sacrifice of bulls and goats, and learned to worship in synagogues in a plainer way. They were in contact with the northern nations, made alliance with Phœnicia, and did business with men of many nationalities in the fishing towns of the Lake of Tiberias. It is possible that through their intercourse with foreigners, a part of their district was called "Galilee of the Gentiles ;" and they seem to have become so different in their dialect or pronunciation that when a man from Galilee opened his mouth in Jerusalem, his speech betrayed him. The Galileans derived at least one advantage from their intercourse with foreigners; it made them less exclusive, and prepared them in a degree for a religion which should be addressed to Jew and Gentile alike. Jesus Christ, when he began his ministry, did not address crowds in Jerusalem, nor seek disciples from among the Scribes and Pharisees, but came into the towns of Galilee, and called fishermen from their humble occupation.

The prophecy in Micah led the Jews to look to Bethlehem Ephrathah as the destined birth-place of the Messiah; and it was made an objection to the claims of Jesus of Nazareth that his home was in Galilee.

Bethlehem is a long white town on a ridge, with terraced olive groves, at a distance of 6 miles from Jerusalem. Here, enclosed within the walls of the Greek convent, is the venerable Church of the Nativity, now parcelled out among the Greek, Latin, and Armenian monks, who house together from necessity in different quarters of the convent. The church, built by Helena, the mother of Constantine, is one of the oldest in the world; and the cave beneath it under the choir is the traditional Cave of the Nativity. It is mentioned by Justin Martyr in the second century; and Origen, in the fourth, says that "there is shown at Bethlehem the cave where He was born, and the manger in the cave." "It is the only sacred place, as far as I know (says Conder), which is mentioned before the establishment of Christianity by Constantine; yet it is remarkable that Jerome found it no longer in possession of the Christians. "Bethlehem," he says, "is now overshadowed by the grove of Tammuz, who is Adonis; and in the cave where Christ wailed as a babe the paramour of Venus now is mourned."

Mr Bartlett, in his "Walks about Jerusalem," deems the

identification of the spot at variance with probability, since, although it may occasionally happen that caverns are used as stables in Palestine, this one is deeper underground than would be convenient for such a purpose. When we consider, in addition, the tendency of the monks to fix the scene of remarkable Scriptural events in grottoes, perhaps from the impressiveness of such spots, the presumption against the site appears almost conclusive.

Palestine exploration was hardly likely to throw any light on this question, which is to be elucidated rather by a study of the causes which led to a confusion between the traditions relating to Christ and the legends told of Tammuz.

The people of Bethlehem are better fed, better dressed, better off in most respects than the people of other small towns in Palestine. The women are remarkable for their beauty, and they wear a peculiar kind of head-dress, adorned with rows of silver coins. It is believed that at the time of the Crusades a good deal of intermarriage took place between Europeans and the women of Bethlehem. The population now is chiefly Christian.

If we attempt to follow Joseph and Mary, returning from Egypt and taking at first the road for Bethlehem, but changing their course when they hear that Archelaus reigns, and withdrawing into the parts of Galilee (Matt. ii. 23), we may suppose that they make their way to the river Jordan, cross by the ford near Jericho, journey on the eastern side and so avoid Samaria, and then, re-crossing by the ford near Bethshan, make their way to Nazareth.

Nazareth, the town in which Jesus was brought up, is also without any Jewish inhabitants at the present day ; the population is about six thousand, of whom one-third are Moslem, while two-thirds are Christians of the Latin, Greek, and other churches. Unfortunately they bear an evil character for their turbulence,

In Nazareth we are shown what purports to be the work-shop of Joseph the carpenter, but we know that this is a modern appropriation, a Latin chapel, built only in 1859. We are asked to look at the *Mensa Christi*, a block of rock, rudely oval, 10 feet across and 3 feet high, in a church built in 1861, but we have no confidence that Jesus and his disciples used it as a table. Making a stronger claim is the house in which the Holy Family lived, or what remains of it, for the legend says that the upper storey or the outer room was carried away by angels through the air, and after lengthy travels was set down on the wooded hill-top of Loretto in Italy. It is a rock-cut grotto under the high altar of the Latin church. A wall of separation makes two chambers of it, the outer being called the Grotto of the Annunciation, and the inner the Grotto of St Joseph. The shaft of a red granite pillar hanging through the roof is believed to be miraculously suspended over the very place where the angel Gabriel stood to deliver his message, From the inner chamber—that of St Joseph—a narrow passage, with seventeen steps, leads up obliquely to the inmost part of the cave, a chamber of irregular shape, traditionally supposed to be the Virgin's kitchen.

Escaping from these places we inquire for that synagogue in which Jesus received instruction when a youth, and "stood up to read" on a memorable occasion after he had become a public teacher. But there are no Jews in Nazareth, and so there is no need of a synagogue now. The Greek Catholics, indeed, tell us that their chapel, in the main street, occupies the very site of the synagogue ; but we find no remains of synagogue architecture. It occurs to us that there is one site, at all events, the features of which could hardly be destroyed or altered, namely, the " brow of the hill on which the city stood," and from which the Nazarenes intended to precipitate the great Teacher after that scene in the Synagogue. But when we have been guided to the "brow," although we see before us a fearful descent of about 1000 feet—which old Maundeville calls "the Leap of the Lord"—we observe that it is 2 miles from the town ; and we cannot understand how it can be the brow of the hill on which the city stood.

In this general uncertainty of things are our explorers able to do anything for us ? Yes, some little, for they are men who use their eyes, and they point out that high up above the present town are numerous old cisterns and tombs. The cisterns would certainly be in close proximity to the dwellings of the people, the ancient Nazareth must therefore have stood higher on the slope ; and so the "brow of the hill" was probably one of the cliffs now above the town.

Conder also points out that the Virgin's Fountain of Nazareth—also called the Fountain of the Annunciation—should be one of the most surely identified places. There is but one spring in the town, and Mary must necessarily have drawn water from it like other women. The Greeks have built their church at the place, and declare it to be the scene of the Annunciation. Their church is dedicated to St Gabriel, and even the Latins admit that it stands on the site where the angel first became visible. "As in the eighth century, so now, the spring is under the floor of the church, which is itself half subterranean. The water is led to the left of the high altar, past a well-mouth, by which it is drawn up for pilgrims, and so by a channel to the masonry fountain, where it comes out through metal spouts under an arched recess broad enough for fifteen women to stand side by side. A pool is formed below at the trough, and here the constant succession of the Nazareth women may be seen all day filling their great earthenware jars, standing ankle-deep in water, their pink or green-striped baggy trousers tucked between their knees; their heads are covered, if Moslems with the moon-shaped tire, if Christians with a gay handkerchief or the hair plaited in long tails. A negress in blue here and there mingles with the crowd, which is chattering, screaming, gossiping, and sometimes fighting.

"The people of the town are remarkable for the gay colouring of their dresses, and the Christian women for their beauty. Many a charming bit of colour, many a shapely figure set off by picturesque costume, many a dark eye and ruddy cheek have I seen in the streets or by the spring. This beauty is peculiar to the Christians of Bethlehem and Nazareth."

Jesus lived at Nazareth until the time arrived for entering upon his public work. The immediate occasion which called him forth from the carpenter's shop was the news that John the Baptist had begun preaching in the wilderness of Judea. The work of the Palestine explorers has thrown important light on the movements and mission stations of John the Baptist.

John appears to have begun his public work at the great ford of the Jordan near Jericho; and there went out to him Jerusalem and all Judea to be baptized. The Jordan at this part is a brown, rapid swirling stream, about 20 yards across, fringed with a jungle of tamarisk and cane and willow, in which the leopard and the wolf find a hiding place. The tradition which says that Jesus was baptized here is at least as old as the fourth century; the Greek and the Latin churches agree in regard to it, and at the present day pilgrims from all churches resort to this spot to bathe in the sacred waters.

Our explorers see no reason to doubt this tradition, and a difficulty which did exist they have been enabled to remove. It is stated in the fourth Gospel (John i. 28), that John was baptizing in Bethabara beyond Jordan, when Jesus came to him; that the Baptist bare testimony to

Christ during two days, and on the third day Jesus was minded to go into Galilee and was present at Cana at the marriage feast. Hostile critics of the fourth Gospel, taking the traditional scene of John's baptizing near Jericho— where Bethabara has usually been placed on the maps— asserted that Jesus would have a journey of 80 miles to accomplish in a single day to reach Cana of Galilee, and that the feat is of course impossible. But there is really no assertion that it was done or attempted. It is only a tradition of the fourth century which fixes Bethabara so far south, or says that Jesus was baptized at Bethabara. A position near Upper Galilee would suit the narrative better as the site of Bethabara. Now the surveyors in the course of their work marked all the fords of the Jordan, and collected all the names. The following winter, when Major Conder was looking through the list in order to prepare an index, he was struck with the presence of the word *Abara*. He saw at once that the house or station at this place would be Beth-Abara, which had thus been discovered unwittingly. He looked it out upon the map, and found it to be one of the principal fords of the Jordan, just above the place where the Jalud river, flowing down the Valley of Jezreel and by Beisan, debouches into Jordan. The distance thence to Cana would only be 22 miles. The fourth Gospel does not say that Jesus was baptized at Bethabara, and so this new discovery does not disturb that part of the tradition which fixes the baptism near Jericho. Jesus, after being baptized, retired into the wilderness, and when he returned to the world he found that John had removed to the more northerly station, and thither he followed him. As Jesus began to make disciples at Bethabara, the events of John i. must have occurred after the Temptation, and so indeed they are placed in the Gospel Harmonies (see Smith's "Dictionary of Bible," p. 721).

The Revised Version reads "Bethany beyond Jordan,"

instead of Bethabara, and this is the reading of the oldest manuscripts. It is gratuitous to suppose any confusion with Bethany near Jerusalem. "Bathania" was a well-known form (used in the time of Christ) of the old name Bashan, a district in Peræa or the country beyond Jordan; and perhaps, as Conder suggests, the original reading was "Bethabara in Bethany beyond Jordan." We must agree with him, too, that this identification of Bethabara is one of the most valuable discoveries resulting from the survey.

That John the Baptist did move from one station to another in pursuance of his mission is shown again by the statement that after these things John was baptizing in Ænon near to Salim, because there was much water there (John iii. 23). Where was Ænon? It used to be assumed that it was of course near the desert of Judea where John first preached. But surely it would be unnecessary to tell us that there was enough water to baptize with in the Jordan, whereas if abundance of water could be found anywhere else in Palestine it would be somewhat remarkable. Now such abundance is found almost in the heart of Samaria. The traveller who rides across from the town of Samaria, passing behind Ebal, or who follows the stony road in the magnificent gorge east of the same mountain, finds himself gradually descending to the springs which lie at the head of the great *Far'ah* valley, the open highway from Shechem to the *Damieh* ford of the Jordan. It was up this valley that Jacob drove his flocks and herds from Succoth to Shalem near Shechem. It was along the banks of the stream that the "garments and vessels" of the hosts of Benhadad were strewn as far as Jordan. It was here also that Israel, returning from captivity (according to the Samaritans), purified themselves before going up to Gerizim to build the temple. But the place possesses a yet higher interest as the probable site of "Ænon near Salem" where John was baptizing, and where a question arose between John's disciples and a Jew about purifying (John ii. 25). The phrase "much water" might fairly be translated many waters or many springs, and in an open valley here the springs are found. The waters gush out over a stony bed and flow down rapidly in a fine stream. The supply is perennial, and a continual succession of little springs occurs along the bed of the valley, so that the current becomes the principal western affluent of Jordan south of the Vale of Jezreel. About 4 miles north of the head springs is a village called *'Ainun*, and about 3 miles south another village called *Salem.* So here we have "Ænon near Salem," and in between the two villages the two great requisites for the baptism of a multitude, namely, an open space in which the crowd could stand, and abundance of water. There are indeed other places called Salem scattered up and down the country, but none of them has an Ænon near to it ; and there is one other place called Ænon, but it has no Salem near to it, besides which, it is away near Hebron, in a district quite out of the question.

It would appear, then, that John began baptizing, in the first instance, near Jericho, and made his appeal to Jerusalem and all Judea ; that next, remembering the other great section of the Jews in Galilee, he removed to Bethabara in the north ; and further, because the reformed religion was not to be for the Jews alone, he entered Samaria itself and baptized at Ænon.

At the head-springs of Ænon we are only about 5 miles from Jacob's Well. Conder and others consider the identity of Jacob's Well beyond question, because Jewish and Samaritan tradition, Christian and Mohammedan tradition all agree about it. The identity is further supported by the proximity of Joseph's Tomb, about 600 yards north of it, a tomb venerated by the members of every religious community in Palestine. A Christian church was built round Jacob's Well before the year 383 A.D., and destroyed before Crusading times, only the vault or crypt remaining. The ruins covered up the well and hid it altogether some few years ago; but Captain Anderson, of the Palestine Exploration Fund, removed them and descended by a rope. The Arabs allowed the rope to twirl and slip, so that Anderson went into a swoon, from which he was awakened by the shock of striking the bottom. He measured the well and found it 7½ feet in diameter and 75 feet deep. Anciently it must have been deeper, for some of the ruins have fallen into it, and every passing traveller throws in a stone to hear it fall. The question arises, why there should be any well at this spot at all, seeing that the valley (between Ebal and Gerizim) abounds in streams of water, and there is one stream only 100 yards from the well itself? The answer given is that the man who dug the well had no right to use the streams; he was a stranger in the land, and felt the need of a supply of water upon his own property.

Jacob's Well is one of the few spots undoubtedly rendered sacred by the feet of Christ. When the Pharisees had heard that Jesus was baptizing more disciples than John, Jesus left Judea for Galilee, "and he must needs pass through Samaria. So he cometh to a city of Samaria called Sychar, near to the parcel of ground that Jacob gave to his son Joseph, and Jacob's Well was there. Jesus, therefore, being wearied with his journey, sat thus by the well. It was about the sixth hour. There cometh a woman of Samaria to draw water," &c. (John iv. 1-7). This woman, we suppose, came from Sychar; but an unaccountable confusion has grown up between Sychar and Shechem. If the woman had come from Shechem she would have to carry her pitcher a mile and a half to the well, passing abundant streams on the way—an apparently needless trouble. But the early Christians used to place Sychar a mile east of Shechem, and our explorers agree with Canon Williams and others in identifying it with the village of 'Askar, which stands within sight of the well, about half a mile distant, on the slope of Ebal. Yet the Crusaders confounded Sychar with Shechem, misleading everybody who came after; the error lasting to our own time, and reappearing even in carefully-written books.

The question arises, why Jesus on this occasion must needs go through Samaria? It has been customary to reply that it was because Samaria lay right across his path in going from Judea to Galilee. But this does not satisfy us when we know that it was a frequent thing to cross the Jordan and travel by the eastern route, because the Jews had no dealings with the Samaritans. I was one day reading the Gospel of St John very carefully in order to compare notes with a friend, and I was struck with the meaning implied in Christ's expression, "One soweth and another reapeth." Jesus says to his disciples, " Say not ye, there are yet four months and then cometh the harvest." We judge that he is pointing to the rich corn-field, where the valley opens out into the Plain of *Mukh-nah;* he remarks that the corn is not ripe yet, and the harvest is not due. Yet he says, " Behold ! Lift up your eyes and look on the fields, that they are white already unto harvest. He that reapeth receiveth wages and gathereth fruit unto life eternal." He is now referring to the spiritual harvest : the people are flocking out of the town to listen to his teaching, they are favourably disposed and ready to be converted. Now, why should they be so ready to listen, seeing that the Jews had no dealings with the Samaritans? Christ himself supplies the answer when he says, "Herein is the saying true, 'One soweth and another reapeth. I sent you to reap that whereon ye have not laboured ; others have laboured, and ye are entered into their labour.'" He cannot mean that he is sowing seed now, by his preaching, for his disciples to reap a harvest of conversions by-and-bye, for he says, "The fields are white already unto harvest. Lift up your eyes and look!" He recognises the truth that sowing and reaping are separated by an interval of time, though at the Harvest-home sower and reaper may rejoice together, as those who have laboured at different seasons for the same result. Some Teacher, therefore, has been sowing seed among these Samaritans before Christ came to Jacob's Well; and who is that likely to have been but John the Forerunner, when he preached at Ænon, and the people of Sychar went to be baptized at the "many waters"? In the light of this reading we may understand how the woman of Samaria so soon grasps the fact that the Jewish stranger at the well is the Christ that John had said was to come after him. If we read the chapter again we shall see how it was through John's baptizing at Ænon that circumstances arose which made Jesus decide to go through Samaria.

It was while John was yet at Bethabara that Jesus went to Cana of Galilee to the wedding feast. There are two rival sites for Cana: one is the ruin of *Kanah*, about 8 miles north of Nazareth, the supposed site in Crusading times; the other is the village of *Kenna*, about 4 miles north-east, which was the accredited site before the Crusaders arrived. The traveller is shown the water-pots at either place. It is difficult in the present instance to decide between rival claims, but the opinion of most writers is in favour of *Kefr Kenna*, and our explorers lean to that, partly for the reason that it is on the high road between Nazareth and Tiberias.

Travelling eastward to Tiberias we see a little way off the road on our left hand a hill of rather peculiar form; it looks as though it might be the crater of a volcano, with two stunted horns, one at either end. This is called the *Horns of Hattin*, and is noted in history as being the place where the Crusaders received their last crushing defeat at the hands of Sal-a-din, the great Saracen general, in the year 1187. But it is still more interesting to us as being the place where Christ preached the Sermon on the Mount. The tradition which makes *Kurn Hattin* the Mount of Beatitudes is of Latin origin, and not older than the twelfth or thirteenth century; but the place is so well adapted for the delivery of a discourse to a large multitude, that in this case we may well believe it was correctly chosen by those who first selected it. When we are at the spot we have no difficulty in reconciling the seemingly inconsistent statements of St Matthew, who says that the sermon was preached on the mount, and St Mark, who says that Christ came down from the mount, and preached in the plain. Sitting on one of the peaks or "horns" aforesaid, Jesus might begin his discourse to his disciples, and when a larger crowd began to gather, might descend to the base of the peak, while still remaining on the mountain of Hattin.

From Hattin we are soon at Tiberias, a town once beautiful and famous, but now notorious for the filth of its streets and the activity of its vermin. The Arabs say that the king of the fleas holds his court there. Josephus tells us that the city was built by Herod Antipas, and named in honour of the Emperor Tiberius. It was therefore a new city in Christ's day, and probably at first inhabited only by Romans, Antipas himself having a palace there, adorned with figures of animals, "contrary to the Jewish law." Moreover, as it was built on the site of an ancient burial ground, it would be regarded by the Jews as a polluted and forbidden locality. These circumstances, taken together, may account for the fact that Jesus Christ does not appear ever to have entered the city.

The former greatness of Tiberias is indicated by the extent of the walls, 12 feet in thickness, which have been traced by Dr Selah Merrill and by Herr Schumacher for a distance of 3 miles, on the south side. In the course of the wall is an old castle on the summit of a hill, 1000 feet above the town. An aqueduct, 9 miles long, brought pure water from a distance, whereas the present inhabitants are content to drink of the waters of the lake. Looking about in the town we notice some traces of its former grandeur; here a magnificent block of polished granite from Upper Egypt, there a hunting scene carved on the surface of a hard black lintel of basalt, besides old buildings, and broken shafts and columns half buried in rubbish.

From Tiberias we go north, and after a ride of 3 miles reach Medjel, which represents the Magdala of Christ's time, and is known wherever the New Testament is read as the home of Mary Magdalene. The village is insignificant, being only a collection of huts and hovels; the people are poor and degraded, and their children half naked. Travellers approaching the place are greeted by the howling of dogs, which rush out as though they would devour them.

Tiberias and Medjel are the only places now inhabited about the lake, and the visitor is impressed with a sense of deadness and desolation. Yet the lake is beautiful, and upon its shores there were in Christ's time no less than nine cities, while numerous villages dotted the plains and hills around. All the surrounding region was highly cultivated, and the lake itself was covered with fishing boats. There are no more than half a dozen boats now— made at Beyrout, or some other seaport town, and brought hither on the backs of camels—but the lake still swarms with fish. When a revolver was fired into the water at random several fishes were killed and floated on the surface.

The lake is surrounded by hills, except at the south end, where it touches the Jordan Valley. These hills are at such a distance from the water as to leave a belt of land,

generally level, all round it, which at some points broadens
out into large plains, such as those of Gennesaret and
Batiha.   Medjel, already mentioned, is at the southern end
of the charming Plain of Gennesaret, about which Josephus
goes into ecstasies on account of its exceeding great
fertility.   He speaks of the palms and figs, olives and
grapes that flourished there, and the fish for which its
streams were far-famed.   The plain is but 3 miles long
by 1 mile wide, and it now looks neglected ; but it might
be made a little paradise again, for the soil is as fertile as
ever.   "As we journey towards the northern end " (says Dr
Merrill) "we observe on our left a strange sight.   The
mountain appears to have parted asunder and left a great
chasm, the walls of which are perpendicular, and full of
caves, which, not long before the birth of Christ, were
occupied by robbers, whom Herod the Great had much
difficulty in subduing.   Along the bottom of that chasm,
ran, in Christ's time, the main road from Cana of Galilee,
Nazareth, Tabor, and the region of the south-west, to the
north end of the lake, and thence to Damascus.   Christ
would pass along this road in going down from Nazareth
to Capernaum."

It was probably in the Plain of Gennesaret that the
multitude stood on the land while Jesus put off in a boat
to be free from the pressure of the crowd while he addressed them (Mark iv. 1).   In this neighbourhood, also,
no doubt, was spoken the parable of the net cast into
the sea.

Of all the nine cities then about the lake we should like
to recover especially the sites of Capernaum and Bethsaida.
Before the Exploration we had to be content with the
vague statement that Capernaum was somewhere north
of Tiberias.   We are now able to point to two sites,
and say that Capernaum was one or other of these,
while these two places are but 2½ miles apart.   One of

these places is *Tell Hum*, at the head of the lake, about 2
miles west of the point where the Jordan enters the lake.
Here we have ruins indicating the former existence of a
town hardly smaller than Tiberias ; we find a regular
cemetery, and within an enclosure we have the remains of
a synagogue. Besides the synagogue ruins the argument
in favour of this site is found in its name : *Tell* means a
heap, such as the place has become, and *Hum* is the
abraded form of the name Nahum. Tradition said that
the prophet Nahum lived and died here, and indeed his
grave was pointed out as late as the fourteenth century·
The village of Nahum would be *Kefr Nahum* in Hebrew ;
Khafarnaum, as Josephus has it ; Capernaum as we are
familiar with it. Sir Charles Wilson is in favour of this
site. On the other hand, Major Conder is in favour of
Khan Minyeh, 2½ miles from *Tell Hum*, along the shore
southward, and right in the corner of the Plain of Gennesaret. Here, again, we have evidences of the former
existence of a town, although we have no synagogue
ruins. The name of the place, in this case also, supplies
a strong argument. It appears that the Jews, who looked
upon Capernaum as the home of Christ and the head-
quarters of his followers, called the disciples " Sons of
Capernaum ; " they also nicknamed them Diviners or
Sorcerers—in their language, *Minai*, a name often appear-
ing in the Talmud. Khan Minyeh, then, would seem
to be the town of the Minai or Sorcerers, the early Jewish
converts to Christianity ; and their mother town was
Capernaum. An objection might seem to lie against
Khan Minyeh because of its situation in the plain, while
it is said of Capernaum, " And thou, Capernaum, shalt
thou be exalted unto heaven ? thou shalt go down unto
Hades " (Matt. xi. 23). Such an expression might be
interpreted morally ; but if it is to be understood literally,
then there is the suggestion that the town was not entirely

in the plain, but spread over the rocky promontory to the north-east. Rev. Henry Brass explored this promontory in the spring of 1890, and on the highest part, about 242 feet above the lake, found " the remains of a fortification—possibly the station of the Roman Centurion (Matt. viii. 5) —and here and there traces of buildings, but everywhere broken pottery, showing that there was formerly a large population. The ruins of the Khan at the junction of the roads from Cæsarea, Jerusalem, and Perea with the great Roman road leading north to Damascus, probably mark the very spot where Matthew sat at the receipt of custom ; and the outlying rocks at the foot of the cliff, to this day the favourite resort of fish, indicate the spot where Peter would naturally go to cast his hook (Matt. xvii. 27)." *

Before quite dismissing Capernaum from our minds, let us inquire about the site of Bethsaida. The name signifies House of Fisheries, and it is recorded that Bethsaida was on the lake and had the Jordan running past it. Before we go further let us recall what occurred after the feeding of the five thousand.

Jesus constrained his disciples to enter into the boat, and to go before him unto the other side to Bethsaida. This is St Mark's account (Mark vi. 45). St John, speaking of the same event, says that the disciples entered into a boat, and were going over the sea unto Capernaum (John vi. 17). It would appear, therefore, that Bethsaida and Capernaum were in the same direction, looking across the lake from the place where the disciples embarked. On the morrow, when the multitude which had been fed found that Jesus and his disciples had gone away, they engaged some small boats which had come from Tiberias, and crossed over to Capernaum, seeking Jesus. They must have had some ground for believing he had gone away in that direction : at any rate, at Capernaum, " on the other side

* " Quarterly Statement," July, 1890.

of the sea," they found him, and so we cannot doubt that the boat had landed him at Capernaum, or near it. When, therefore, two Evangelists tell us that they came to the shore at Gennesaret, and moored the boat there (Matt. xiv. 34 ; Mark vi. 53), it seems plain that Capernaum itself was in the land of Gennesaret, as it would be if situated at Khan Minyeh. And yet, considering that the disciples had been instructed to go "unto the other side, to Beth-saida," and perhaps only deviated a little through the stress of the storm, and landed at Capernaum, we can hardly doubt that Bethsaida was close by. In fact the ruins at *Tell Hum* may very well mark the site of Beth-saida, especially as their position agrees with the descriptions of early travellers who place Bethsaida north-east of Capernaum. For example, Willibald (A.D. 722) says, "And thence (from Tiberias) they went round the sea, and by the village of Magdalum to the village of Caper-naum, where our Lord raised the prince's daughter. Here was a house and a great wall, which the people of the place told them was the residence of Zebedæus and his sons John and James. And thence they went to Bethsaida, the residence of Peter and Andrew, where there is now a church on the site of their house. They remained there that night, and next morning went to Chorazin, where our Lord healed the demoniac, and sent the devil into a herd of swine. Here was a church of the Christians." They afterwards went on to the sources of the Jordan at Banias.*

Chorazin, 2 miles north-west of *Tell Hum*, is called *Kerazeh*, a name easily confounded with *Khersa*, in the Gadarene country east of the lake ; and this mistake Willibald appears to make.

The question is much discussed whether there were not two Bethsaidas ; and those who believe there were, call the

* "The Recovery of Jerusalem," p. 284.

second one "Bethsaida Julias," and place it on the eastern side of the Jordan, not far from the north end of the lake. Josephus says that Bethsaida was a village raised to the dignity of a town by Philip the Tetrarch, who rebuilt it and changed its name to Julias in honour of the daughter of the Emperor. Philip built himself a tomb there, and was buried there.

The question between *Tell Hum* and *Khan Minyeh* as the site of Capernaum has been made to turn partly on the presence of synagogue ruins at the former place and their absence from the latter. But this can have little or nothing to do with the decision, for the best judges believe that the synagogues date only from the second century A.D.

Nevertheless, the existence of synagogue ruins in Galilee is a very interesting fact; and it is probable that those erected in the second century would be modelled after the pattern of those which preceded them and in which Christ, in so many instances, read and taught. The synagogue ruins at *Tell Hum* are a shapeless heap, but the stones have been carefully examined and measured, and it becomes possible theoretically to reconstruct the building. Similar ruins are found at seven or eight other places in Galilee, and some of them—especially those at *Kefr Birim*—are in a better state of preservation. (*See* Frontispiece.) Examination shows that the Jewish synagogues were not the plain barn-like structures some people had imagined. The building faced the south, looking towards Jerusalem, the holy city. Four rows of columns ran from one end to the other, dividing the building into five aisles. At Kefr Birim one synagogue was furnished with a porch. A smaller building, at a little distance from the village, has two lambs sculptured on the lintel of the door, and beneath them is an inscription in He-brew. The inscription has been thus read by Renan, " Peace be to this place, and upon all the places of God. Joseph the Levite, the son of Levi, put up this lintel. A blessing rest upon his work." At the synagogue ruins of *Nebartein*, north-east of *Safed*, on the lintel of the main entrance, is a representation of the seven-branched candlestick, similar to those in the catacombs at Rome and on the rocks in the wilderness of Sinai. Here, again, is an inscription in Hebrew. During the excavations at *Tell Hum* synagogue a lintel of one of the side entrances was found, and on its face a vase—perhaps the pot of manna—and on either side a rod or reed. Along the head is a scroll of vine leaves and grapes. The dimensions of this synagogue were 74 feet 9 inches by 56 feet 9 inches. The material was white limestone, brought from a distance, while the stone used at Kerazeh was the hard black basalt of the neighbourhood.

As already remarked, *Kerazeh* (Chorazin), north-west of *Tell Hum*, has sometimes been confounded with *Khersa*, which was on the eastern side of the lake. Khersa is Gergesa, where Christ was met by the two demoniacs coming out of the tombs (Matt. ix. 1). It is situated on the left bank of *Wady Semakh*, and at the point where the hills end and the plain stretches out towards the lake. Sir C. Wilson is of opinion that there is only one spot where the herd of swine could have run down a steep place into the lake. It is a place about a mile south of Khersa, where the hills, which everywhere else on the eastern side are recessed from a half to three quarters of a mile from the water's edge, approach within 40 feet of it, and *there* do not end abruptly but descend in a steep, even slope. Some time after Sir C. Wilson's survey, the eastern coast was carefully examined by Mr Macgregor in his canoe, and he came to exactly the same conclusion.

A difficulty has arisen with regard to this locality in consequence of the different readings in the three Gospels. In Matthew Christ is said to have come into the country of the Gergesenes ; in Luke and John into that of the

Gadarenes. . The old MSS. do not give any assistance here, but the similarity of the name Khersa to that of Gergesa is, as Dr Thomson points out, in "the Land and the Book," a strong reason for believing that the reading of Matthew is correct ; and we have also the testimony of Eusebius and Origen that a village called Gergesa once existed on the borders of the lake. Perhaps the discrepancy may be explained by supposing that Gergesa was under the jurisdiction of Gadara. Gadara itself, now *Umm Keis*, is a good two hours' distance from the lake, else here we find rock-hewn tombs which are actually occupied by fellahin, while there do not appear to be any such at Khersa. To meet the difficulty which might be felt from the absence of tombs at Khersa, Sir C. Wilson has suggested that the demoniacs may have lived in a tomb built above ground, like one still existing at *Tell Hum*, a rectangular building, capable of holding a large number of bodies, and which appears to have been whitewashed within and without. It is possibly this description of tomb to which our Lord refers in Matt. xxiii. 27, where he compares the Scribes and Pharisees to "whited sepulchres," beautiful in outward appearance, but within "full of dead men's bones."

Dr Merrill, speaking of Chorazin, Bethsaida, Capernaum, and other places now desolate by the Lake of Galilee, remarks that the contrast between the present and the former condition of this region is painful to one who knows its history. Nevertheless, he says, "this region is to me one of the most sacred and delightful on earth. No place that men have consecrated brings me so near to Christ as a day spent in walking and meditating on these lonely shores."

"Christ also visited Perea, the country east of the Jordan. Doubtless he followed the main road to the hot springs on the Yarmuk, and thence to the beautiful city of Gadara, on the mountain above them. He may have gone

X

a little farther east, past *Capitolias* and *Dium*, cities belonging to the Decapolis, and turned south through a densely populated region to Geraza, whence, by one of the two routes before indicated, he would return to the valley after his mission had been accomplished. It was in Perea that the 'seventy disciples' were commissioned to labour, and their welcome and success must have been unusual, for it is reported of them that they 'returned again with joy, saying, Lord, even the devils are subject to us through thy name' (Luke x.). The connection of our Saviour with this region opens up an interesting field of inquiry. He may have foreseen that in its rich cities, and among its throngs of human beings, his Gospel was soon to triumph in a remarkable manner, for it is true that in Bashan, a country which we are now accustomed to speak of as a desert, Christianity, in the early centuries of our era, had one of its most important strongholds."

Jesus Christ at one time, either for quietness or for safety, went away into the borders of Tyre and Sidon, and there entered into a house and would have no man know it (Mark vii. 24). A similar reason may have led him to visit Cæsarea Philippi (ancient Paneas and Dan) at the extreme north-east corner of the Holy Land, where the Jordan springs forth a full-grown stream, under the slopes of Hermon. It is generally accepted now that Hermon, and not Tabor, was the Mount of the Transfiguration (Luke ix. 29). Hermon was once *Shenir*, the " Shining," a name made appropriate by its cap of snow; and some writers imagine a connection between this and the raiment that became white and dazzling.

There is one remarkable natural peculiarity of Hermon still to be noticed (says Conder) namely, the extreme rapidity of the formation of cloud on the summit. In a few minutes a thick cap forms over the top of the mountain, and as quickly disperses and entirely disappears.

In the accounts of our Lord's transfiguration, we read that whilst staying at Cæsarea Philippi, he retired with his disciples to "a high mountain apart," and there can be but little doubt that some part of Hermon, and very probably the summit, is intended. From the earliest period the mountain has been a sacred place; in later times it was covered with temples; to the present day it is a place of retreat for the Druzes. This lofty solitary peak seems wonderfully appropriate for the scene of so important an event; and in this connection the cloud formation is most interesting, if we remember the cloud which suddenly cleared away, when they found "no man any more, save Jesus only, with themselves" (Mark ix. 8).

After these things it occurred, as Christ and his disciples "were on the way to Jerusalem, that he was passing through the midst of Samaria and Galilee" (Luke xvii. 11). Some critics have cited this text as a proof that St Luke was ignorant of the country about which he wrote. Seeing that Galilee is north of Samaria, they think that a journey from north to south should rather be described as a passing through the midst of Galilee and Samaria. Moreover, they point out that, according to Matt. xix. 1 and Mark x. 1, Jesus did not pass through Samaria at all, but crossed the Jordan, and travelled by the eastern route. Notwithstanding the neatness of this indictment, it is easy to show that St Luke's statement may be perfectly correct. Jesus intended to go up to Jerusalem to the feast, and as he did not share the Jewish prejudice against the Samaritans, he contemplated going through Samaria. He sent some of the disciples before him to prepare his way, and they entered into a Samaritan village; but they could not succeed in obtaining accommodation, because the object of the Master was to go through to Jerusalem (Luke ix. 52). The chronic feeling of enmity between Samaritans and Jews was naturally stirred into greater heat by the sight of pilgrims going up to the festival; for then the question was revived whether men ought to worship at Jerusalem or Mount Gerizim. Being refused a passage through Samaria, and yet still intent upon going up to Jerusalem, Jesus Christ would turn eastward, and journey along the border, which led straight to the Bethabara ford of the Jordan. Travelling thus, with Samaria on his right hand and Galilee on his left, it is surely not incorrect to say that he was passing through the midst of Samaria and Galilee; or, as we have it in the margin of the Revised Version, he passed *between.* It seems to have been at one of the border villages that he was met by ten lepers, one of whom was a Samaritan (Luke xvii. 12); and where would he be more likely to find Jewish and Samaritan lepers in one group than on the border line of the two provinces? He is following this line eastward, and accordingly, when Matthew and Mark say that he crossed the Jordan and came into the borders of Judea, by the eastern route, it is in perfect accordance with the statement in Luke. In further confirmation, we read in Luke xviii. 35, as well as in the other Evangelists, that the route taken brought Jesus through Jericho. To approach Jerusalem from Jericho was a matter of course with the pilgrims from Galilee who had travelled by the eastern route.

The Jericho road was the scene of the parable of the Good Samaritan. "A certain man went down from Jerusalem to Jericho." The actual descent would be about 3000 feet; and every expression of that kind in the Scriptures, as of "going down" or "going up," is always true to the features of the ground. The man "fell among thieves." So likely a district is it, that in the days of the Crusaders nine knights banded themselves together to defend pilgrims going down this dangerous pass: and hence arose the Order of Knights Templars. "There came by a priest and a Levite." Jericho was a sacerdotal city, and priests and Levites were continually passing and repassing between Jericho and Jerusalem. In going down the Jericho road the traveller has often a wide prospect on either side; but it is, for all that, a mountain pass, with no way of escape if one were attacked; and the Bedawin, whose black tents may be seen in the distance, are the very fellows to attack the traveller now, if they dared.

The road up from Jericho brings us past Bethany—a village now of about forty small dwellings—and over the Mount of Olives, to Jerusalem.

[*Authorities and Sources* :—" Tent-Work in Palestine." Major Conder. " The Sea of Galilee." Sir Charles Wilson. (In vol., " Recovery of Jerusalem.") " East of Jordan." Dr Selah Merrill. " Survey Memoirs." Vol. of Special Papers. " Quarterly Statements of P. E. Fund." " Galilee in the Time of Christ." Dr Selah Merrill. " Twenty-One Years' Work in the Holy Land." P. E. Fund.]

2. *Christ in the Capital.*

The Jerusalem of Christ's day was the city as it existed in the days of Herod the Great. East and west it was no wider than at present; southward it covered the high south-western hill and a good part of the slope of Ophel; north-ward the third wall was not yet built, but there were suburban buildings outside the second. The Temple area had been so enlarged by Herod as to include all, or nearly all, the present Noble Sanctuary ; and there were approaches from the west, one of which led over Robinson's Arch. A main street from the Valley Gate led eastward to the Temple, passing over Wilson's Arch. Another main street, running north and south, passed under Wilson's Arch and Robinson's Arch, and led to a gate in the south wall. In the north-western part of the High Town was Herod's palace, with the three strong towers near the Valley Gate which defended it. The Tower of Antonia occupied the site of the present Turkish barracks, north-west of the Temple ; and when Pontius Pilate was governor he occupied it. Westward of the city the *Birket Mamilla* existed as a reservoir of water, and supplied the palace and towers : but the *Birket es Sultan*, or so-called Lower Pool of Gihon, had not been made. The Pool of Siloam was well known, and of course the spring-head which supplied it. The traditional Pool of Bethesda did not exist, but the true Bethesda—now buried under ruins—exhibited its five porches, and was in favour as a healing fountain. For the rest we may say that although all the valleys were deeper than they are now, the streets and bazaars probably followed in most instances the lines which they still preserve, and were just as narrow as they are at present.

In the High Town, called in Josephus' day the Upper Market Place, there would be an open space somewhere, actually used for a market ; and here, we may conjecture, Jesus would sometimes teach. The very circumstances of the spot would suggest the parable of the Labourers, some of whom stood idle till the eleventh hour. Christ also taught in the ample spaces of the Temple courts (John vii. 14) ; and in the last days of his ministry, at any rate, used to retire from the city before the gates were closed at sunset (Luke xxi. 37). Whether he ever lodged within the city we cannot tell, but that he had no home there and no friend in whose house he was sure of a welcome, may perhaps be inferred from the fact that a guest-chamber had to be engaged when he desired to eat the Passover (Mark xiv. 12).

The **Pool** *of Bethesda.*—It is not doubted that when Christ told the blind man to " **Go, wash in** the Pool of Siloam," he

was sending him to the very pool which still bears that
name. About the Pool of Bethesda, "by the sheep *gate*"
(John v.), there has not been the same assurance and unan-
imity. The traditional pool occupies what was once a valley north of the Temple; but as the valley itself was there
when Titus sought to attack the Temple from the north, we
judge the pool to be a later construction. The two arches
at the western end of it, with their staircases now buried in
rubbish, are not the same as "five porches." Again, several
writers have supposed that the so-called Virgin's Fountain
might be the true Bethesda, because it is an intermittent
spring, and because the modern Jews believe the water of
this pool to be a sure cure for rheumatic complaints. They
often go in numbers, men and women together, and stand
in their clothes in the pool, waiting for the water to rise.
But the Virgin's Fountain is too far away from the Sheep-
gate to be the pool which the Evangelist refers to.

It was pointed out some years ago by M. Clermont
Ganneau that the Pool of Bethesda should be sought near
the Church of St Anne, where an old tradition has placed
the house of the mother of Mary, calling it *Beit hanna*,
"House of Anne." This expression is exactly identical
with *Bethesda*, both expressions signifying *House of Mercy*,
or *Compassion.** This anticipation has been verified; for
in the year 1888 the ancient pool of Bethesda was found
a short distance north-west of the present Church of St
Anne. Certain works carried on by the Algerian monks
laid bare a large tank or cistern cut in the rock, to a depth
of 30 feet, and Herr Schick recognised this as the Pool of
Bethesda. It is 55 feet long from east to west, and
measures 12½ feet in breadth. A flight of twenty-four
steps leads down into the pool from the eastern scarp of
rock. Herr Schick, who at once saw the great interest of

---

* "Quarterly Statement," 1872, p. 116.

this discovery, soon found a sister-pool, lying end to end, 60 feet long, and of the same breadth as the first.   The first pool was arched in by five arches, while five corresponding porches ran along the side of the pool. At a later period a church was built over the pool by the Crusaders, and they seem to have been so far impressed by the fact of five arches below, that they shaped their crypt into five arches in imitation.   They left an opening for getting down to the water ; and further, as the crowning proof that they regarded the pool as Bethesda, they painted on the wall of the crypt a fresco representing the angel troubling the water of the pool.

All this appears to agree very well with what Eusebius says in his " Onomasticon," concerning a pool which he calls Bezatha—"a pool at Jerusalem, which is the *Piscina Probatica*, and had formerly five porches, and now is pointed out at the twin pools there, of which one is filled by the rains of the year, but the other exhibits its water tinged in an extraordinary manner with red, retaining a trace, they say, of the victims that were formerly cleansed in it." Here we have a sheep pool, in which the sacrificial victims used to be washed, and close by it (so that they constituted twin pools) a second, which must have been intermittent, the very character attributed to those waters which, at a certain season, were troubled.*   Eusebius gives no clue to the situation of the twin pools, but the Bordeaux pilgrim, who visited Jerusalem in A.D. 333, after speaking of two great pools at the side of the Temple, one on either hand as he entered Jerusalem from the east side (apparently at St Stephen's Gate), refers to the twin pools as being more within the city. They "have five porches" (he says), " and are called Bethsaida. Here the sick of

---

* It would be legitimate to read " by the sheep-pool " instead of " by the sheep-gate."

many years were wont to be healed. But these pools have water which, when agitated, is of a kind of red colour."

There had been a disposition in recent years to identify these twin pools with two souterrains or tunnels existing under the Convent of the Sisters of Sion at the north-west corner of the Haram area, but that fancy is now dissipated. The manner in which most of the previous speculations have been set aside by the actual discovery of the Pool of Bethesda is an instructive testimony to the value of excavation work in Jerusalem.

A Tablet from Herod's Temple.—Josephus, in his "Antiquities of the Jews,"[*] after describing the cloisters of the Temple and the Court of the Gentiles, goes on to describe the inner court, and the middle wall of partition which divided Jews from Gentiles. He says, " Thus was the first enclosure ; in the midst of which, and not far from it, was the second, to be gone up to by a few steps. This was encompassed by a stone wall for a partition, with an inscription which forbade any foreigner to go in under pain of death." Again, in his work on the " Wars of the Jews,"[†]—" When you go through these first cloisters, unto the second court of the Temple, there was a partition, made of stone all round, whose height was three cubits. Its construction was very elegant ; upon it stood pillars, at equal distances from one another, declaring the law of purity, some in Greek, and some in Roman letters, that no foreigner should go within the sanctuary,—for that second court of the Temple was called the Sanctuary, and was ascended to by fourteen steps from the first court."

In the year 1871, M. Clermont Ganneau had the good fortune to discover one of these pillars or tablets, partly buried in the foundations of a building not far from the

---

[*] xv. 11. 5.   [†] v. 5. 2.

Haram area.   It bears the following inscription in Greek, in seven lines :—

ΜΗΘΕΝΑΑΛΛΟΓΕΝΗΕΙΣΠΟ
ΡΕΥΕΣΘΑΙΕΝΤΟΣΤΟΥΠΕ
ΡΙΤΟΙΕΡΟΝΤΡΥΦΑΚΤΟΥΚΑΙ
ΠΕΡΙΒΟΛΟΥΟΣΔΑΝΛΗ
ΦΘΗΕΑΥΤΩΙΑΙΤΙΟΣΕΣ
ΤΑΙΔΙΑΤΟΕΞΑΚΟΛΟΥ
ΘΕΙΝΘΑΝΑΤΟΝ

The translation is :—" No stranger is to enter within the balustrade round the Temple and enclosure.   Whoever is caught will be responsible to himself for his death, which will ensue."

M. Clermont Ganneau remarks that the episode in the Acts of the Apostles (xxi. 26, *et seq.*) throws great light on this precious inscription and receives light from it.   Paul, after purification, presents himself in the Temple ;   the people immediately rise against him, because certain Jews of Asia believed that Paul had introduced a Gentile— Trophimus of Ephesus—and had thus polluted the sacred place.   They are about to put him to death when the Tribune commanding at Fort Antonia intervenes and rescues him.   The people demand of the Tribune the execution of the culprit, *i.e.*, the application of the law.

This inscription, and probably this very stone, was almost certainly seen and read by Christ ;   and it would be likely to impress him painfully with the exclusive spirit of the Jews.   It certainly could not meet with the approval of the Teacher who preached to Samaritans at Jacob's Well, and laboured more in the half-Gentile town of Capernaum than in Nazareth, defending his course by quoting the example of Elijah who went to Sarepta a city of Zidon.   Christ declared himself the Light of all the World, and the

Shepherd who had other sheep not of the Jewish fold. It was the work of Christ, before it became the work of Paul, to break down the middle wall of partition between Jew and Gentile. There can hardly be a question, then, that the sight of this inscription would intensify his desire to see this Temple destroyed and the Jewish ritual abolished, that he might rear upon its ruins a spiritual temple for all nations.

At the beginning of the week of his passion, Jesus Christ came up the steep ascent from Jericho, the road bringing him at last to Bethany. One night he halted in the village, as of old; the village and the desert were then all alive, as they still are once every year at the Greek Easter, with the crowd of Paschal pilgrims moving to and fro between Bethany and Jerusalem. In the morning he set forth on his journey. Three pathways lead, and probably always led, from Bethany to Jerusalem; one, a long circuit over the northern shoulder of Mount Olivet, down the valley which parts it from Scopus; another, a steep foot-path over the summit; the third, the natural continuation of the road by which mounted travellers always approach the city from Jericho, over the southern shoulder, between the summit which contains the Tombs of the Prophets and that called the Mount of Offence. "There can be no doubt" (says Dean Stanley) "that this last is the road of the entry of Christ, not only because, as just stated, it is, and must always have been, the usual approach for horsemen and for large caravans, such as then were concerned, but also because this is the only one of the three approaches which meets the requirements of the narrative which follows.

"Two vast streams of people met on that day. The one poured out from the city, and as they came through the gardens whose clusters of palm rose on the south-eastern corner of Olivet, they cut down the long branches, as was their wont at the Feast of Tabernacles, and moved upwards towards Bethany, with shouts of welcome. From Bethany streamed forth the crowds who had assembled there on the previous night, and who came testifying to the great event at the sepulchre of Lazarus. The road soon loses sight of Bethany. . . . Gradually the long procession swept up and over the ridge, where first begins 'the descent of the Mount of Olives towards Jerusalem.' At this point the first view is caught of the south-eastern corner of the city. . . . It was at this precise point that the shout of triumph burst forth from the multitude, Hosanna to the Son of David ! . . . Again the procession advanced. The road descends a slight declivity, and the glimpse of the city is again withdrawn behind the intervening ridge of Olivet. A few moments, and the path mounts again, it climbs a rugged ascent, it reaches a ledge of smooth rock, and in an instant the whole city bursts into view. . . . Immediately below is the valley of the Kedron, here seen in its greatest depth as it joins the valley of Hinnom, and thus giving full effect to the great peculiarity of Jerusalem, seen only on its eastern side—its situation as of a city rising out of a deep abyss. It is hardly possible to doubt that this rise and turn of the road, this rocky ledge, was the exact point where the multitude paused again, and ' He, when he beheld the city, wept over it.' Nowhere else on the Mount of Olives is there a view like this."*

On one of those last days the Great Teacher, leaving the city a little before sunset, sat on one of the rocky banks of Olivet, over against the Temple. The mountain rises 150 feet above the level of the city ; the city has the appearance of being tilted up on its western side, so that from the mountain you can look down into its streets. The Temple courts would be in the foreground, with Solomon's Porch on the eastern side. Perhaps the 80 feet of rubbish

* "Sinai and Palestine."

which now rests against the wall had not yet half accumulated; and in that case the stones which Solomon laid down would be still visible—blocks 20 cubits long by 6 cubits thick, and extending a length of 400 cubits. The disciples had been calling their Master's attention to the goodly stones and buildings of the Temple, as they came along, and he had declared that they would one day be thrown down; and now, sitting on Olivet he prophesies the end of the age.

From the Mount of Olives it was but a short way to Bethany, to spend the night. A wild mountain-hamlet, perched on its broken plateau of rocks, Bethany is screened by a ridge from the view of the top of Olivet. The modern name of the village—El-Azarieh—connects it with Lazarus, whose traditional house and grave are still exhibited, as well as the traditional house of Simon the leper. The welcome which awaited Christ in the home of Mary and Martha and Lazarus must have been very grateful after the day's teaching and turmoil in the noisy city.

It is hopeless to try and identify in Jerusalem the house or the street in which the disciples made ready the Passover for their Master. The Garden of Gethsemane, which was visited afterwards, may probably have been at or near the place which is now pointed out on the slope of Olivet.

When Christ was brought before Pilate it would be at the Tower of Antonia, north-west of the Temple, on the site now occupied by the Turkish barracks.

Outside the barracks, on the north side, is the street now called the *Via Dolorosa*, because tradition says that Christ passed along it in going from the Judgment Hall to the place of crucifixion, marked now by the Church of the Holy Sepulchre.

The True Site of Calvary.—The question has been much debated whether the Church of the Holy Sepulchre occupies the true site of Calvary or not. We know that

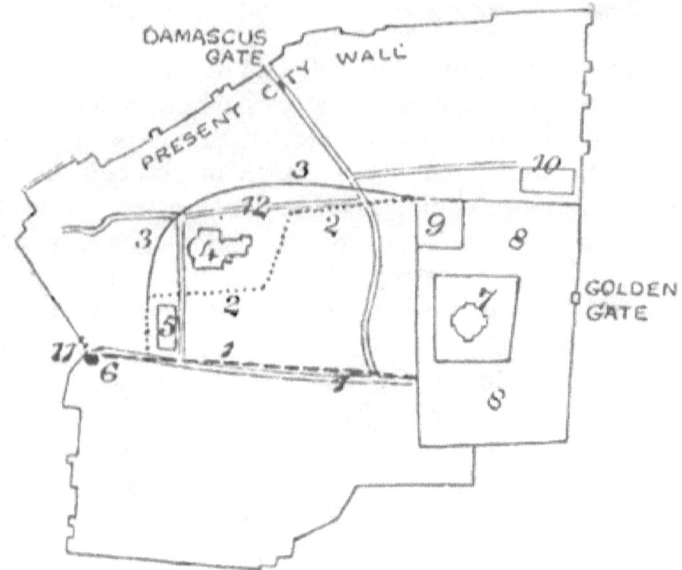

OUTLINE PLAN OF JERUSALEM.

1 North wall of Upper City, probable course.
2 Second wall, so drawn as to exclude the Church of the Holy **Sepulchre.**
3 Second wall, including the Church.
4 Church of the Holy Sepulchre.!
5 Pool **of Hezekiah.**
6 Citadel.
7 Dome of the Rock (Site of the Temple).
8 Haram-area or Noble Sanctuary.
9 Tower **of** Antonia, now Turkish Barracks.
10 Birket-Israel (Traditional Bethesda.)
11 Jaffa Gate.
12 Via Dolorosa.

Jesus suffered and was buried at some spot outside the city, for it was " as they came out " that they found Simon of Cyrene, and compelled him to go with them to bear the cross. The Church of the Holy Sepulchre is almost in the heart of the present city ; but we have to remember that at the date of the crucifixion the third wall was not yet built. The first question to be settled is the course of the second wall, and the point whether it included the site of the church or not. In this connection the discovery of a portion of the second wall, running north-west, along by the Greek Bazaar, was very important : only it was not followed far enough to remove all doubt. If we adopt Herr Schick's line for the second wall, the Church of the Sepulchre would be outside : but this is not enough. If the site were within the second wall it could not be Calvary ; if it was outside the wall it may be Calvary or may not. The Church is closer to the wall than we should expect the place of execution to be ; and unless Calvary were further away there would hardly seem to be reason enough for pressing Simon of Cyrene into service to carry the cross.

But another discovery must be mentioned which has some bearing on the question. A little way east of the church, on a piece of ground belonging to the Russians, the excavators passed through the remains of some bazaars which were known to have existed there in the middle ages, and below these they came upon a Byzantine pavement, which appears to be the one laid down by Constantine around the buildings which he erected. Thus it becomes morally certain that the Church of the Holy Sepulchre stands on the spot where Constantine built his church, believing it to be Calvary. But between the days of Christ and the days of Constantine there was time and room for mistake to arise. Jerusalem was destroyed in the year 70, the Christians did not return to it until.

eighty years after, and by that time it might be difficult to identify the sacred sites. When Constantine came to build his church he found the site occupied by a temple of Venus, a circumstance which may argue the traditional sacredness of the site, but scarcely the tradition that it had been the Jewish place of execution. Major Conder says he could devoutly wish that the site may turn out not to be genuine, because it is disgraced by the scenes that occur there.

Passing through the doorway we enter the vestibule, in which is the Stone of Unction, a slab of marble which is devoutly kissed by pilgrims. Passing round it to the left, the rotunda of the church is reached ; to the right a narrow passage with small chapels runs behind the apses of the Greek church, and here a flight of steps leads down to the subterranean Chapel of Helena with its picturesque lighting and heavy eighth century basketwork capitals. Beneath this, again, is the dark cave so suggestively named the Chapel of the Invention of the Cross. The rotunda is well lighted with a dome light blue in colour, and covered with golden lilies and arabesques. In the centre rises the old Chapel of the Sepulchre, dark and gloomy, of marble discoloured by age, surmounted by a queer cupola of Italian taste, and ornamented all along the top with gilt nosegays and modern-framed pictures. Stooping to enter, we pass into the vestibule or Chapel of the Angel, walled with marble slabs, and thence into the inner Chapel of the Sepulchre itself, where the darkness is only relieved by the glowing lamps over the altar on the tomb. The most impressive portion of the church is, however, the nave east of the rotunda, belonging to the Greeks, with its great screen in front of the three eastern apses. The floor is unoccupied, save by the short column marking the " centre of the world." The dome above is poor, rudely white-washed, and painted in fresco ; but the glory of the place consists in the large screen and the panelling of the side walls.*

On Sundays the Christians of various churches—Greek, Latin, Armenian, Coptic—hold their services simultaneously, under the dome and in the side chapels which open off it. On one occasion when I was present the Greek patriarch was preaching under the dome of the rotunda, at the east end of the Chapel of the Sepulchre when suddenly the Latins struck up their instrumental music and singing, drowning the preacher's voice. I was prepared to sympathise with the Greeks, when presently they formed a procession and marched round the rotunda, passing right through a little band of Copts who were engaged in their own way of worship at the west end of the Chapel of the Sepulchre. This want of consideration for the members of other churches seemed so calculated to lead to quarrels that I was not surprised to find a hundred Turkish soldiers drawn up in front of the church to keep the peace. This was a fortnight before Easter. At Easter time itself, when the so-called miracle of the "holy fire" is enacted, and Christians of all churches struggle with one another to be the first to light their tapers at the sacred flame, quarrels do actually arise, and the place is a pandemonium. Woe to the owner of the taper first lit; it is snatched from him, and extinguished by having a dozen others thrust into it. Strong men struggle with one another, and even delicate women and old men fight like furies. We may well join with Conder in wishing that the evidence may finally prove Calvary to have been somewhere else.

For some years past a site has been coming into favour, outside the present north wall, not far from the Damascus Gate. Here is a rounded knoll with a precipice on the south side of it, containing a cave known to Christians as Jeremiah's Grotto, from the tradition that Jeremiah lived

* Conder's "Tent Work."

Y

in it and composed his Lamentations there. When this
knoll is looked at from the south-east, especially from the
southern shoulder of the Mount of Olives, it appears to
many observers to bear a striking resemblance to a huge
skull. As long ago as 1871, Mr Fisher Howe of Brooklyn
proposed the identification, in a little book called "The
True Site of Calvary," published in New York.* Dr
Chaplin and Major Conder have given additional probability to it by bringing into prominence the Jewish tradition which regards this knoll as the place of public
execution. When the death was by stoning, the condemned person was hurled from the top of the cliff, which
is about 50 feet high, and if he was not killed by the fall,
stones were cast at him till he died. The place was called
the House of Stoning, and Christian tradition has regarded
it as the place of the martyrdom of Stephen. The circumstance that Jesus Christ was put to death in the Roman
manner, being crucified and not stoned, makes little difference to the argument for the site of Calvary, since there
is no reason to suppose that Jerusalem possessed two
places of execution. It may be added that the surface
of the knoll is now used as a Mohammedan burial ground ;
and this may also have been its character in Jewish times.
About 200 yards west of the Grotto, Conder made the
interesting discovery of an indisputably Jewish tomb
judged to belong to the centuries immediately preceding
the Christian era. It would be bold to hazard the suggestion that this is the very tomb in which the body
of Christ was laid—the new tomb in the garden belonging
to Joseph of Arimathea—yet its position so near the
old place of execution is certainly remarkable. "Thus,"
says Conder, " to ' a green hill far away, beside a city wall,'

* See a paper by Rev. Charles S. Robinson, in the *Century Magazine*,
November, 1888.

we turn from the artificial rocks and marble slabs of the monkish chapel of Calvary."

[*Authorities and Sources:* — "Tent Work."   Major Conder.   "The Recovery of Jerusalem."   Colonels Warren and Wilson.   "Sinai and Palestine."   Dean Stanley.   "Walks about Jerusalem."   W. H. Bartlett. "Quarterly Statements of Palestine Exploration Fund."]

CHAPTER V.

1. *Assyria.*

MESOPOTAMIA—"the Land between the Rivers"—is a tract of country nearly 700 miles long, and from 20 to 250 miles broad, enclosed between the Euphrates and the Tigris, and extending from the mountains of Armenia to near the Persian Gulf. It is for the most part a vast plain, but is crossed near its centre by a range of hills running almost east and west—from Hit on the Euphrates, famous for its bitumen pits, to Samarah on the Tigris. North of this line the country, though dry and bare, is undulating, and rises occasionally into mountains, while south of it the region is flat and consists of rich, moist, alluvial land, formed by the rivers themselves. This land of alluvium was Babylonia, and its capital Babylon; the country north of it was Assyria, with its capital Nineveh. But the extent of both countries varied from time to time, according to the power of various monarchs and their successes in war.

The beginnings of the Assyrian and Babylonian empires are lost in obscurity, and no records exist among the people themselves accounting for their origin. Yet the account given in the Bible agrees so well with what is known from the records that there can be no reasonable doubt that in it there is a true history of the rise of these two nations, which were in after time to wield the power of the then known world. This Biblical account, borne out and amplified as it is by the late discoveries, forms one of the most interesting and instructive links in the history of the human race and its progress in civilisation.

"Taking, then, the account as it stands in the Bible,"* says Mr Budge, "it appears that the descendants of Ham, the third son of Noah, were Cush, Mizraim, Phut, and Canaan. The lands of Cush and Mizraim have hitherto been identified with Ethiopia and Egypt respectively; Phut was regarded as doubtful, and Canaan was the country with which we are so well acquainted from the frequent occurrence of the name in the Bible. The identification of the first-named and most important of these districts, the land of Cush, has been regarded by many as unsatisfactory: for Nimrod, judging from the names of towns said to have been founded by him, could hardly have been an Ethiopian, though, according to the Bible story, he was a descendant of Cush.

Amongst the treasures of the Assyrian excavations there has luckily been found a tablet, giving, in a list of the nations, &c., along the Taurus range of mountains, a country bearing the name of Kusu, the same word as is used in the inscriptions to denote the country of Ethiopia; and from this and from other sources it is clear that two countries of this name were known to the people of the ancient world, the one being Ethiopia and the other Cappadocia or its immediate neighbourhood. It seems therefore likely that Nimrod and his followers, for some reason unrecorded, left his home in the land of Cush or Cappadocia, and journeying in a south-easterly direction, came to the land of Sumer or Shinar. There meeting perhaps with the Semitic population of the country, he did not go any farther, but settled there with his followers, and built Babylon, and Birs-Nimroud, the supposed Tower of Babel.

In course of time the new comers began to mingle with

* Genesis x. 6.

the original (Semitic) inhabitants of the country, and both races were obliged, for the purpose of trade and intercourse, to learn each other's language, so that there must have been for several hundreds of years two tongues in use at the same time in Mesopotamia, and it was not until the twelfth or even perhaps the tenth century before Christ, that the Akkadian was entirely supplanted by the language of the Semitic Babylonians. The Norman invasion in England is a case parallel to the above, but with this difference, that whilst the invasion of England by the Normans was a conquest, the entry of these people (afterwards known as Akkadians and Sumerians) into Babylonia seems to have been otherwise ; and the Babylonian language, therefore, while admitting very many Akkadian and Sumerian words, has not suffered, with regard to the grammatical forms, to the same extent as the English language.

The entry of the Akkadians into Babylonia was the beginning of civilisation in that country, for they brought with them, along with their religion, their legends and traditions, their laws, their art, building knowledge, agricultural skill, and that great civiliser of nations, the art of writing. From this union of the intellectual Akkadian race and the warlike Babylonians arose the two nations of whom both tradition and history have preserved the record, as having been the mightiest of the nations of the ancient world, namely, Babylonia and Assyria, of whom so many tales are told, and whose power and high civilisation amongst the barbarism of the early ages of the world made so great an impression during the time of their supremacy.

After the mingling of these two races, but long before the Akkadian language had died out, the Babylonians, as they will be henceforth called, sent out colonies northwards and founded the great cities of Assyria—Ninua (Nineveh), Resin, Kalhu (Calah), Assur, &c.

The religion of the Assyrians was derived from Babylonia, and remained very similar to that of the latter country. Both countries worshipped the same deities, but the Assyrians made some changes in the system, especially in introducing the worship of Assur. Assur was worshipped as "king of the gods," "father of the gods," " the deity who created himself." Among the other principal gods of the Assyrians were Nebo, the god of writing ; Merodach, or Bel, a companion deity to Nebo ; Shamas, the Sun-god, and Sin the Moon-god ; Ishtar, corresponding to Venus ; Nergal and Ninip, gods of hunting ; Vul the storm god, Anu, king of heaven, and Hea, the lord of the under world.

The government of Assyria was monarchical, and the power of the king was absolute, though in practice his rule was tempered by the advice of counsellors. The commander-in-chief of the army was called the Tartan, and here was also a high officer called the Rabshakeh (2 Kings xviii. 17). Judges decided cases in the gate of the temple or the palace, and there was an appeal from them to the governor or king. The priests were a privileged class ; they lived on the revenues of the temples and the offerings of worshippers. The Assyrian months were lunar, and the 7th, 14th, 21st, and 28th days were Sabbaths of rest : extra work and even missions of mercy were forbidden, certain foods were not to be eaten, and the king was not to ride in his chariot. The laws of the country resembled in many respects those of Israel : a father was supreme in his household, and a husband had the power of divorcing his wife. Slavery was in vogue, and whole families were sometimes sold together. Various trades were practised, including weaving, dyeing, manufacture of iron goods, copper, and bronze goods, sculpture, and building, &c. But the most remarkable feature of Assyrian civilisation was their literature and libraries of clay tablets, and it is to these that we owe most of our present knowledge of this great people.

Before the days of Moses there was friendly intercourse, as we have seen, between Mesopotamia and Egypt. In later ages Assyria and Egypt were frequently at war with one another. The hostile armies were obliged to march through Palestine; and it became very difficult for the kings of Israel and Judah to look on with equanimity and preserve a strictly neutral attitude. Yet if they favoured one of the great powers they of course gave umbrage to the other; besides which, Assyria, in the days of its power, could hardly brook to leave any small kingdom independent. At length Samaria was conquered, and its inhabitants deported, by Shalmaneser or by Sargon; and afterwards Judea also, by Nebuchadnezzar.

Speaking of the captivity of Israel in Babylonia as a providential event, a great German writer, Lessing, says, —"When the child, by dint of blows and caresses had come to years of understanding, the father sent it at once into foreign countries, and here it recognised at once the good which in its father's house it had possessed but not been conscious of."* Again he says,—"The child, sent abroad, saw other children, who knew more, who lived more becomingly, and asked itself in confusion, why do I not know that too? why do I not live so too? ought I not to have been taught and admonished of all this in my father's house?"

It is because of this sojourn abroad of the Jews, and the influence of other nations upon them, that the exploration of these eastern countries is a matter of such importance to Bible students. In Assyria, Babylonia, and Egypt we get into by-paths of Bible history, and the old records when unearthed, read sometimes like new chapters of the Bible.

The land of Mesopotamia, not inaptly called a grave-yard of empires and nations, is now neglected and desolate, under Turkish misrule. "The monotony of the landscape would be unbroken" (says Zénaïde A. Ragozin) "but for

* Lessing : "Education of the Human Race."

certain elevations and hillocks of strange and varied shapes, which dot the plain in every direction ; some are high and conical or pyramidal in form, others are quite extensive and rather flat on the summit, others again long and low, and all curiously unconnected with each other or with any ridge of hills. This is doubly striking in Lower Mesopotamia or Babylonia, proverbial for its excessive flatness. The few permanent villages, composed of mud-huts or plaited reed-cabins, are generally built on these eminences ; but others are used as burying-grounds, and a mosque, the Mohammedan house of prayer, sometimes rises on one or the other. The substance of these mounds being rather soft and yielding, their sides are still furrowed in many places with ravines, worn by the rushing streams of rain-water. The rubbish washed away lies scattered on the plain, and is seen to contain fragments of bricks and pottery, sometimes inscribed with arrow-headed characters ; in the ravines themselves are laid bare whole sides of walls of brickwork and pieces of sculptured stone."

The Arabs never thought of exploring these curious heaps. Their law forbids them to represent the human form either in painting or sculpture, lest it should lead the ignorant into idolatry. They are superstitious, and look on relics of ancient statuary with suspicion amounting to fear, and connect them with magic and witchcraft. It is therefore with awe not devoid of horror that they tell travellers of underground passages in the mounds, haunted not only by wild beasts, but by evil spirits, strange figures having been dimly perceived in the crevices. Better instructed foreigners have long ago assumed that within these mounds must be entombed whatever ruins and relics may be preserved of the great cities of yore.

The first European whose love of learning was strong enough to make him disregard difficulty and expense, and use the pick-axe upon these mounds, was an Englishman named Rich. This was in 1820 : but Mr Rich was not very successful, and it was literally true that up to 1842, "a case 3 feet square enclosed all that remained, not only of the great city Nineveh, but of Babylon itself." In 1842 M. Botta, a French Consul stationed at Mosul on the Tigris, began to dig, and after fruitless labour at the mound of Kouyunjik, opposite Mosul, was directed by a native to Khorsabad, and there, on cutting a trench, entered a hall lined all round with sculptured slabs, representing battles, sieges, and similar events. A new and wonderful world was suddenly opened, and he walked as in a dream. The discovery created an immense sensation in Europe, and the spirit of research and enterprise was effectually aroused.

The investigation was soon taken up by Mr Austen Henry Layard, our own countryman, and the objects found were brought to the British Museum, which now boasts a splendid collection. After getting over preliminary difficulties—the interesting story of which may be found in his volumes on "Nineveh and its Remains"—Mr Layard obtained a grant of money from the Museum, with full licence from the Turkish Government, and then succeeded in organizing a band of Arabs to work willingly and well, and from that moment made new discoveries every day.

One morning, as he was going to the scene of operations —they were digging in the mound of Nimroud—two Arabs galloped up to him, and said, " Hasten, O Bey, hasten to the diggers, for they have found Nimrod himself! Wallah, it is wonderful, but it is true; we have seen him with our eyes! There is no God but God!" What they had seen was a sculptured human head, which, upon removing more earth, was seen to belong to a winged quadruped—one of those colossal "bulls" since deposited at the British Museum. A "bull" we say, but really a monster with the body of a bull (sometimes the body of a lion), the head of a man, and the wings of an eagle—the Assyrian idea of the cherubim.   Many of these objects were surrounded by writing in the curious cuneiform or arrow-headed character.

Besides these so-called bulls, Mr Layard found obelisks of black basalt, with figures in low relief representing tribute being brought to the Assyrian kings.   On the black obelisk in the British Museum — found in the

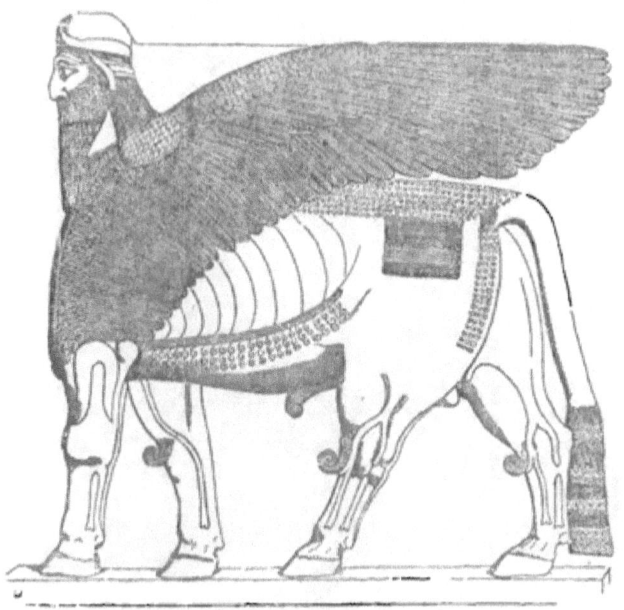

WINGED HUMAN-HEADED BULL.   (N.-W. Palace, Nimrod.)

central mound of Nimroud, amid the ruins of Shalmaneser's palace—occurs the name and figure of Jehu, king of Israel, as bringing tribute to Shalmaneser II. (about B.C. 842).   The mistake indeed is made of calling him " Jehu, son of Omri ; " Jehu sat upon the throne of Omri, but he was a usurper and not of Omri's house.   The tribute bearers on this obelisk carry golden cups and goblets, bars of the precious metals, and other valuable things.   Rev. H. G. Tomkins, speaking of these Assyrian sculptured portraits of Jehu and his princes, says they have "strong aquiline features, and that peculiar shrug or quirk of the nostril which gives a shrewd and

BLACK OBELISK.

sinister look to many a Jew of London streets.   In drawing one of these familiar faces from the monument, I was ready to believe that it belonged to a lineal ancestor of the London 'Clo' men.'   The bag falling down the stooping back deepened this impression." *

* "Journal of the Anthropological Institute," February, 1889.

In addition to these things Mr Layard brought home a large number of alabaster slabs sculptured with battle scenes, lion hunts, and the representation of sacred trees to which winged figures are making mysterious offerings. It was the custom of these Assyrian kings to have the halls and chambers of their palaces lined with plain alabaster slabs, and after each new victory to have the story engraved in a separate room, so that in one chamber we get an account of a battle in Babylonia, in another the story of the siege of Lachish near the Philistine country, and so on.

But the reader—who has no doubt visited the British Museum and looked at all these things—may perhaps ask why we repeat the familiar story. It is in order to give completeness to the picture, and also to induce young visitors to the Museum to look *into* things as well as look at them. Where did the antiquities come from? How have the inscriptions been deciphered? What do they say? Although many of them were brought to the Museum years ago, the writing was not immediately read; the process of decipherment is still going on, and hardly a year passes without startling discoveries being made in the Museum itself. In the year 1872 Mr George Smith there, taking up a clay tablet that had been neglected, deciphered the inscription, and found it to be the Chaldean story of the Flood. In 1873, going out to Assyria for the purpose, he actually discovered the missing portion of the tablet. Such facts are intensely interesting to the student of the Scriptures, and they attract us to give a portion of our attention to the legends and the literature of the Assyrians and the Chaldeans.

Nineveh, we read, was a city of three days' journey. It actually extended 20 miles in length by 10 miles in breadth, and was surrounded by a great wall upon which three chariots could be driven abreast.* Within this cir-

* It is right to say that some writers are not convinced that Nineveh was 60 miles round. They regard Nimroud, Kouyunjik, &c., as so many separate cities.

cumference great mounds exist, as those referred to at Nimroud, Khorsabad, and Kouyunjik. Within these mounds have been discovered six palaces and three temples ; although only one of these buildings—the palace of Sennacherib, at Kouyunjik—is in a decent state of preservation. The restoration of this structure by Mr J. Ferguson, the architect, prefixed as an illustration to Layard's " Nineveh," shows it to have been a very magnificent pile. A second palace found at Kouyunjik belonged to Assurbanipal, the grandson of Sennacherib.

Sennacherib himself we are familiar with through the Bible. He was that monarch who so terrified the good king Hezekiah, when he sent him a blasphemous message and threatened to come and destroy Jerusalem. What the Jews of Jerusalem had to fear if he should come they knew too well; and we know now, for Sennacherib had been besieging Lachish (2 Kings xviii.; Isaiah xxxvi.) in Palestine, and we have recovered the record of that siege. It is inscribed on one of the bulls discovered at the largest of the royal buildings, and shows the monarch seated on his throne, while the

SENNACHERIB BEFORE LACHISH.

writing around says, " I, Sennacherib, the great king, the king of Assyria, seated on the throne of judgment before Lachish, I give permission for the slaughter." Before him are the miserable captives, having rings fixed into their noses or lips, with bridles attached, so that their heads may be held facing forward while the king puts out their eyes with a pointed instrument. Captives are there having their tongues torn out, others being stripped naked and flayed alive, while human heads are piled up into pyramids.

All these tortures the Jews themselves had to fear if Sennacherib should take Jerusalem. It was doubtless a day of terrible suspense in the Holy City, and a night in which few dared go to sleep. But the early morning brought the tidings that the army of Sennacherib was destroyed, that the angel of the Lord had gone forth and slain in the camp of the Assyrians a hundred four score and five thousand men. We knew the Scripture story of the deliverance, but we can realise it better now when we have the record of the siege of Lachish, and know what fate threatened the Jews of Jerusalem.

Moreover, we have recovered Sennacherib's own account of this very campaign, in which he tells us that he had taken forty-six fenced cities in Judea, and that he shut up Hezekiah in Jerusalem "like a bird in a cage." He forbears to tell us why he failed to capture the bird ; he glosses over the disaster which befell his army; and he seems even to misrepresent the facts by declaring that, after this, Hezekiah sent him splendid presents to Babylon, for the presents of Hezekiah were sent before this, when Sennacherib was down by Lachish, and sent with the hope of buying him off, which there was no need to do after his retreat.

A great difficulty in the Book of the Prophet Isaiah is also satisfactorily cleared up by these inscriptions. Sennacherib, coming from the Philistine country to Jerusalem, would have to travel from the south-west, whereas, in an earlier chapter, Isaiah had told us that the Assyrian invader came down from the north, that he captured Carchemish in his way, and conquered Damascus, and took Samaria, and then, after crossing the gorge at Michmash, encamped at Nob, outside Jerusalem on the north. Moreover, the prophet intimates, he is likely to take the city; whereas, in the later chapter, he says, " He shall not take it, nor so much as shoot an arrow against it." It was a great difficulty, and it appeared to be a contradiction; but it is now satisfactorily explained, for we find from the Assyrian inscriptions that there had been an earlier campaign, conducted by Sargon, the father of Sennacherib, ten years before, and that he it was who actually came by the northerly route, and did capture Carchemish, &c., on his way. There can be no doubt that if we read the 10th chapter of Isaiah with Sargon in our minds, and not Sennacherib, all difficulty disappears.

In the 20th chapter of Isaiah there is an incidental mention of this Sargon, " In the year that the Tartan (*i.e.*, the commander-in-chief) came unto Ashdod, when Sargon, the king of Assyria, sent him," &c.; and for twenty-five centuries this had been the only evidence that any such monarch had lived. Not unnaturally the evidence was thought insufficient—this isolated reference standing like a doubtful fossil in old-world rocks—and many historians and critics wished to identify Sargon with Shalmaneser, Sennacherib, or Esarhaddon. Some said that Isaiah had made a mistake. But Nineveh is disinterred, and it turns out that Sargon was a very great king, and not even the first of that name, for there had been two Sargons, heroes of antiquity, before him. M. Botta finds at Khorsabad the palace of Sargon; and it appears that he was the successor of Shalmaneser, he was the father of Sennacherib, and he reigned for seventeen years. Among the treasures which Mr George Smith recovered from the ruins of Nineveh is the royal seal of Sargon, with his name and date.

As soon as Sargon ascended the throne he prosecuted the Syrian war with vigour, keeping up the siege of Tyre, storming the city of Samaria, and subduing the whole country of Israel. The kingdom of Samaria was put an end to, the people being carried into captivity and spread over the northern provinces of the Assyrian empire and in the cities of the Medes. It appears to be Sargon who is referred to in 2 Kings xvii. 6, and xviii. 11 (although the passages had hitherto been understood of Shalmaneser), where "the king of Assyria" took Samaria and carried Israel away, placing in their cities men from Babylon, from Cuthah, from Avva and Hamath and Sepharvaim.

In the eleventh year of Sargon the people of Ashdod in Philistia deposed the ruler whom Sargon had placed over them, and set up a man named Yavan, whose chief recommendation was his hostility to Assyria. Yavan made league with Hezekiah, king of Judah, with Moab, and with Edom, and led the Philistines to revolt. The leaguers sent an embassy to Egypt, asking aid, and Pharaoh held out encouragements, but did not give any assistance when the hour of danger came. Sargon, learning of the revolt, came to Palestine ; Yavan fled into Egypt, the rebellion collapsed, and the cities of Ashdod and Gimtu were taken by the Assyrians. Yavan ultimately delivered himself up to the king of Meroe, or Ethiopia, who bound him and sent him in chains to Sargon.

The expedition against Ashdod took place in B.C. 711, during the reign of Hezekiah, king of Judah, and is the one referred to in the twentieth chapter of Isaiah, where the prophet denounces the conduct of Egypt. The way in which Isaiah speaks of the Egyptians and the Ethiopians, in this and other chapters, is remarkably justified by the account given in the Assyrian inscriptions. Egypt is described in the annals of Sargon as a weak power, always stirring up revolts against Assyria, and unable to help or shield the revolters. "In those days" (remarks Mr George Smith, from whose larger work we are here quoting) "Egypt was truly a broken reed.   The account which Sargon gives of the turning of the fountains and water-courses to protect the city of Ashdod strikingly parallels the similar preparations of Hezekiah (2 Chron. xxxii.); and it is a curious fact that Hezekiah's preparations had been made only two years before, according to the ordinary chronology."

As remarked by Mr St Chad Boscawen, the political significance of the embassy of Berodach Baladan (2 Kings xx. 12) is at once apparent when viewed in the light of the monumental inscriptions ; and the atmosphere of intrigue, rebellion, and stern vengeance is very clearly apparent in the writings both of the Hebrew and the Assyrian scribe. It was this embassy, in B.C. 712, which brought about the invasion of Judea and the siege of Jerusalem in B.C. 711, by Sargon.   The prophecies of Isaiah (chapters x. and xi.), so long unsolved mysteries, are now found to be clear and detailed records of this lost incident in Oriental history.

"Sargon" claimed descent from an ancient hero named Bel-bani ; and he assumed the name of an old Babylonian monarch—Sargon of Agadé, who was worshipped as a demi-god—but his own name was not really Sargon.   When he stormed the city of Samaria, he carried away, he tells us, 27,000 of the Israelites into captivity.   The kingdom of Samaria was suppressed, and those Israelites who were not deported were placed under an Assyrian governor.   Thus the Bible account of the captivity of the ten tribes is confirmed.   And as to Judah, when we come to the Babylonian annals of the conquest by Nebuchadnezzar, we find confirmation of the statement that he destroyed Jerusalem, and carried the inhabitants of that city into captivity.

These, then, are some instances of the light that is being thrown upon the Scriptures by these Assyrian writings—of the manner in which the Bible narrative is being filled out and illustrated with new and copious details, and on the whole, as all critics are bound to say, is being confirmed in its statements.

Besides Ahab and Omri, Jehu and Hezekiah, the cuneiform tablets mention Menahem, Pekah, and Hoshea, kings of Israel ; and Azariah, Ahaz, and Manasseh, kings of Judah. Ahaz is called Jehoahaz, his name, like so many more, being compounded with the name of Jehovah ; and it would seem that on account of his perversion to foreign worship the Bible writers would not use the Lord's name in such association. Further, the kings of Assyria and Babylon spoken of in the Bible come before us again in the cuneiform texts, with many particulars of their warlike expeditions, — Sennacherib, Esarhaddon, Shalmaneser, Tiglath-Pileser, Nebuchadnezzar, &c. Tiglath-Pileser, we find, was not the first of that name, for there had been a monarch so designated as early as 1300 B.C.

The other palace found at Kouyunjik belonged, as stated before, to Assurbanipal. He was the Sardanapalus of Greek writers and was a great conqueror. His date is about 640 B.C. Mr Rassam, the native co-worker with Mr Layard, was fortunate enough to discover Assurbanipal's library—the library of the Assyrian kings. The "books" of the Assyrians differed very much from our own. They used to take a tablet of clay, to write upon it with an iron stylus, bake it into terra cotta, and then place the record on the library shelf. These clay tablets were more durable than leaves of paper or rolls of parchment, and the Assyrian records, covered up more than two thousand years ago, are in many cases so well preserved that scholars can read them.

As progress was made in deciphering the inscriptions, it was found that new and remarkable light was being obtained regarding the history and civilisation of half-forgotten empires. Collections of inscribed tablets had been made by Tiglath-Pileser II. (B.C. 745), who had copied some historical inscriptions of his predecessors. Sargon, the father of Sennacherib (B.C. 722), had increased this library by adding a collection of astrological and similar texts; and Sennacherib himself (B.C. 705) had composed copies of the Assyrian canon, short histories, and miscellaneous inscriptions to add to the collection. Sennacherib also moved the library from Calah, its original seat, to Nineveh, the capital; and Esarhaddon, the son of Sennacherib, added numerous historical and mythological texts. All the inscriptions of the former kings, however, were nothing compared to those written during the reign of Assurbanipal, the grandson of Sennacherib, who not only recorded the events of his own reign, but collected literature from other countries, and caused translations to be made of Babylonian records which were then ancient. Thousands of inscribed tablets were collected and copied, and stored in the royal library at Nineveh; and it is this royal library which has been found.

The amount of Assyrian literature now in our possession is more than equal to the entire contents of the Old Testament. It includes religion, astronomy, mythology, history, geography, natural history, royal decrees and private letters, legal decisions and deeds of sale, lists of tributes and taxes, precepts for private life, &c. Among the sacred legends are stories of the Creation and the Deluge. These narratives did not originate with the Assyrians, for they received their religious system by inheritance from the Babylonians. But neither did they originate with the Babylonians; for we learn from their own records that this learning and these traditions were brought into their country by the Akkadians.

Assurbanipal, when he made raids into Babylonia and acptured a city, would carry off the sacred writings to enrich the royal library at Nineveh. When they were brought to Nineveh they were copied by the priests, and they were sometimes translated into the Assyrian tongue, although Assyrians who professed to be well educated used to learn the Akkadian language, much as English boys learn Latin, or theological students study Hebrew and read the writings in the original. It is very interesting to find that these old Assyrians and these ancient Chaldeans had their own version of the Creation, the Deluge, the Building of Babel, &c., which they venerated as being ancient even then, and regarded as most sacred.

The Chaldean narratives differed in minor particulars from those in the Bible. The Chaldean Deluge, for instance, lasted only seven days, instead of the greater part of a year ; the vessel was not an ark, but a ship, of proper ship shape, with a pilot on board to navigate it, and other people on board besides the family of Noah. The Chaldean Noah, when the waters were subsiding, sent out not only a raven and a dove, but a swallow as well ; and in the end of the event he was translated that he should not see death ; and this in the Bible does not occur to Noah, but to Enoch. Nevertheless, with these and other differences, we have the grand fact that the cycle of narratives preserved in the early chapters of Genesis are not mere ingenious inventions on the part of Hebrew writers, but had their parallel in early Chaldea. The key to their exact meaning is for the present lost ; but we may hope that it will be recovered, and then there will be an end to the controversy between Geology and Genesis.

2. *Babylonia.*

Babylonia comprehended the country from near the Lower Zab to the Persian Gulf, about 400 miles long ; and from Elam, east of the Tigris, to the Arabian Desert, west of the Euphrates, an average breadth of 150 miles.

Its history begins very early, for one of its kings—Sargon of Accad—is believed to have reigned in 3800 B.C. The circumstance to which we owe the discovery of this remarkable fact is thus related in Dr Sayce's "Hibbert Lectures": The last king of Babylonia, Nabonidos, had antiquarian tastes, and busied himself not only with the restoration of the old temples of his country, but also with the disinterment of the memorial cylinders which their builders and restorers had buried beneath their foundations. It was known that the great temple of the Sun-god at Sippara, where the mounds of Abu-Hubba now mark its remains, had been originally erected by Naram-Sin, the son of Sargon, and attempts had been already made to find the records which, it was assumed, he had entombed under its angles. With true antiquarian zeal Nabonidos continued the search, and did not desist until, like the dean and chapter of some modern cathedral, he had lighted upon 'the foundation stone' of Naram-Sin himself. This foundation-stone, he tells us, had been seen by none of his predecessors for 3200 years. In the opinion, accordingly, of Nabonidos, a king who was curious about the past history of his country, and whose royal position gave him the best possible opportunities for learning all that could be known about it, Naram-Sin and his father, Sargon I., lived 3200 years before his own time, or 3750 B.C."

The date is so remote and so contrary to all our preconceived ideas regarding the antiquity of the Babylonian monarchy, that it was not received without hesitation ; but it appears to be supported by other evidence, and is now generally accepted. It is believed, indeed, that the monuments found at *Tell-lo,* including statues of diorite, a material foreign to Babylonia, are earlier still, and must be regarded as pre-Semitic.

It may be asked, what interest can we have in people and things so remote ? the Babylonians and their religion have long since perished, and have no influence upon the world of to-day. To this it is replied that through the providential circumstances of the Captivity the Jews were brought into contact with the Babylonians; the Jewish religion in its turn influenced Christianity, and all Christians should be concerned to know what the Jews learned in their exile. In the view of Hebrew prophets the Jews were "sent into foreign countries" to receive education and discipline; the Assyrian conqueror was the rod of God's anger (Isaiah x. 5), and the Babylonish exile was the punishment meted out to Judah for its sins. The captives who returned again to their own land came back with changed hearts and purified minds, intent upon re-establishing Jerusalem as the home of a righteous people. And they had done something more than learn to abominate idolatry, they had been led to weigh the value of the religious beliefs and practices of the nations they had lived with during seventy years.

But it was not only through the Babylonian exile that the religious ideas of the Babylonian and the Jew came into contact with each other. "It was then, indeed" (says Dr Sayce), "that the ideas of the conquering race were likely to make their deepest and most enduring impression; it was then, too, that the Jew for the first time found the libraries and ancient literature of Chaldea open to his study and use." But old tradition had already pointed to the valley of the Euphrates as the primeval cradle of his race. We all remember how Abraham, it is said, was born in Ur of the Chaldees, and how the earlier chapters of Genesis make the Euphrates and Tigris two of the rivers of Paradise, and describe the building of the tower of Babylon as the cause of the dispersion of mankind. Now the Hebrew language was the language not only of the Israelites, but also of those earlier inhabitants of the country whom the Jews called Canaanites and the Greeks Phœnicians. Like the Israelites, the Phœnicians held that their ancestors had come from the Persian Gulf and the alluvial Plain of Babylonia.   The tradition is confirmed by the researches of comparative philology.   Their first home appears to have been in the low-lying desert which stretches eastward to Chaldea—in the very region, in fact, in which stood the great city of Ur, the modern Mugheir.

The earliest known kings of Shumir resided in Ur, and besides that, it was the principal commercial mart of the country.   For, strange as it may appear, when we look on a modern map, and observe the ruins 150 miles from the sea, Ur was then a maritime city, with harbour and docks. Through the accumulation of alluvium brought down by the two great rivers, the Babylonian territory has steadily increased from age to age, and the waters of the Gulf have been pushed back.   There was, in early times, a distance of many miles between the mouths of the Tigris and Euphrates, and Ur lay very near the mouth of the latter river.   The platform of the principal mound which marks the site is faced with a wall 10 feet thick, of red kiln-dried bricks, cemented with bitumen.   The mound has something of the shape of a pear, and measures about 2 miles in circumference.   This mound representing the town, the suburban district is full of graves of all ages, showing the long period through which the city flourished.

It appears from the inscriptions found at Ur that the city was devoted to the worship of the Moon-god Sin, frequently called "the god Thirty," in allusion to his function as the measurer of time by months.   Here stood the great temple of the god, which was partially explored by Mr K. Loftus—a temple built in stages, of which two remain.   The bricks of the temple are inscribed with the name of Ur-Bagas, its founder, the first monarch of united Babylonia of whom we know.   Some of the hymns used in the ritual service of the temple, or at any rate composed in honour of the god, were obtained by Assurbanipal, and translated by his scribes out of the Akkadian language into the Assyrian. One of them begins thus :—

"Lord and prince of the gods who in heaven and earth alone is supreme !

"Father Nannar, Lord of the firmament, prince of the gods !

"Father Nannar, Lord of heaven, mighty one, prince of the gods !

"Father Nannar, Lord of the moon, prince of the gods !"

It was from a city where such hymns were repeated in praise of the Moon-god that Abraham was called to rise up and go forth. With Terah, his father, and a tribe of servants and adherents, he started for new lands.

The distance from Ur of the Chaldees to Haran in northern Mesopotamia was considerable, but it lay along the line of the river and by the common route of travel. It is remarkable that Haran, like Ur, was a city of the Moon-god, who appears at one time to have taken primary rank among the Babylonians. Nabonidos restored the temple at Haran, and it is thus that he celebrates the event :—"May the gods who dwell in heaven and earth approach the house of Sin, the father who created them. As for me, Nabonidos, king of Babylon, the completer of this temple, may Sin, the king of the gods of heaven and earth, in the lifting up of his kindly eyes, with joy look upon me month by month at noon and sunset : may he grant me favourable tokens, may he lengthen my days, may he extend my years, may he establish my reign, may he overcome my foes, may he slay my enemies, may he sweep away my opponents. May Nin-gal, the mother of the mighty gods, in the presence of Sin, her loved one, speak like a mother. May Samas and Istar, the bright offspring of his heart, to Sin, the father who begat them, speak of blessing. May Nuzku, the messenger supreme, hearken to my prayer and plead for me."

There would seem to be as much reason for Abraham
to leave Haran as there was for his leaving Ur; and the
Bible actually represents the stay in Haran as only a stage
in the migration. Canaan was the land which God had
"told him of;" and there, building altars successively at
Shechem and Bethel and in the oak-grove of Mamre, he
realized that the Lord could be approached in every place
by those who worshipped in spirit and in truth.

Terah and Abraham had come out of Chaldea with a
large family and numerous following. "For years," says
Ragozin, "the tribe travelled without dividing, from pasture to pasture, over the land of Canaan, into Egypt
and out of it again, until the quarrel occurred between
Abraham's herdsmen and Lot's, when Lot chose the
Plain of the Jordan and Abraham remained in the
centre of the country. After the battle of four kings
against five, in the Vale of Siddim, when Lot was taken
prisoner, Abraham pursued the victorious army, now carelessly marching homewards, with its long train of captives
and booty, and produced a panic among them by a sudden
and vigorous onslaught. Not only was Lot rescued, with
his women folk and his goods, but all the captured goods
and people were brought back too. Chedorlaomer, of whom
the spirited Bible narrative gives us so life-like a sketch,
lived, according to the most probable calculations, about
2200 B.C. In the cuneiform inscriptions he is called
Khudur-Lagamar; and among the few vague forms
whose blurred outlines loom out of the twilight of those
dim ages, he is the second with any flesh and blood
reality about him, probably the first, conqueror of whom
the world has any authentic record."

It is supposed that the "Amraphel, king of Shinar," who
marched with Khudur-Lagamar as his ally, was no other
than a king of Babylon, one of whose names has been read
Amarpal, while "Ariokh of Ellassar" was an Elamite, Eri-

aku, brother or cousin of Khudur-Lagamar and king of Larsam. At Larsam the Elamite conquerors had established a powerful dynasty, closely allied by blood to the principal one, which had made the venerable Ur its head-quarters.

Babylon was a very ancient city of Babylonia, and is first mentioned in the inscriptions of Izdhubar,* a mythical hero, whose name is connected with the Chaldean story of the Flood. It remained for some centuries of secondary importance, but became at length the capital of the country. The native name, Bab-ilu, signifies the Gate-of-God, corresponding to Beth-el, the House of God, in the land of Palestine. According to Herodotus, the city stood in a broad plain, and was an exact square, measuring 15 miles each way. It was surrounded, he says, by a broad and deep moat, full of water, behind which rose a wall 50 royal cubits in breadth and 200 in height. In digging the moat the alluvial clay was at once made into bricks and baked in kilns; and with these the walls were built, the cement being hot bitumen. "On the top, along the edges of the wall, they constructed buildings of a single chamber, facing one another, leaving between them room for a four-horse chariot to turn. In the circuit of the wall are a hundred gates of brass, with brazen lintels and side-posts."

The broad stream of the Euphrates passed through the city, dividing it into two parts, and the centre of each division was occupied by a fortress. In the one stood the palace of the kings, surrounded by a wall of great strength and size; in the other was the sacred precinct of Jupiter Belus, a square enclosure, 2 furlongs each way, with gates of solid brass. "In the middle of the precinct," says Herodotus, "there was a tower of solid masonry, a furlong in length and breadth, upon which was raised a second tower, and on that a third, and so on up to eight. The

* Or Gilgames. (See *Academy*, Nov. 8th, 1890.)

ascent to the top is on the outside, by a path which winds round all the towers. . . . On the topmost tower there is a spacious temple, and inside the temple stands a couch of unusual size, richly adorned, with a golden table by its side. Below, in the same precinct, there is a second temple, in which is a sitting figure of Jupiter, all of gold." Other historians make the circuit of the city from 45 to 48 miles, instead of 60 ; and it is hardly necessary to say that modern writers question both its extent and the height of its walls.

The god whom Herodotus calls Jupiter-Belus was Bel-Merodach. Babylon was called "the dwelling-place of Bel" and the "town of Marduk." The temple of Bel is represented by the ruin of Babil, a mound on the eastern side of the stream. Some writers believe this to be the site of the Tower of Babel. Others, including Sir Henry Rawlinson, have identified the Babel tower with the ruin of Birs Nimroud, the ancient Borsippa, on the western side of the river. Birs Nimroud is one of the most imposing ruins in the country, standing in the midst of a vast plain, with nothing to break the view. Sir H. Rawlinson excavated at the site, and discovered that the tower was built in seven stages, the material being brick-work on an earthen platform. The first stage was an exact square, 272 feet each way, and 26 feet high, the bricks blackened with bitumen. The higher stages were of course successively smaller, but they were not placed in the centre of those on which they rested, but considerably nearer to the south-western end which constituted the back of the building. The bricks of the lowest stage being blackened, those of the second stage were orange-coloured, of the third red, the fourth it is supposed were plated with gold. Seven colours were used, emblematic of the planets, and the building was called the Temple of the Seven Spheres. On the seventh stage there was probably placed the ark or tabernacle, which seems to have been again 15 feet high, and must have nearly covered the top of the seventh story. This temple was sacred to Nebo, the Babylonian Mercury, the inventor of the alphabet, "the writer," "the prophet," "the author of the oracle." Assurbanipal is never weary of telling us, at the end of the documents which his scribes had copied from Babylonian originals, that Nebo and Tasmit had given him broad ears, and endowed him with seeing eyes, so that he had written and bound together and published the store of tablets, a work which none of the kings who had gone before him had undertaken, even the secrets of Nebo!

From receptacles at the corners of the stages above described, Sir H. Rawlinson obtained inscribed cylinders, stating that the building was the Temple of the Seven Planets, which had been partially built by a former king of Babylon, and having fallen into decay, was restored and completed by Nebuchadnezzar. It was at Birs Nimroud that Mr Hormuzd Rassam found a leaf of metal with some writing on it, which proved to be a dedication by Nebuchadnezzar to the god Nebo for his restoration to health. If this relates to Nebuchadnezzar's recovery from his madness, it is an interesting confirmation of the story in the Book of Daniel.

"The secrets of Nebo" referred to by Assurbanipal, were astronomical records and other writings stored up in Nebo's temple. The religion of the Babylonians was based on a study of the heavenly bodies, and was so intimately connected with astronomy that it was necessary for the priests to be astronomers. There were observatories at the principal temples; observations of the heavens were regularly made, and naturally the records were preserved in the temple chambers, and became the nucleus of large libraries. It was the good fortune of Mr Rassam to discover one of the most important of these libraries, at

Abu Hubba—about 30 miles south-east from Bagdad— on one of the canals branching eastward from the Euphrates. Abu Hubba proves to be the ancient Sippara, the Biblical Sepharvaim, whence some of the people were taken, to re-people Samaria after the ten tribes of Israel were carried away. The Hebrew name being in the dual form, and signifying the two Sippars, we look for duality in the ruins, and we find them actually on the two sides of the stream. Sippara, we knew from Berosus, was a great seat of sun-worship; the temple of the god Shamas was here, and it was here that Xisuthrus, the Chaldean Noah, was said to have buried the records of the antediluvian world. The explorations of Mr Rassam have restored to us the remains of the Sun-god's temple.

The citadel occupies the southern portion of the *enceinte*, and its highest point on the south-west face was once on the banks of a stream, either the Euphrates itself or a broad canal communicating with the river. The trenches exca- vated in the mound soon struck the walls of a building, and by following the line of this wall the outer face of a large square edifice was uncovered. Trenches and shafts sunk in the interior showed that within the outer rampart there were more than one hundred chambers ranged round a central court. In the central portion of the mound an important pair of chambers were found, and in the centre of one of them a large brick altar platform, about 30 feet square, upon which it was evident that the altar of burnt-offering had stood, for there were charred fragments about. The axis of this chamber was north-east and south-west, and at the north-east end a doorway was found, leading into a smaller chamber, the floor of which was paved with a material resembling asphalt. Under this floor Mr Ras- sam discovered a terra cotta box containing three inscribed records, namely, a stone tablet with a sculptured panel, representing the worship of the Sun-god, and two cylinders.

The cylinders were found to bear inscriptions of Nabonidos, king of Babylon, B.C. 555, recording the restoration of this temple in the year B.C. 550; and the stone tablet bore a long and important record of the restoration of the temple by Nabu-abla-iddina, king of Babylon, whose date may be given as about B.C. 852. Above the figure of the Sun-god on this tablet were the words—" The statue of the Sun-god—the great lord—dwelling in the House of Light, which is within the city of Sippara." But the statue and other objects of value had been removed. From the cylinder of Nabonidos, as previously stated, we learn that the temple had been restored by Naram-Sin, the son of Sargon I., in the year 3750 B.C. It was of very great interest to find in the lower strata of the temple area a small ovoid of pink and white marble, bearing an inscription of Sargon I., of such archaic character as to appear to confirm this date.

The temple was called by many titles—as, " Palace of the God," " High Place," " Dwelling of the God," " Resting-Place of the God,"—and, among others, the " House of God," in Akkadian, E-Din-gira, in Semitic Babylonian, Bit-ilu, in Hebrew, Bethel.

The city of Akkad or Agadé, built by Sargon I., seems to have been a part of the double Sippara, and here Sargon founded the celebrated library which contained among its treasures a great work on astronomy and astrology, in seventy books. Around this nucleus other writings aggregated, and the temple of Shamas became the great record office of the state. Mr Rassam found at Abu Hubba some thousands of tablets relating to fiscal, legal, and commercial transactions; and it would thus appear that all documents of this character were preserved by the priests. A remarkable example of the careful preservation of the writings committed to their charge was furnished in the course of the excavations. On the south-east side of the large quadrangle was a smaller square, in which were a series of chambers, evidently offices of the temple. In one of these over 30,000 tablets were found stored. They were packed by Mr Rassam as he found them, and removed to England without any disturbance of their order; and when the cases came to be examined it was found that the majority of the tablets were arranged chronologically. Ranging as these tablets did from B.C. 625 to B.C. 200, they must have lain for nearly 2000 years quite undisturbed in the ruins.

A Babylonian temple was also the court of justice, and as the Jewish Sanhedrim met in the temple at Jerusalem, so did the council of the grey-haired ones meet in the courts of Chaldean temples to answer judgment. Dr Oppert has translated some contracts and legal decisions relating indubitably to captive Jews who had been carried to Babylon after the destruction of Jerusalem. One of the most interesting of them is a law-suit commenced by a Jewish slave named Barachiel in order to recover his freedom. The case was as follows :— Barachiel—who bears the same name as the father of Elihu in the Book of Job (xxxii. 2-6),—had been the property of a wealthy person named Akhi-nuri, who had sold him to a widow of the name of Gaga, about 570 B.C. He remained in the house of this lady as a slave, with the power of liberating himself by paying a sum equal to his *peculium* or private property, which he had been allowed to acquire, like a slave in ancient Rome ; but it seems that he was never fortunate enough to be able to afford the sum of money required. He remained with Gaga twenty-one years, and was considered the *res* or property of the house, and as such was handed over in pledge, was restored, and finally became the dowry of Nubti, the daughter of Gaga. Nubti gave him to her son and husband in exchange for a house and some slaves. After the death of the two ladies he was sold to the wealthy publican, Itti-Marduk-baladh, from whose house he escaped twice. Taken the second time, he instituted an action in order that he might be recognised as a free-born citizen, of the family of Bel-rimanni ; and to prove that he was of noble origin he pretended that he had performed the matrimonial solemnities at the marriage of his master's daughter, Qudasa, with a certain Samas-mudammiq. Such a performance, doubtless, implied that the officiating priest was of free birth, and no slave or freed-man was qualified to take part in it.

The name Barachiel, says Dr Oppert, is evidently that of a Jew. He is called "a slave of ransom ; " that is to say, not a slave who has already purchased his freedom, but a slave who was allowed by special laws to employ his private fortune in the work of liberating himself. He professes to have been the "joiner" of the hands of bride and bridegroom at a wedding which must have taken place before the thirty-fifth year of Nebuchadnezzar's reign, when he still belonged to the house of Akhi-nuri, "the seller of the slave," as he is called at the end of the text.

The judges, after perusing all the evidence, do not find any proofs that Barachiel was a man of free birth, and accordingly say to him :—" Prove to us that you are the descendant of a noble ancestor." Thereupon Barachiel confesses that he is not free-born, but has twice run away from the house of his master ; as, however, the act was seen by many people, he was afraid, and said he was the son of a noble ancestor. " But I am not free-born," he confesses, and then gives an account of the events of his life. The judges decided that Barachiel should be restored to his condition as a slave of ransom.*

Such a story as this serves to show what the life of many an Israelite may have been during the Captivity.

* " Records of the Past." New Series, Vol. i.

3. *How the Writings were Read.*

To the ordinary visitor to the British Museum, looking at the cuneiform inscriptions—nothing but arrowhead characters variously grouped—it seems wonderful that they should constitute a language, and incredible that they should be read. The question is often asked, "How can we trust the translations put before us ? How do we know that they are any more than guesses?" It may be well, therefore, to relate how the key to the lost character was obtained, and how the decipherment proceeded until now the translation of narrative texts can be made with as much certainty as translations from the Hebrew of the Old Testament.

The clue was obtained from the Behistun inscriptions, through the energy of Sir Henry Rawlinson ; and the records of the successive steps of the discovery will be found in the *Journal of the Asiatic Society*, in the *Quarterly Review* for March 1847, and in such popular works as Mr Vaux's " Nineveh and Persepolis." The process of deciphering cuneiform texts was already well advanced when Sir Henry Layard and Mr Rassam discovered such abundant treasures in the mounds on the Tigris. The inscriptions which are now known to record the personal history of Darius, the son of Hystaspes, are almost always in three forms of the cuneiform character, which may be described as Persian, Median, and Assyrian, and were addressed to different races of his subjects. The most extensive monument of the kind is found on a rock escarpment at Behistun, on the frontiers of Persia, a place on the high road from Babylonia to the further east. The rock is almost perpendicular, and rises abruptly from the plain to the height of 1700 feet, an imposing object which must always have attracted the attention of travellers. It was known

BEHISTUN SCULPTURE.

to the Greeks, who erected on the top of it a temple to Zeus; and it had probably been sacred to Ormazd, the supreme deity of the Persians. High up on the face of this rock, 300 feet above the plain, there are two tablets, one of them containing sculptured figures and nearly a thousand lines of cuneiform character. The sculptured portion of the rock represents a line of nine persons united by a cord tied round their necks, and having their hands bound behind their backs, who are approaching another of more majestic stature, who, holding up his right hand in token of authority, treads on a prostrate body. His countenance expresses the idea of a great king or conqueror, and behind the king stand two guards with long spears in their hands.

The reign of Darius was disturbed by many revolts, and the insurrectionary attempts of many impostors and pretenders. It is these impostors who are represented as prisoners in the sculpture, and over the head of each figure we find his name and description. The first one, the prostrate figure, is "Gomates, the Magian, an impostor," who said, " I am Bartius, the son of Cyrus; I am the King," and so on. The inscription is by far the largest and most important record which has been preserved of the greatness of Darius, and of the Persian state and system. The lines over the monarch himself would read in English as follows :—

" I am Darius the king, the great king, the king of kings, the king of Persia, the king of the (dependent) provinces, the son of Hystaspes, the grandson of Arsames, the Achæmenian," &c.

It will be noticed here how the word king is repeated ; as the inscription proceeds the name Darius is repeated also. A German scholar, Professor Grotefend, had observed that such inscriptions generally begin with three or four words, one of which varies while the others do not. He suspected that the word which changes would be the king's name—as different inscriptions would relate to different kings—and that the other words gave the king's titles. He felt convinced that a word which was constantly repeated signified "king," and conjectured that when two kings were mentioned they were probably father and son. Finding that the names of Cyrus and Cambyses would not suit, because no two names in the inscription he was dealing with commenced with the same letter, he tried others. Cyrus and Artaxerxes seemed equally inapplicable, because of their unequal length, the two names he was dealing with being of six letters each. The only names remaining were those of Darius and Xerxes; and these on further comparison appeared to agree so exactly with the characters that he did not hesitate at once to adopt them. Having thus found out more than twelve letters, among which were precisely those composing the royal title, the next business was to give these names their original Persian form, in order that by ascertaining the correct value of each character, the royal title might be deciphered. From the "Zeudavesta" of Anquetil du Perron, M. Grotefend found that the Greek form Hystaspes was originally represented in Persian by Gustasp, Kishtasp, or Wistasp. The first seven letters of this name were at once discovered, while a comparison of all the royal titles led him to the conclusion that the three last formed the inflection of the genitive singular, corresponding to the Latin Hystaspis. Thus did Grotefend proceed step by step, his ingenuity and perseverance being beyond all praise. Meantime Sir Henry Rawlinson, although stationed in Persia and cut off in a great degree from the results of European scholarship, was devoting himself with ardour to the study of the Behistun inscription, and making independent progress.

It turned out that of the three forms of arrow-headed

character in this class of inscriptions the Persian was the easiest to decipher, being an alphabetic language, and that the other two were not purely alphabetic. Still, a sure clue was obtained, and the key being applied by an increasing number of investigators, the Median and the Assyrian in the course of time yielded up their secrets. At length, in 1857, to put the method of decipherment to a test, the inscription of Tiglath-Pileser I. was submitted to four eminent Assyriologists, namely, Sir H. Rawlinson, Dr Oppert, Mr Fox Talbot, and Dr Hincks, who made translations of it independently, and sent them, under seal, to the secretary of the Royal Asiatic Society. When they were opened and compared it was found that they exhibited a remarkable resemblance to one another, much greater, in fact than could have been the case if the method of decipherment had not been sound. Since 1857 immense advances have been made, until now, as Dr Sayce confidently declares, it is possible to translate an ordinary Assyrian text with as much ease and certainty as a page of the Old Testament.

[*Authorities and* **Sources** : — " Assyrian Discoveries." By **George** Smith. "**The** Chaldean Genesis." **By** George Smith. "Ancient History from the Monuments : Assyria." By George **Smith.** "Ancient History **from** the Monuments : Babylonia." **By Rev. Dr** A. H. Sayce. "**Nineveh and** its Remains." **H. A.** Layard. " Nineveh **and Persepolis."** W. S. W. **Vaux.** " Guide to the **Kouyunjik Gallery." British Museum.** " The **Story of the Nations : Assyria." By Zénaïde A.** Ragozin. "**The Story of the Nations : Babylonia."** Zénaïde **A. Ragozin.** "**Hibbert** Lectures." Dr **A.** H. Sayce. " **Records of** the **Past."** " Transactions of **the** Society of **Biblical** Archæology." Smith's " Dictionary **of the Bible." " From** Under **the Dust** of **Ages."** St Chad Boscawen.]

THE VANDALISM OF THE ORIENTALS.

IT seems to be quite providential that the calamities of cities and the burial of treasures of art and knowledge should result in their preservation, and contribute to the education of the world. It is remarkable also that the explorers of the buried cities of the East should be the Christian nations of the West, and that such a wealth of discovery should enrich this nineteenth century. Through the catastrophe which overwhelmed Pompeii, and preserved it under volcanic ashes for 1700 years, we have become better acquainted with the private life of the Romans than would have been possible by any other means. The fugitive from Pompeii, in the hurry of escape, abandoned articles of intrinsic value, and could not pause or stoop to pick them up; yet they were saved from the hand of the robber that they might give instruction to the world many centuries afterwards. The golden diadems, ear-rings, and bracelets which Dr Schliemann found in a great silver vase on the supposed site of Troy had been packed in the greatest haste, and the fair owner, unable to return to them, no doubt gave them up for lost; but she was an instrument in the hand of Providence, and knew not what she did. By the recovery of the Assyrian royal library, we are being informed concerning the religion and mythology, as well as the history, of early nations, about whom we knew too little through the ordinary channels of history. Think of Assurbanipal's librarian at Nineveh speculating on the ultimate destiny of the records under his care! How could he guess that when the empire was passed away, its kings forgotten, its gods put aside as mythical inventions, there would come scholars from beyond the pillars of Hercules and learn to decipher its records?

How disappointing is it, then, to all lovers of knowledge, as well as to all students of Bible antiquities, to know that, now, when the existence of these treasures is known, there is too little enterprise in our people to go and reap the harvest of them ; and while we wait they are being carelessly or wantonly destroyed ! One explorer tells of an Arab who found an entire black statue, and because it was too heavy to carry away bodily, broke off its head and carried that away first.   Palaces and temples, when unearthed, are used as quarries for the building stone. Limestone slabs, covered with precious sculptures and inscriptions, are burnt for the sake of the lime.   Decaying mounds of bricks, because they contain nitre, are carted off as manure for the fields ! The following are a few instances of the vandalism which seems to be defeating the apparent intention of Providence.

The beautiful sanctuaries " erected by Amenhotep III. in the island of Elephantine, which were figured by the members of the French expedition at the end of the last century, were destroyed by the Turkish governor of Assouan in 1822."—*Professor Maspero.*

The great Sphinx at Gizeh,—" The nose and beard have been broken off by fanatics."—*Professor Maspero.*

Sebakh diggers ply their occupation in the midst of the mounds of the ancient city of Thebes.   "*Sebakh,* signifying ' salt,' or ' saltpetre,' is the general term for that saline dust which accumulates wherever there are mounds of brick or limestone ruins.   This dust is much valued as a manure or ' top-dressing,' and is so constantly dug out and carried away by the natives, that the mounds of ancient towns and villages are rapidly undergoing destruction in all parts of Egypt."—*Miss Amelia B. Edwards.*

" Prisse d'Avennes relates that when he visited, in 1836, Behbeit el Hagar, the site of the old Heb, in the Sebennyte nome, near the present city of Mansoorah, he went away disgusted, seeing the regular trade that was carried on in the most beautiful sculptures of the ruined temple, which was besides used as a quarry by the inhabitants of the spot."—*M. Naville.*

" When the sheikh on whose land I was excavating became reassured as to the object of my researches, he told me that some twenty years ago a great number of inscribed stones were unearthed on that spot [site of Goshen] ; but since that time they had disappeared, most of them having been used for building purposes. The great number of broken pieces which are built into the walls of the houses prove that the sheikh spoke the truth." —*M. Naville.*

At Babel there are four wells scientifically built. When Mr Rassam cleared one of them of *débris* he came to water at the bottom. Each stone is 3 feet in thickness, is bored, and made to fit the one below it so exactly that you would imagine the whole well was hewn out of the solid rock. Yet the Arabs break up these stones for the sake of making lime."—*Transactions of the Society of Biblical Archæology,* viii. 185.

" In 1815 Lady Hester Stanhope conducted excavations at Ascalon, and found a colossal statue of a Roman emperor, thought possibly to have been that of Augustus, erected by Herod. It was unfortunately broken up by the workmen in search of treasure supposed to be concealed within."—Conder's " *Syrian Stone-lore.*"

" At Cæsarea a broad street has been laid out (by the recent immigrants from Bosnia) which passes directly over the remains of the Roman temple built by Herod in honour of Cæsar and of Rome (the finely dressed white stone being turned to good account by the colonists), and over the

Crusaders' Cathedral, the foundations and walls of which also furnish splendid building material."—"*Quarterly Statement* of Palestine Exploration Fund," July 1884.

"I pointed out that while the objects underground would keep a few years longer, the march of civilisation was rapidly erasing all records of the past above ground. The ancient ruins were being burnt into lime, the old names were giving way to modern appellations, and the records of the past were disappearing."—*Colonel Sir Charles Warren.*

"Of Memphis there is at present hardly a trace left; and other great cities known to ancient travellers have disappeared with their monuments. Mummy cases and coffins with most interesting inscriptions have for centuries been used as fuel. And innumerable manuscripts have suffered the same fate. . . . The tombs are convenient abodes for Arab families, who destroy the paintings and inscriptions either by the dense smoke of their fires or by actually pulling down walls. I was taken to see the 'Lay of the Harper,' one of the most interesting remains of Egyptian poetry, which was published a few years ago by Dr Dumichen, but we found the walls on which the poem was written a mere heap of ruins. But the vandalism of European and American travellers is most fatal to the monuments. There is, or rather was, a famous picture at Beni-hassan, which was formerly thought to represent Joseph presenting his brethren to Pharaoh. An English lady has been heard to request her guide to cut out for her the face of Joseph!"—*P. Le Page Renouf.*